BREAKING THE BARRIERS

The Incredible Story of Tennis, Race and Innovation

ABSOLUTELY AMAZING eBOOKS

Habent Sua Fata Libelli

ABSOLUTELY AMAZING eBOOKS

Manhanset House
Shelter Island Hts., New York 11965-0342

bricktower@aol.com • tech@absolutelyamazingebooks.com
• absolutelyamazingebooks.com
All rights reserved under the International and Pan-American Copyright Conventions. No part of this publication may be reproduced, stored in a retrieval system, or transmitted in any form or by any means, electronic, or otherwise, without the prior written permission of the copyright holder.
The Absolutely Amazing eBooks colophon is a trademark of
J. T. Colby & Company, Inc.

Library of Congress Cataloging-in-Publication Data
Caldwell, Dale G.
Breaking The Barriers, The Incredible Story of Tennis, Race and Innovation
p. cm.

1. Sports & Recreation / Tennis. 2. Biography & Autobiography / Sports. 3. Biography & Autobiography / Cultural, Ethnic &Regional / African-American & Black.
Non-Fiction, I. Title.
ISBN: 978-1-955036-09-2, Trade Paper

Copyright © 2021 Dale G. Caldwell
and the International Tennis Hall of Fame
Electronic compilation/ paperback edition
copyright © 2022 by Absolutely Amazing eBooks

August 2022

BREAKING THE BARRIERS

The Incredible Story of Tennis, Race and Innovation

Dr. Dale G. Caldwell

"The history of tennis cannot be fully understood without understanding the contributions of African Americans. *Breaking The Barriers* illuminates the stories, memorable moments, and contributions of African Americans on the game of tennis in a heartfelt and informative way." —Douglas Stark, Museum Director, International Tennis Hall of Fame.

"Dr. Caldwell's pioneering work, *Breaking The Barriers* is transformational. Regardless of your race and/or background, this book will interest anyone that loves the sport of tennis. It is a fascinating read." —D.A. Abrams, Founding Board Member, Black Tennis Hall of Fame and Former Chief Diversity Officer, United States Tennis Association

"In *Breaking the Barriers*, Dr. Dale Caldwell provides us with a compelling look at the rich history of Blacks in tennis and a compelling personal story of his lifelong love of the sport. You will learn a great deal." —Cecil Harris, author of *Different Strokes: Serena, Venus, and the Unfinished Black Tennis Revolution*

"Black tennis history and the history of *Breaking the Barriers* tennis reflects the best of American history. The dignity, strength and perseverance of the individuals and their supporters is inspiring. As this wonderful book shows, the journey has been spectacular. I learned more about wonderful people and events from Dr. Caldwell's book. What a great pleasure to read. Read this book, be informed and inspired by the stories." —George F. A. Parnell, General Counsel of the United States Professional Tennis Association, Inc., Former Division 1 Tennis Player (Howard University) and Nationally Ranked Men's Player

"The greatest gift that one generation, one culture can give to another is the lessons and memories of perseverance, courage and triumph. Dr. Dale Caldwell's book *Breaking the Barriers*, is such a gift."
—Frank Adams

"Dr. Dale Caldwell has written a must-read extraordinary book for anyone who values the history of tennis and race in America. The reader is taken on a powerful journey to learn that we must first remove the barriers that divide us to find common ground."
—Roxanne Aaron, President, American Tennis Association

DEDICATION

I have been blessed to work with many wonderful people in the tennis world. They are the reason that I wrote this book. I thank former International Tennis Hall of Fame (ITHF) President Tony Trabert and former CEO Mark Stenning for supporting my request to develop an exhibit on black tennis history in 2007. I will be eternally indebted to Gary Cogar and Art Carrington for their passionate work on the Breaking the Barriers exhibit and to Doug Stark and Nicole Markham for their extraordinary efforts to update and digitize the exhibit. I am truly grateful to ITHF CEO Todd Martin for encouraging me to write this book; Bob Davis for being the first person to support and give his heart and soul to growing the Black Tennis Hall of Fame; D.A. Abrams for his early advocacy of the organization; Ann Kogar for her years of tremendous support and Executive Director Shelia Curry for leading the organization to new heights of success. I dedicate this book to my daughter Ashley Marie Caldwell, to my mother Grace Estelle Dungee Caldwell, to my father Reverend Gilbert Haven Caldwell, Jr., to my brother Paul Douglass Caldwell, to my high school tennis coach and mentor Bill Ewen and to all the people who have made tennis the most popular individual sport in the world.

Also by Dr. Dale G. Caldwell

Fruit of the Spirit Hymnal and Calendar
Fruit of the Spirit Poems and Hymns
Intelligent Influence
Intelligent Influence in Baseball
School To Work To Success
Tennis in New York
The Influence of Socioeconomic Factors on Student Achievement

Table of Contents

About the Author
Acknowledgments 1
Foreword 5
Introduction 7
Ch 1, My Family's Tennis Journey 1
Ch 2, How Tennis Got its Scoring 45
Ch 3, How Tennis Got Its Name 53
Ch 4, The Birth of Lawn Tennis 65
Ch 5, Tennis Becomes a Global Sport 75
Ch 6, The United States National Lawn Tennis Association..87
Ch 7, The US National Championships 97
Ch 8, The West Side Tennis Club 105
Ch 9, The International Tennis Hall of Fame 123
Ch 10, ITHF Barrier Breakers 131
Ch 11, Tennis in the Black Community 155
Ch 12, Breaking the Barriers Timeline 165
Ch 13, Breaking the Barriers Exhibit Panel 1 199
Ch 14, Breaking the Barriers Exhibit Panel 2 215
Ch 15, Breaking the Barriers Exhibit Panel 3 239
Ch 16, Black Tennis Hall of Fame Inductees 251
Epilogue 323

Dale G. Caldwell, Ed.D.
Author of *Breaking the Barriers*

Dr. Caldwell worked closely with International Tennis Hall of Fame (ITHF) Museum Director Gary Cogar and Co-curator Art Carrington to create the International Tennis Hall of Fame's (ITHF) groundbreaking *Breaking the Barriers* touring exhibit. This exhibit, which was produced by the ITHF and partially funded by the United States Tennis Association (USTA), has become the most popular touring exhibit in the museum's history. The success of this exhibit,

which presents a fascinating portrait of black tennis history, convinced Dr. Caldwell to found the Black Tennis Hall of Fame, Inc. (BTHOF.org) in 2007 to recognize and record "the incredible accomplishments of individuals who broke through barriers of race and class in tennis." This organization, which was expertly managed by President Bob Davis since 2009 and Executive Director Shelia Curry since 2019, has become the premier black tennis history organization in the world.

Dr. Caldwell made tennis history on his own when, in 2006, he became the first African-American to serve as the president and chief executive officer (CEO) of the USTA Eastern Section and, in 2011, by becoming the first and only African-American to serve as a USTA Section president and CEO and then as a member of the USTA board of directors. The success of the BTHOF inspired him to establish the Black Entrepreneurship Hall of Fame (BEHOF.org) in 2019 and the Black Inventors Hall of Fame (BIHOF.org) in 2020. These extraordinary organization are celebrating the incredible accomplishments of people who have been overlooked in the history books because they were black.

Dr. Caldwell graduated from Princeton University with a BA degree in Economics, the Wharton School of the University of Pennsylvania with an MBA degree in Finance, and Seton Hall University with an Ed.D. degree in Educational Leadership. He co-authored the book *Tennis in New York* with Nancy Gill McShea in 2010 and founded the *New York Open* professional tennis tournament at the legendary West Side Tennis Club in Forest Hills in 2013. Dr. Caldwell is also an accomplished tennis player who earned national rankings as a junior in the 18 and under division of the ATA and in the 40 and over division of the USTA. In addition, he has had USTA sectional rankings in the Men's Open, 25, 30, 35 and 40 singles divisions.

Dr. Caldwell has been a certified Professional 1 tennis teaching professional with the United States Professional Tennis Association (USPTA) for more than 40 years and certified teaching professional with the Professional Tennis Registry (PTR) for 7 years. In 2010, he was awarded the *Tennis Educational Merit Award* by the ITHF for his volunteer work on the *Breaking the Barriers* exhibit and with the USTA. In 2020, he was awarded the Sportsmen's Tennis and Enrichment Center *Distinguished Alumni Award*. Dr. Caldwell was inducted into the Black Tennis Hall of Fame in 2015 and the USTA Eastern Tennis Hall of Fame in 2021.

Acknowledgments

I would first like to thank Todd Martin, International Tennis Hall of Fame (ITHF) chief executive officer (CEO), for supporting my idea of a *Breaking the Barriers* book that is based on the ITHF touring exhibit of the same name. I would also like to thank Doug Stark, ITHF Museum director, and Nicole Markham, ITHF curator of collections, for their incredible support of the *Breaking the Barriers* exhibit over the last 10 years. I am grateful to Gary Cogar, who, when he was the ITHF Museum director, lead in the development of the *Breaking the Barriers* Exhibit. It was a true pleasure to help him develop this groundbreaking historical exhibit. I have found each of the members of the ITHF family that I have worked with to be amazing people.

Throughout my tennis life I have been helped by many more people than I can list in this section of the book. However, I am especially grateful to the following people and organizations:

My parents Gilbert and Grace Caldwell, for introducing me to the sport of tennis; my brother Paul Caldwell, for motivating me to push myself athletically.

Legendary Boston-based grassroots tennis instructor Jimmie Smith, for being my first professional tennis coach.

The American Tennis Association (ATA), for providing a place where a young black kid from poor urban communities can develop and test his tennis skills.

The federal Comprehensive Employment and Training Act (CETA), for giving me my very first job as a tennis instructor in New Haven, Connecticut.

Harry Hopman, the greatest professional tennis coach in history, for teaching me that I had the skills to be one of the best players in the world in my age group if I wanted it badly enough.

Bill Ewen, for being an amazing high school tennis coach, teaching me the importance of spiritual, mental and physical excellence and serving as a lifetime mentor.

David Benjamin, for making the Princeton Men's Tennis Team one of the best college teams in the country and serving as a mentor and advisor for the last 20 years.

Eve Kraft, for hiring me as a tennis pro for the Princeton Community Tennis Program when I was a Princeton student.

Jonathan Haines, for hiring me as a tennis teaching professional at Racquet Club West in Mechanicsburg, PA and encouraging me to become a certified United States Professional Tennis Association (USPTA) tennis teaching professional.

Tom Sweitzer, for hiring me as a tennis teaching professional at the Hershey Racquet Club.

Arthur Ashe, for allowing me to teach tennis with him during a New York Black MBA Association tennis outing.

Larry Dillon, for introducing me to grassroots tennis organizing and the volunteer world of the USTA.

Gene Scott, Skip Hartman and all of the other volunteers who helped to elect me as the first African-American president of the USTA Eastern Section.

D.A. Abrams, for being an amazing executive director of USTA Eastern when I was president and CEO and for hiring me to do consulting work for the USTA.

Art Carrington, for his incredible research that helped us develop the *Breaking the Barriers* Exhibit.

Bob Davis and now Shelia Currey, for being an outstanding Executive director of the Black Tennis Hall of Fame that I founded to continue the research on Black tennis history.

The USTA 2009-2010 nominating committee, for selecting me for the 2011-2012 USTA board of directors.

The ITHF, for awarding me the *2010 Tennis Educational Service Award*.

Breaking The Barriers

Nancy McShea, for co-authoring the book *Tennis In New York* with me.

2011-2012 USTA president Jon Vegosen, for being a mentor and naming me the head of the USTA Board Strategic Planning Committee.

Seth Abraham, David Dinkins, Billie Jean King and Ilana Kloss, for being outstanding mentors during my tenure on the USTA board of directors.

Todd Martin, for his support of this book and for telling me I had an excellent one-handed topspin backhand when we were playing tennis during a USTA board retreats.

Mark McIntyre, for his guidance and support in the founding of the New York Open professional tennis tournament.

Sandy DeShong and Deepak Trivedi, for their volunteer help in establishing the New York Open.

Herb Glenn, for inspiring me to start the Newark Open professional tennis tournament.

My daughter Ashley Marie Caldwell, for serving as the vice president of the New York Open at age 9 and reigniting my love for the game because of her interest in tennis.

I feel like my tennis career is entering an amazing new phase so I would also like to thank, in advance, all of the people that will help me in tennis in the future.

Foreword

I have had the opportunity to see the sport of tennis through many lenses. As a ball boy at a professional tournament in Cleveland in the late 1970s, a nationally ranked junior, slowly but surely progressed in my pursuit of excellence in tennis. As a player on the ATP Tour, I discovered how hard one has to work to "make it" and how much harder the work is to sustain an elite level, ultimately reaching the finals at the Australian and US Opens and achieving a ranking of number 4 in the world. In my role as the CEO of the International Tennis Hall of Fame (ITHF), I have continued to discover things that make tennis so special. Since the sport's inception in 1874, it has attracted a very diverse group of exceptional people who made history both on and off of the tennis court.

Dr. Dale Caldwell, in this groundbreaking book, shares the stories of some of the most extraordinary people who have ever been connected to the amazing sport of tennis. Dale, when he was the first black president of the United States Tennis Association (USTA) Eastern Section, brought the idea of doing an exhibit on the first 100 years of tennis in the African-American community to the ITHF. He worked as the curator of the resulting *Breaking the Barriers* exhibit on US black tennis history that was viewed by more than 25,000 people at the 2007 US Open.

This book builds on that exhibit by providing information on tennis legends of all races and backgrounds who accomplished remarkable feats. Dale introduces readers to legends like Ora Washington who was the best black female athlete in both tennis and basketball in the US. Dale also shares the amazing story of William Agustus Larned, a white tennis player who won a record seven US National Championships and became the first top player to use a metal racket in 1922. These stories, combined with the history of tennis, the ITHF, the United States Tennis Association (USTA), the American Tennis Association (ATA) and the Black Tennis Hall of Fame (BTHOF), make this book a must-read for anyone who loves tennis or fascinating history.

Todd Martin
CEO
International Tennis Hall of Fame
May 2021

Introduction

A Unique Book on Tennis History

The *Breaking the Barriers* exhibit that International Tennis Hall of Fame (ITHF) Museum director Gary Cogar and his talented staff, co-curator Art Carrington and I developed in 2007 chronicling the history of black tennis players in the United States, has been the most successful touring exhibit in the history of the ITHF. The success of this exhibit and the demand for more information on tennis history, inspired me to write this book about people of all races and backgrounds who broke through barriers of race, class and ability. The primary purpose of this book is to introduce readers to the fascinating stories of accomplishment explored in each of the three tennis history panels in the exhibit. However, in documenting my findings, I learned that writing a book about the history of discrimination and classicism in sports is not easy. It is much easier to celebrate wonderful athletic accomplishments and ignore the ugly aspects of sports history.

In my research, I discovered that there have historically been two types of books written about black history and racial discrimination. The first type is one that focuses primarily on teaching readers about the suffering of blacks and exposing the people that were the cause of discriminatory practices. The second type is one that, instead of shaming people, celebrates the accomplishments of African-Americans who succeeded in spite of the problems of racism. These two types of books are extremely important. Unfortunately, they do not reach a diverse audience because they are only of interest to those individuals who want to learn about black history.

I have chosen to write a third type of book that describes black tennis history and, at the same time, celebrates this history in the context of all tennis history. This book is different than the other two types of black history books because it not only celebrates black history, it recognizes the achievements of people of different races and backgrounds who broke new ground in the sport. This new type of black history book has relevance to all readers and provides a more complete context in which to view the incredible sport of tennis.

Why is tennis so incredible? Those of us who grew up playing tennis are aware of the unique aspects of the sport. Tennis not only provides tremendous exercise for people of all ages, it helps players manage their emotions. This co-ed activity is the second most popular participation sport in the world. Research suggests that high school tennis players in both suburban and urban communities have higher grade point averages than participants in any other sport. Tennis is a very popular spectator sport. The United States Open (US Open) tennis tournament is the largest annually occurring sport in the world in terms of attendance. This two-week tournament is so popular, it has greater economic impact on New York City than all of the home Yankee, Knicks, Rangers and Mets games combined

Some people do not see the value in telling the stories of black tennis players who played a long time ago. These individuals often believe that the racial discrimination of the past was unfortunate, but it should be forgotten. They feel that those people who experienced discrimination simply had bad luck because they were victims of the influences of the times in which they lived. I have always liked Edmund Burke's famous quote, "Those who don't know history are doomed to repeat it." I therefore believe that it is extremely important to share stories about history that may have been lost because of racial discrimination. These stories are often fascinating and educational. More importantly, too often, victims of past discrimination have been forgotten or relegated to the back pages of history. In 2006, to ensure that the stories of these fascinating individuals become permanent, I convinced the International Tennis Hall of Fame to fund the creation of the *Breaking The Barriers* exhibit on Black tennis history. I had the honor of serving as the co-curator of that exhibit. I then founded the Black Tennis Hall of Fame to honor people who broke through barriers of race and class to achieve success in tennis. This book is an expansion of my efforts to memorialize this fascinating history.

Breaking The Barriers

As a black tennis player who has benefitted socially and athletically from the sacrifices of many of these heroes, I feel an obligation to tell the world their stories of perseverance through incredible barriers. However, I wanted this book to be different than other books describing black history. I have focused this book on telling the complete story of tennis and the black and white players who broke through extraordinary barriers to make tennis the popular global sport it is today. I believe that readers of all races and backgrounds will find these diverse tennis stories to be fascinating. Unfortunately, bias against people because of their race and religion was prevalent in the sport of tennis. People who were Jewish were denied admission to certain country clubs. People of Latino descent were treated as second class citizens. Some of these individuals were able to "pass" because they looked like the white members and players. However, people of African descent, because they had darker skin and different facial features were singled out as people who did not belong in white country clubs or tennis tournaments.

What Inspired Me To Write This Book?

On August 1, 2006, eight months after becoming the first African-American president of the historic United States Tennis Association (USTA) Eastern Section, I wrote a letter to former world number 1 and 1970 International Tennis Hall of Fame (ITHF) inductee, Tony Trabert, the president of the ITHF at the time. In the letter I requested that the Hall of Fame dedicate a section honoring black players who, because of discrimination, were never allowed to "*Compete in tournaments required for induction into the ITHF.*" In response to my letter, Tony Trabert, Mark Stenning (the ITHF chief executive officer at the time), and the board of trustees supported the creation of a traveling exhibit at the 2007 US Open honoring black players who were American Tennis Association (ATA) champions.

Dr. Gary Cogar, the ITHF Museum director, led the project and, since it was my idea, I was selected as the curator of the exhibit. We had a lot of fun during the first few weeks of the project. However, I felt that it was important to have another expert on black tennis history so Gary and I agreed that legendary ATA Men's Singles Champion (and one of my tennis heroes growing up) Art Carrington become co-curator of the exhibit. I am confident all readers will find that the information in this book, generated largely by the work of Gary, the ITHF staff, Art, Black Tennis Hall of Fame executive director Bob Davis and me, to be fascinating and eye opening. After discussing this book idea with legendary pro tennis player and current ITHF CEO Todd Martin, I embarked on writing about the incredible history of the great sport of tennis in a way that will introduce the world to many of the forgotten legends of black tennis history.

In 2012, I wrote a popular book on leadership called *Intelligent Influence*[1] (www.IntelligentInfluence.com) that explains that the secret of success in life is managing how we have been influenced and how we influence others. In my research for the book, I learned that all people "*Do what they do, think the way they think, and, accomplish what they accomplish because of influence.*" No human being in history has ever been successful solely because of their efforts alone. A person's success, or lack thereof, is largely the result of the people and events that influenced them. I therefore felt that it was important to introduce this book by talking about the influences in my life and tennis that "influenced" me to "influence" the ITHF to create an exhibit that has "influenced" thousands of people to celebrate black tennis history.

I begin this book by sharing the story of the ways in which I, as an African-American and a passionate tennis player, was influenced by playing tennis and studying the sport's history. I feel that this information will help people develop greater understanding of why I am convinced that the ITHF *Breaking the Barriers* exhibit is important to both the tennis world and to society as a whole. I believe that my story, and the story of my family, which is similar to that of many other tennis lovers of all races and backgrounds, will help to convince readers that celebrating black tennis history is important. My hope is that Chapter 1 will inspire people from all walks of life to think deeply about the influence of tennis and discrimination in their lives and the lives of people they know.

---

[1] Dale G. Caldwell, *Intelligent Influence: The 4 Steps of Highly Successful Leaders and Organizations* (New Brunswick: Intelligent Influence Publishing Group, 2012)

CHAPTER 1: My Family's Tennis Journey

My Parents' Honeymoon

One of the early family stories that helped me develop a deeper understanding of the significance of racial discrimination was the story of my parents' honeymoon in 1957. Three years before I was born, my mom and dad, who lived in segregated Greensboro, North Carolina, got married in Greensboro, North Carolina. They had a beautiful wedding and were excited about beginning their life together.

From left to right, Bishop Edgar Amos Love (one of the founders of the fraternity Omega Psi Phi), my Mom and my Dad

They had read many wonderful things about racial integration in the North and the world famous Mount Airy Lodge in the Pocono Mountains of Pennsylvania. The literature convinced them that it would be the perfect place for them to spend their honeymoon Several months before the wedding my dad called the hotel to make reservations for December 1-3, 1957 in a honeymoon suite. He was thrilled that they had available rooms and was extremely excited about spending his honeymoon with his bride at this famous resort.

From left to right, my Aunt Margaret Alexander, my Aunt Phoebe Bell, my Mom, my Dad, Junior, my Grandmother Julie Estelle Brown Caldwell and my Grandfather Gilbert H. Caldwell.

Like any other new husband, my dad looked forward to the wedding, the reception afterwards and the honeymoon and was anxious to start a new life with his wife. He therefore saved his money to ensure that everything was perfect for my mom. The more my mom learned about this trip the more excited she became to go to this special place to kick-off their life together. My parents were exhausted after their wedding on November 30, 1957 and stayed in North Carolina on their wedding night. The next day, December 1, 1957, they drove eight

Breaking The Barriers

hours from Greensboro, North Carolina to Mount Airy Lodge in the beautiful Pocono Mountains of Pennsylvania.

They arrived at the resort late in the day drained from the emotional toll of their wedding, exhausted from the reception the night before, and, sleepy from the long drive. When my father reached the magnificent grounds of the resort he was overjoyed about spending a few days in this beautiful hotel. He could not wait to get to his room and relax with the love of his life. My dad therefore quickly got out of the car and anxiously approached the reception desk to pay for the room and pick up the room keys. He was clearly exhausted but extremely excited to have finally arrived at this legendary resort.

From left to right, my Aunt Mary Dungee, my Uncle Clyde Dungee, my Father, my Mother, my Aunt Cora Lee Boyd, my Uncle John Dungee and my Grandfather John Edward Dungee.

His excitement turned to shock when, to his amazement, he was told by the person at the front desk that they had no available rooms for him. My dad presented confirmation of his reservation and, in as pleasant a tone as possible given the situation, explained that there must be some kind of mistake. Initially he never considered that this mix-up was based on his race because he was in the North where he naively thought racism was virtually nonexistent.

The person at the front desk insisted, in spite of my dad's evidence to the contrary, that there were no available rooms and that he did not have a reservation. Growing up in the segregated South my dad instinctively knew the limits of how hard he could challenge the authority of a white person before the police got involved. Finally, after my father pressed the front desk clerk and the manager (in as nice a way as he possibly could given his intense anger) for a more definitive answer as to why he was not allowed to stay in the hotel he was told that, "We don't accept black people because it would be uncomfortable for many of our guests."

After attempting to challenge this policy with no success my father was crushed. I can only imagine the intensity of my dad's emotional pain and embarrassment in front of his new wife. Here he was, an educated young minister with a very bright future and a deep desire to provide the best for his wife, being humiliated by an insensitive hotel staff and a discriminatory corporate policy simply because of the color of his skin. My mom and dad experienced a lot of discrimination in the South. However, this discrimination was made even more painful because it took place in the supposedly desegregated North at a time when my mom and dad were happier and more optimistic than ever about their future.

My wonderful mother Grace, who is the personification of her name, did everything she could to make my dad feel better. However, the emotional scar that resulted from this indignity will never disappear. They were forced to leave the hotel and contact a local United Methodist Minister who helped them find a black owned hunting lodge in New York State where they spent their honeymoon devastated emotionally by the experience at Mount Airy Lodge.

Rectifying a Wrong

Throughout his life my father has had the opportunity to speak to many different groups around the world. He was an extraordinary speaker who was very comfortable talking about growing up in the South and his work as a "Foot Soldier" in the Civil Rights Movement.

Breaking The Barriers

However, because of the permanent emotional scars of his honeymoon experience, he has been reluctant to tell the story of the racism they experienced on their honeymoon. Nonetheless, this story would take on new life when my parents were invited, in honor of Black History Month, to speak at the Bear Tavern Elementary School in Hopewell Township, New Jersey. The pre-kindergarten to fifth grade school was approximately 85% white, 12% Asian and 3% other races. There were very few black students at the school so my parents had no idea how their stories of racism would be received by the students and administrators. I drove my 83 year-old parents to the school and on the way, encouraged them to share their honeymoon story with the students. At first, they were reluctant to tell this emotionally draining story, but they agreed to discuss it briefly. We would never have predicted what would happen as a result of them deciding to tell their honeymoon story.

When we got there the gym was packed with hundreds of students anticipating my parents' speech. These were clearly a bright group of students who were anxious to hear from someone who had lived the black history that they had learned from their outstanding teachers. The Principal, Chris Turnbull, made a few introductory remarks and introduced my parents by showing a wonderful video of their wedding and pictures of my dad and Dr. King that they had asked me to secretly supply to them before the presentation. My mom does not like public speaking, so my dad did most of the talking. He began by talking about his experience as a "Foot Soldier" in the Civil Rights Movement marching alongside well-known people like Dr. Martin Luther King, Jr., Ralph Abernathy, Jesse Jackson, etc. He brought people to tears by talking about feeling less valuable than white children because he was forced to drink out of the "colored" water fountains. My dad discussed the emotional "scars" that have stayed with him as a survivor of being treated like an animal in a segregated world.

These stories seemed to be interesting to the students. They had difficulty understanding why government set up colored and white water fountains if the water came from the same source. However, their eyes lit up when my dad shared the story of their honeymoon. Many of the students were moved to tears when they heard that story. Even though the story clearly connected with the students we had no idea that they would take action in response to what they heard. The 5th graders in attendance were so inspired by the honeymoon story that they wrote letters to the manager of Mount Airy Lodge asking the hotel to make amends by allowing my parents to celebrate their 60th wedding anniversary for free at the newly renovated hotel. To everyone's surprise, Mathew Magda, the VP of Mount Airy Casino Resort Operations, agreed to provide an all-expense paid 60th Honeymoon in November of 2017. My friend Bill Klun, who was a fan of my parents, convinced CBS News to do a story about their special 60th anniversary honeymoon. Sunday Morning assigned CBS News correspondent Steve Hartman to interview my parents when they arrived at the Mount Airy Lodge. The 3-minute story on my parents' honeymoon went viral. More than 6 million people not only watched this video, but they were moved to tears because of the passion that these young people had to right a wrong.

Civil Rights Leaders

Over the years, my parents have told me many stories about the discrimination that they faced growing up in North Carolina, South Carolina and Texas. However, their honeymoon story moved me the most because it occurred during what was supposed to be one of the happiest moments in my parents' life. I am proud to say that, in spite of the racial discrimination that they faced throughout their life, my parents were both extremely successful. My mother became an outstanding public school teacher in Boston, New York, New Haven, Wilmington and Denver. My dad, a legendary United Methodist Minister, knew and marched with Dr. Martin Luther King, Jr. He met Dr. King at Boston University Divinity School where he was a student and Dr. King was a recent graduate. Together, they organized a march to integrate the Boston Public Schools in 1965. My favorite picture is the one included below where my dad, on the left, is at a press conference preceding the Boston march with Rev. Ralph Abernathy and Dr. Martin Luther King, Jr.

Breaking The Barriers

My Father Reverend Gilbert H. Caldwell, Jr.,
Reverend Ralph D. Abernathy and Reverend Dr. Martin Luther King, Jr.

My dad went on to march and work with Dr. King and other Civil Rights Leaders on some of the best known events in US history (the Selma to Montgomery March, the March on Washington, the Mississippi Freedom Summer and the Poor Peoples Campaign, among others). I was too young to join my father on Civil Rights marches, rallies or discussions. However, his stories about these critical events in American history influenced me to develop a passion for black history. Amazingly, my love for tennis was influenced by racial discrimination. My Dad's inability to play tennis on the "White Only" tennis courts when he was young convinced him to make his firstborn son a tennis player.

My Parents' Love for Tennis

In the early 20th century, tennis became a very popular sport for ministers, doctors, teachers and lawyers in the black community. My grandfather, Reverend Gilbert H. Caldwell, a successful Methodist Minister in Texas, North Carolina and South Carolina, enjoyed tennis and taught my dad to play. My father was a good athlete who used to play touch football with legendary professional baseball player and

1977 Major League Baseball Hall of Fame Inductee Ernie Banks in Texas when they were both kids. He really enjoyed playing tennis so much he wanted to play with anyone anywhere he could. However, in the segregated South at the time, he was restricted from playing with white players on the nicest tennis courts in his community because he was black. He had become accustomed to being treated like a second-class citizen. However, there was something even more disturbing about not being able to play his favorite sport because he was black. This added to the emotional scars he had developed because he was a black person in the segregated South.

Growing up in the South in the 1930s, 40s and 50s, my dad experienced racial discrimination on a daily basis. He could not drink from the same water fountains or go to the same bathrooms or restaurants as people who happened to be white. However, there is something even more disturbing about being denied the right to play a sport because of one's race. Good athletes naturally seek out other good athletes so that they can test themselves against the best. They don't care what color a person is or where they live or how much money their family makes. They know that the only way for them to get better is to play with the best people around. The segregation of tennis courts created an unnatural relationship between good athletes because it prevented the best white and black players from pushing each other to become even better tennis players. The scar of racial discrimination in tennis has left an emotional scar on my dad that will stay with him for the rest of his life.

My father was the first person to teach me tennis as a small child. My Dad was the Senior Pastor of Union United Methodist Church in Boston where I was born. He passed his love for this amazing game on to me when I was 5 years old. As a typical boy who was easily influenced by his peers, I preferred the sports that most of my friends liked. I was therefore much more interested in basketball and football than tennis at the time. However, I loved hitting tennis balls with my dad in Franklin Park in Boston. Back then, playing tennis on public parks was a time consuming endeavor. We could not just walk on the courts and start hitting tennis balls. We had to bring and set up our own net on the courts. However, that activity helped to make this bonding time with my dad very special.

Breaking The Barriers

It has taken me many years to realize that one of the main reasons that I was inspired to play tennis throughout my life was because of my dad's stories of growing up in the segregated South and being denied the right to play on many tennis courts because he was black. His emotional tales about living in Dallas and Galveston, Texas in the 1940's where he would peak through the fence of the local "Whites Only" tennis club dreaming that one day he could play on those very same courts inspired me to take tennis very seriously. He had an unfulfilled passion for the sport of tennis that motivated him to ensure that his first born son would be given opportunities in tennis that he did not have. There are many reasons why I love tennis. One of them is that, as the oldest son, I have subconsciously felt an obligation to make tennis my passion and make my mom and dad proud of my tennis accomplishments. However, I have come to genuinely love playing and watching tennis as well as volunteering my time to influence others to love the sport as much as I do.

As civil rights activists, my parents were clearly influenced to be extremely conscious of racial discrimination. They never encouraged me to become a radical activist for human rights. Instead, they taught me to treat all people the same regardless of their race, gender, background, financial circumstances or personal limitations. They went out of their way to expose me to both black and white communities to ensure that I could survive in very different racial environments. They also taught me to be proud of my racial background and know black American history.

Early School Life

My school life began when my parents moved to a predominantly black section of Boston called Roxbury. My dad was the Assistant Pastor of the Union United Methodist Church in Boston and, to ensure that the family had enough money to survive, he took a job as the Executive director of the United Methodist Church-supported early childhood center called the Cooper Community Center. I then attended first grade at a local public school in Boston called the Prince School. Unfortunately, the public schools in the area did not provide the kind of education that my mom (as a public school teacher) wanted for me so I was sent to an excellent private school called the Advent School in the wealthy Beacon Hill Section of Boston.

It was at that time that I began the challenging dual life that defines me even today. As a black resident of a predominantly black community, I was influenced to speak and act in a more informal way because I was laughed at for speaking the "Queen's English." As a student in a predominantly white elite private school, I was influenced to speak more formally because I would be laughed at for speaking casual English. Unfortunately, I was insecure and uncomfortable in both communities. This feeling of being out of place threatened to make me a loner with no friends in my neighborhood or at school. However, when I discovered that I was better than most kids my age in tennis everything changed. This discovery gave me the confidence I needed to develop friends and do well in school.

The Importance of Race and Tennis in My Life

Fortunately, race relations in America have improved exponentially since the 1960s. However, when I was young, a person's race played a critical role in determining where they lived, shopped and worshiped. Back then, because of redlining (where blacks are limited by real estate agents and politicians to live in the "black" community instead of the "white" community) and job discrimination, blacks lived in one section of town while whites lived in another section. Schools and churches were largely segregated. As a result, there was little sustained positive interaction between blacks and whites. Going to an elite white school while living in a poor black community gave me entree into two very different worlds. Therefore, early in life, I had a chance to observe how different types of people lived their lives. The older and more experienced I became at observing different people, the more I realized that in spite of economic and cultural differences, black people and white people were very much alike. People in both communities valued family, education and positive human interactions with people they trusted. However, they refused to interact on a regular basis as equals because they assumed that "those people" were very different.

Breaking The Barriers

One of the wonderful things about writing a book on the history of a particular subject is that it inspires you to think about your personal history as well as the history of your subject. As I was writing about the history of tennis in New York City in the book *Tennis in New York*[2], I was inspired to think about the role of tennis in my personal development. Through this reflection, I discovered that tennis provided the emotional, physical and intellectual foundation that I needed to get through the many challenges of living in poor black communities and going to rich white schools. Thus, you could say that for me, tennis was "the great equalizer."

I took tennis for granted early in my life because I did not realize how it gave me the confidence to manage my emotions in a way that enabled me to deal with the teasing I endured in the black community and at a white school. I was laughed at by black friends because I went to a white school and didn't hang out with them. I was teased in the white school because I lived in a black community and enjoyed different entertainment. I did not realize how tennis helped my footwork, hand-eye coordination and flexibility so I could be one of the best basketball players in the community and at school. Most importantly, I did not realize how tennis helped me learn to focus in a way that enabled me to succeed academically. This self-reflection has convinced me that being a very active United States Tennis Association (USTA) and American Tennis Association (ATA) volunteer as well as writing about tennis history has been my way of giving back to a sport that has been one of the main reasons that I have had a wonderful life.

Learning Tennis

As the son of a United Methodist Minister who moved frequently, I had the unique opportunity to live in black communities, white communities, multi-racial communities, very poor communities and middle class communities. I first hit a tennis ball when I was 5 years old. However, my deep love for tennis developed around age 6 or 7 when my Dad and I would hit the ball regularly on the Carter

---

[2] Dale G. Caldwell and Nancy Gill McShea, *Tennis in New York*, (New Brunswick: Intelligent Influence Publishing Group, 2011)

Playground tennis courts in Franklin Park on Columbus Avenue in Boston (the courts where we had to bring our own net) in the 1960's.

My parents enrolled me as one of the first students in Jimmy Smith's urban tennis camp in Boston in the 1960's. Jimmy Smith (who was inducted into the Black Tennis Hall of Fame in 2013) became a legend as one of the first black tennis pioneers in Boston. He was passionate about the sport and wanted to identify future tennis stars in the black communities of Boston. He therefore established a local community tennis program in the predominantly black Dorchester section of Boston that eventually led to his founding of the famous Sportsman's Tennis Club. As a child, I was very shy and reserved both on and off of the tennis court. However, Mr. Smith and his team of great coaches helped me develop the confidence in my ability to successfully compete with other tennis players in the program and beyond.

Most kids feel out of place when they are very young. I was no different. If I had not been a very good tennis player when I was young I probably would not have had many friends in either the black or white community. Tennis was the source of the little confidence I had at that time in my life. Any success that I had socially, academically and athletically growing up was rooted in my ability to play tennis. However, my confidence in tennis gave me confidence in basketball and academics. I therefore did well in both.

Most tennis players remember the first time that they beat their parents in the sport. I am no different. My mom was a very good athlete and a good tennis player. However, she did not play tennis as often as she wanted to because of her focus on taking care of me and my younger brother Paul. I enjoyed hitting tennis balls with her as a child. However, my most vivid memory of playing tennis with my mom occurred when she offered to buy me a metal tennis racket if I beat her. I was 10 years old at the time. I still remember playing her at the YMCA in Greensboro, North Carolina (near the place where she grew up and went to college). I was motivated to win that racket and did whatever I needed to do (short of cheating) to beat her and win a metal tennis racket. My mom was extremely devoted to her children and did not seem to be bothered in the least by my victory (probably because it made me so happy). This experience was one of my first tennis based life lessons. Through this informal family competition my mom taught me the importance of being focused on a tangible goal. That lesson has helped to guide me for the last 45 years.

The Significance of the ATA

As a junior player, I played in a lot of New England Lawn Tennis Association (NELTA) sanctioned tournaments. NELTA is one of the 17 sections of the USLTA (which is now the USTA and the official governing body of tennis in the US). Even though tennis was integrated at the national level at that time, local USLTA tournaments still presented problems for black players. As an African-American junior player playing tournaments in the 1970s in New England, I often felt uncomfortable playing matches at beautiful country clubs that had no black members. As the only black player in most of these tournaments, I often felt that I did not belong. Many of the tournaments were in very exclusive country clubs throughout the richest communities in New England.

Frequently, the draws were somewhat suspect. There were rarely more than one or two black players in a tournament draw. Defying probability, I would sometimes play the only other African-American player in a tournament in the first round. In addition, in tournaments where I was the only African-American player, I would draw a top seeded player in the first round seemingly more often than other players of the same ability. I may have been experiencing discrimination or I may have just had extremely bad luck. Nevertheless, these experiences, combined with my lack of confidence as a black tennis player in a white tennis world, ensured that, all too often, I had lost a match in my mind before I even entered the match warm-ups.

My performance on the court, therefore, did not match my ability to play tennis. I had the skills necessary to win many matches and achieve a high ranking sectionally and even nationally. However, I did not have the confidence I needed to win in tournaments where I was usually the only black player in a field of 32 or 64 boys. I therefore lost a lot of matches I should not have early in my tournament career. Fortunately, like many other black players facing similar challenges, I had the opportunity to play in American Tennis Association (ATA) tournaments.

It is hard for me to convey in words how important the ATA was to the development of my self-awareness and self-confidence. The ATA is the oldest black sports organization in the United States. It was founded in Baltimore, Maryland on November 30, 1916 to provide an association dedicated to growing tennis in the black community because blacks were excluded from participating in the "White Only" USLTA at that time.

Even though tennis was an extremely popular sport in the black community in the first half of the 20th Century, blacks were not allowed to participate in USLTA tournaments or serve as leaders of the USLTA. Since the tournament was filled with players who looked like me, I found the ATA tournaments to be a lot more fun than the NELTA tournaments. However, the incredible history of ATA made playing in their regional tournaments a very special experience for me even as a young child.

In the early part of the 20th century, the ATA provided an important opportunity for blacks to compete and experience fellowship around the sport they loved during a time when segregation was commonplace throughout the United States. This unique alliance of people from around the country rapidly became one of the most powerful organizations in the black community because the sport appealed to the most influential people in black society in much the same way that it appealed to the most successful people in white society. Tennis, in both black and white communities, was a passion of successful business leaders, doctors, lawyers, professors and ministers. Local ATA chapters were established throughout the country where people of all ages were given an opportunity to learn the sport and test their skills against each other. The first ATA National Championships took place in 1917 in Baltimore and quickly became one of the most celebrated national sporting events in the black community.

> *"My mom taught me the importance of being focused on a tangible goal."*

Fortunately, we now live in a world were racial discrimination is the exception and not the rule. Racism is still quite prevalent today.

However, in the past, virtually every person who considered themselves white had some racist views. Now, people who hold those views are less common and visible in society. It is therefore very hard for many people to understand or believe that racism was a powerful part of the American culture in both the North and the South. They have forgotten, or never knew, that there was a time when racism was the rule and integration was the exception. There is a tendency for many people to ask themselves "How bad could racism have been in the North? Places like New York City were tolerant of all people. Weren't they?" However, tragically, racial discrimination was an accepted norm in organizations like the United States Lawn Tennis Association (USLTA). This was clearly demonstrated in the minutes of a USLTA executive committee meeting in 1922 in New York City as described in the panel below.

Black Tennis History Reflection

To ensure the accuracy of historical records, the USLTA used a stenographer to keep meticulous minutes of Executive Committee meetings. The Executive Committee, comprised primarily of the officers and representatives from different regions of the country, had the final say on the decisions and actions of the organization. A review of their minutes provides valuable insight into the decisions that the leaders of the organization made over the years.

The USLTA (now the USTA) has made extraordinary efforts in the last 20 years to increase the diversity of its membership. However, the leaders of the organization in the 1920s did not see value in diversity. One of the most unfortunate exchanges in USTA history are found in the USLTA minutes of February 1922[3]. In this exchange, members of the Executive Committee, led by USLTA president (and 1963 International Tennis Hall of Fame Inductee) Julian S. Myrick discussed the application of Howard University (one of the most prestigious historically black colleges in the United States) for membership in the USLTA. The recorded minutes were written as follows:

---

[3] Official February, 1922 Minutes of the Executive Committee of the United States Lawn Tennis Association (USLTA).

Julian Y. Myrick: *"We have a request from Howard University for membership in the U.S.L.T.A"* (Howard University is a historically black university located in Washington, DC.)

R. N. Williams: *"I move that they be asked to join the American Tennis Association (ATA)"*

Stewart: *"We had this thing come up in Chicago. A colored club with very good courts applied for membership in the Western Association. The application was received and we sent somebody out to look over the grounds and situation, and it seemed to be in what we term the "Negro Belt." We asked one of their members to appear. We told him we would take it up and report to him later. We decided in view of the fact that they would be able to enter any tournament in the country, that their application should be turned down. They had a perfect right to enter the Public Park Tennis Association. We cancelled two tickets they bought to go to our Annual Banquet."*

Julian Y. Myrick: *"Why not do as Mr. Williams suggested? Tell them they probably should have written to the American Lawn Tennis Association?"*

Abner Y. Leech: *"Could we possibly refer it to the Membership Committee and let an indefinite period pass?"*

P. B. Williams: *"So far as the American Tennis Association is concerned, the secretary of that organization came into the office and he asked me what the attitude of this Association would be if they applied for membership. I told him I would never make application. I said southern clubs would "see red" on that. I told him there would be no chance in the world of a club of negroes getting membership in the Association."*

Stewart: *"I move that their application be refused. Carried"*

The person taking the minutes provided the following note: *"It was suggested that a letter be sent to the various sectional associations advising them of the actions of this Association and saying that this establishes the policy of the Association toward a club of this kind. Carried"*

Fortunately, the views of the leadership of the USTA have progressed to the point where African-Americans have held the positions of president and CEO, vice-president and secretary-treasurer of the board of the USTA. Unfortunately, it took 144 years before Katrina Adams (2013 Black Tennis Hall of Fame Inductee) became the first black president and CEO of the USTA in 2015.

* * *

Discrimination in the early part of the 20th Century therefore made the ATA a necessary organization in the black tennis community. It gained global prominence by playing a central role in the development of Althea Gibson who became the first black international tennis star (and one of the first American female athletes to gain global prominence). In 1947, Althea Gibson won the first of ten straight ATA National Championships. The color barrier in tennis in the US was broken when, largely because of the public criticism of the USLTA for excluding black players by white tennis champion Alice Marble, Althea Gibson was given the opportunity to compete at the US National Championships at Forest Hills in 1950. In 1951, she became the first black person to participate at Wimbledon in England. In 1957, she won both the Wimbledon and the US National Championships at Forest Hills and became the first black player to win a major international tennis championship.

Arthur Ashe was another product of the ATA. He was a star junior player who won the ATA 18 and under National Championships in 1960. Ashe went on to win the 1960, 1961 and 1962 ATA National Championships. His place as an icon in tennis history was secured when he won the very first US Open in 1968. Ashe's unique ability to connect with people of all ages and races helped to increase interest in the sport around the world (especially in the black community). He was my favorite athlete and my sports role model growing up. Ashe had an incredibly calm temperament (in contrast to many other top players) and amazingly smooth and natural strokes. To this day, I am amazed that he could remain so calm on the court in spite of the racism that he faced on the pro tour and throughout his life. Tragically, Ashe was not allowed to stay in many of the hotels where the pro tennis tournaments were played. In addition, in many tournaments he would have to suffer through racist comments in the middle of a match. He became one of the best players in the world in spite of dealing with racism. Young athletes today should follow his lead and focus on excellence in their chosen sport—not on public displays of anger or euphoria. "Arthur," as he is affectionately known in the black tennis community, transcended the sport of tennis and became a global ambassador fighting injustice around the world until his untimely death in 1993 at the young age of 49.

Ashe was, without question, the individual that I admired the most when I was a teenager. His extraordinary success on the tennis court convinced me for the first time that a black man could compete with the best white players in the world. Ashe influenced me to play as a many ATA tournaments as I could in the hope that, just as he did, I would gain the confidence and skills necessary to compete successfully in USLTA tournaments.

I did well in tennis. However, I never gained the full confidence in my ability to beat anyone at any time on the tennis court. Great athletes have an unwavering belief in their athletic abilities. This self-view is the secret of success of every extraordinary athlete. If I had developed that kind of belief in my abilities, I would have had the confidence to try my luck on the men's professional tennis tour. Even though that never happened, my ATA experience helped me become successful at school and in life. I really enjoyed playing ATA tournaments as a teenager because I felt that I had a chance to compete based solely on my tennis skills and not on some other factors unrelated to tennis (like my race). The confidence I developed in ATA tournaments helped me become much more successful in USLTA tournaments than I would have been otherwise. The ATA served as a launch pad for many black players for more than 100 years. I was fortunate to be one of them.

Tennis and Life Balance

My first major tennis breakthrough came at the ATA Baltimore Tennis Championships in 1974. My Dad and I traveled all the way to Baltimore, Maryland from New Haven, Connecticut where we lived at the time to play in one of the regional junior tennis championships on the ATA circuit. I played the best tennis of my life to that point and won the 14 and Under Division of the tournament. I will never forget the feeling that I had holding the beautiful wooden champion's trophy with the gold tennis player on top.

This victory was my first lesson about the role that tennis can play in life balance. As a newly crowned tennis champion, I had the confidence to say to myself, "Yes I can" every time I walked onto the tennis court. More importantly, this accomplishment helped me begin to develop the confidence to say, "Yes I can" to any challenge that I faced. It may sound silly. However, much of my confidence during this awkward time in my dual life in black and white communities came from this accomplishment. Whenever I felt down or disappointed this trophy would cheer me up and give me the confidence to turn my emotions around. Since that time, I have learned how to effectively use tangible symbols of accomplishments (like plaques, certificates, trophies or medals) to inspire me to push myself beyond my comfort zone in order to pursue challenging goals.

The confidence that I have gained from tangible symbols of accomplishments over the last 40 years has inspired me to: write six books; finish three marathons (New York, San Francisco and Athens, Greece); complete three 500 mile bike rides; become a certified lay minister, certified financial planner, certified management consultant, school board master board member and a certificated housing authority official; graduate from Princeton, Wharton and the Harvard senior executives in state and local government programs; become the New Jersey School Board Member of the Year and the Charter School Administrator of the Year; and, gain national and sectional rankings in tennis, duathlon and triathlon.

My success in the ATA Baltimore tournament led to winning or becoming a finalist in ATA tournaments in Massachusetts, New Jersey and New York. The confidence that I gained from my success on the ATA junior tennis circuit helped me become a sectionally ranked player in the NELTA and a top scholastic player in the New England private school circuit.

My confidence was tested because, as the son of a United Methodist Minister (which at that time had an informal policy of moving ministers to different churches every 5 years), I moved quite frequently. It was therefore very hard for me to develop close friendships knowing that I might move in the near future. I had to learn how to develop new friends much more frequently than most young people. This was especially difficult because I was a young black man attending white private schools where I felt like a fish out of water. By the time I was 18 years old, my family had moved thirteen times because the United Methodist Church placed great emphasis on ensuring that a congregation's relationship is with God, not with the minister. Many of the church leaders believed that in too many denominations ministers and the congregation (when they are together for many years) get too comfortable with each other. Some leaders of the church therefore made the decision to place ministers in different churches after approximately 5 years. My Dad enjoyed trying different things so he moved even more frequently than most Methodist pastors. He therefore was the pastor of 8 churches and held several other senior administrative positions within the church.

Four of the churches my dad led were comprised of almost all white members and four of the churches were comprised of almost all black members. For most of my life I lived in predominantly black neighborhoods but attended predominantly white private schools with national reputations for scholastic excellence. As I mentioned previously, as a young African-American in this unique situation I often felt uncomfortable. I felt like I was "too white" for many of the people who lived in my community and "too black" for many of my classmates at school. Tennis therefore became my foundation. My tennis skills helped me gain the much sought after respect that I needed from people in both black and white communities. I derived great moral support and confidence from the many compliments on my tennis skills that I received playing on tennis courts in both black and white communities in Connecticut, Massachusetts, New York and North Carolina (where I went every summer for several weeks).

> *"Great athletes have an unwavering belief in their athletic abilities...the secret of success of every extraordinary athlete."*

Breaking The Barriers

Tennis and Success

I attended Hopkins Grammar Day Prospect Hill School (Hopkins) from 8th grade through high school. Founded in 1660 in New Haven, Connecticut, Hopkins is the third oldest high school in the United States. Even though it is located in the same town as the prestigious Yale University, it was actually founded as a prep school for Boston's Harvard University because Yale was not founded until 1701. I grew to love this school because it pushed me to excel academically and athletically. However, when I first attended the school I felt I did not belong at such a prestigious and historic school.

In many people's lives there are mentors that influence them to get the most out of their skills and abilities. One such mentor was my 8th grade math teacher and tennis coach Bill Ewen. Mr. Ewen was an excellent teacher who helped me develop a deep love of math in 8th grade. He was also the Hopkins varsity tennis coach and an accomplished player who had very high rankings in the New England Section of the USLTA. In addition, he was a very religious man and was the first white person in the tennis world that I met who viewed people as exactly the same regardless of their race or economic status. He not only helped to improve my tennis game, he taught me that I was no different than any of the white players at the school. I played on the junior varsity tennis team in 9th grade and the varsity team in the 10th, 11th and 12th grades. I went on to become the number 1 tennis player for part of my junior year and all of my senior year. As captain of the tennis team my senior year, I gained great confidence in my leadership skills and led the team on the first spring trip. This position was the start of a lifetime of significant leadership positions in business, government, education and nonprofits, as well as tennis.

My success in tennis at Hopkins played a vitally important role in my success as a student. Hopkins is so well respected that an amazingly high percentage of students are accepted at Yale, Harvard and Princeton. Fortunately, all of the students in my senior year went on to great colleges. This included eleven students attending Yale (11% of the class), five attending Harvard (5% of the class) and two of us attending Princeton (2% of the class). Unfortunately, there were very few African-American students at the school. In my class, the class of 1978, only three black students (all men) graduated in a class of 100 boys and girls.

Amazingly, in elementary and high school, I never had a black or Hispanic woman in my class. Fortunately, the school has done a wonderful job of increasing diversity since I left. Hopkins is clearly one of the best high schools in the US. However, it was a challenge being one of the only African-American students in the school in the 1970s. I never felt comfortable "hanging out" with my classmates and I was often reluctant to speak up in class (even if I knew the answer to a question). Tennis played a critical role in helping me overcome my insecurities in this seemingly "foreign" environment.

Black Tennis History Reflection

As a history student, I learned about the significant role that tennis played in the lives of extremely successful white and black leaders. This knowledge gave me great insight into the very important ways that tennis helps people achieve extraordinary things outside of tennis. Very few people know that some of the best white and black tennis players were very accomplished in fields outside of the sport. For example, Frederick Winslow Taylor was an expert in industrial efficiency who created business process analysis. He is the author of *The Principles of Scientific Management* and is frequently referred to as the "Father" of the extremely influential management consulting profession. However, he made tennis history by winning the first US Nationals Men's Doubles Championship with Clarence Clark in 1881.

A mathematician, inventor and the author of one of the most popular children's books in history, *Alice's Adventures in Wonderland*, Lewis Carrol (whose real name was Charles Lutwidge Dodgson) is credited with creating the seeding system used in tennis tournaments. US President Teddy Roosevelt loved tennis so much that he formed an informal "Tennis Cabinet" with people in his administration.

In the black community, the winner of the Women's Singles division in the first American Tennis Association (ATA) National Championships, Lucy Diggs Slowe, was the founder of the Alpha Kappa Alpha Sorority (one of the most influential organizations in black society). Eugene Kinkle Jones was one of the seven founders of the legendary Alpha Phi Alpha Fraternity and the first executive secretary of the National Urban League. He won the 1920 ATA Men's Doubles Championship with B.M. Clark. The legendary black leader, educator, author, orator and presidential advisor Booker T. Washington was such a fan of tennis that he had a tennis court (the first at a black college) put into the president's residence at Tuskegee Normal and Industrial Institute.

* * *

I gained a deeper appreciation for the significant role tennis played in my accomplishments when I learned that tennis provided a foundation that helped to produce both white and black leaders. Many people who grew up playing tennis at a high level have become successful in society because the sport has a unique way of developing a person intellectually, emotionally and physically. I am clearly not as accomplished as the legends I mention in the panel. However, tennis has played a vital important role in every accomplishment in my life.

Harry Hopman's Tennis Camp

My success playing tennis at Hopkins convinced me that I was a good player. However, it was clear that I was not fully utilizing all of my skills on the tennis court because I did not have a chance to play against the best players in my age group. My parents and I therefore decided that I should attend a national tennis training camp to test my tennis abilities against some of the best junior players in the world. Unfortunately, as a minister and teacher they did not have much extra money so they made some incredible financial sacrifices so that I could attend a legendary tennis camp in Florida for a week.

My Mom taught me that I should always strive to be around the best and most successful people I can find. Therefore, after a great deal of reflection and research, we agreed that I should go to the best tennis camp we could find. Attending a tennis camp was a big decision for me because I had never been away from home. My parents were very protective of me. Consequently, even though I was 16, I was very dependent on my parents and had little interest in traveling on my own. However, we all agreed that this experience would, at a minimum, help me as I prepare to make the transition from living at home to living on a college campus.

I therefore went to Harry Hopman's world famous tennis camp at the Bardmoor Golf and Tennis Club in Largo, Florida in the summer of 1976 (between my sophomore and junior year of high school). Harry Christian Hopman is considered by many to be the best tennis coach in history. He was without question the most successful Davis Cup Captain/Coach in history. The Davis Cup is an international men's team tennis competition among countries. It is now the largest international team sports competition in the world (in terms of country participation). Harry Hopman was inducted into the International Tennis Hall of Fame (ITHF) in 1978 because he was an accomplished player (winning the 1939 US Nationals Mixed Doubles title and the Australian 1930, 1936-37 and 1939 Mixed Doubles title) who led his native country Australia to a record 16 Davis Cups between 1939 and 1967.

He was born in 1906 and evolved into one of the first coaches in sports to put an intense emphasis on physical and mental fitness. He pushed his players physically, mentally and emotionally morning, noon and night until they had the skill and drive that they needed to became world champions. Hopman was the first tennis coach to make exceptional physical fitness a priority. He put his players through grueling off court exercises and intense on-court drills. He helped his players enhance their focus in a match by making them play when they were exhausted. The Australian players he helped to develop included ITHF Inductees (alphabetically with their year of induction in parenthesis) Roy Emerson (1982), Lew Hoad (1980), Rod Laver (1981), John Newcombe (1986), Tony Roche (1986), Ken Rosewall (1980) and Fred Stolle (1985), among others. He moved to the US in the late 1960s to help to start a tennis camp at the Port Washington Tennis Academy in New York where he helped to guide the development of legendary tennis pros Vitas Gerulitis and John McEnroe. In the 1970s, he opened the Harry Hopman Tennis Academy in Largo, Florida. My time in this special camp changed my life.

When I first arrived at the camp I remember stating quietly to myself, "This place is one of the largest and most beautiful sports complexes that I have ever seen." The Har-Tru clay tennis courts seemed to go on forever. The golf course was immaculate. I thought that the swimming pool and dining areas were among the nicest in the world. I was initially intimidated by the magnitude and design of this incredible facility. In addition, because of my insecurity about my tennis game and the extremely obvious fact that I was the only African-American at the camp, I was very nervous about my ability to fit in both on and off of the tennis court. However, the warmth of the other players and the coaches put me at ease immediately.

After the meeting the evening before our first morning workout, I knew that I could fit in off of the court. However, I was at the camp with many nationally and internationally ranked junior players so I had no idea if I could fit in on the tennis court. At that first meeting, I distinctly remember how the coaches emphasized discipline, timeliness and exercise. The rigid daily schedule was a 5:20 AM wake-up call, 6:00 AM breakfast, 6:45 AM exercise, 7:30 AM-11:30 AM tennis training, 12:00noon-12:30 PM lunch, 1:00 PM-4:00 PM tennis training, 4:00 PM-6:00 PM free practice or recreation time, 6:00 PM-7:00 PM dinner, 9:30 PM strictly enforced lights out. I also remember the coaches saying that we should feel free to use the game room, pool or golf course during our free time (knowing that we would not have the time or energy to do anything else other than sleep, eat and play tennis). I was so exhausted from the training that I never used the pool, golf course or game room.

The first day of the camp was the most important because they evaluated everyone's tennis ability and potential. Their plan was to divide the players into three co-ed groups based entirely on tennis ability. I was one of the few students there who did not have a national or sectional ranking so they had no idea of my skills. Frankly, because I had never been in a situation with so many great tennis players I had no idea of my level. Much to my surprise, and probably to the surprise of the coaches, my skills on the tennis court put me in the top group.

As expected, the training for this group was very intense. Harry Hopman and his team of outstanding coaches put great emphasis on conditioning and movement rather than the mechanics of tennis strokes. The focus of our instruction was on footwork, striking the ball effectively, court strategy and endurance. The fact that the summer temperatures often hit 90 degrees in Florida in July did not prevent them from pushing us as hard as they possibly could on the court. I was amazed how rapidly my game improved. I was not only able to compete with the top players, I became one of the better players there. Clearly, if I had this type of training regularly I could have been a highly ranked national or international player.

Black Tennis History Reflection

Years later, as I was researching black tennis history and reflecting on the incredible growth of my tennis game at Harry Hopman's camp, I realized how discrimination limited the ability of black players to improve their skills by regularly competing with the best white players in the world. There has been a lot of attention paid to the ways that racial discrimination limited the ability of black players to enter Grand Slam and other tournaments. However, there has been very little focus on the ways that racial discrimination prevented the global ascendance of black players capable of winning Grand Slam tournaments prior to the amazing careers of Gibson, Ashe, Yannick Noah and Venus and Serena Williams.

Every great tennis player in history developed their skills by competing against the best players in their respective country when they were growing up. Players like Don Budge, Rod Laver, Margaret Court, Billie Jean King, Jimmy Connors, Chris Evert, Bjorn Borg, John McEnroe, Stefi Graf, Monica Seles, Roger Federer, Rafael Nadal and Novak DJokovic became great because they regularly practiced and played against people that pushed them to raise their tennis skills to levels that even they might not have thought they could achieve. Racial prejudiced denied black players that opportunity. Many black tennis players who might have become legends never had a chance to maximize the development of their skills by competing on a regular basis with the best white players in the world who had access to the best coaching, conditioning and competition.

* * *

Breaking The Barriers

I attended the camp the summer before Hopman protégé John McEnroe surprised the world by going through qualifying to get to the semi-finals of Wimbledon. John's success at Wimbledon and beyond helped to increase the reputation of the camp. I also had the great honor of visiting briefly with Harry Hopman and his wife Lucy at their condo on the grounds of the camp. They were truly wonderful people. Hopman was in his late 60s at the time. However, he could still hit the tennis ball very well. He was also a very gracious person who respectfully pushed people to get the most out of their skills and abilities. I am convinced that if Harry Hopman had been a little younger at the time, John McEnroe's success on the professional circuit would have inspired more top players to come to the camp and it would have produced more champions than any tennis camp in history. Unfortunately, Harry Hopman passed away in 1985 at the age of 79 and has been missed dearly by those in the professional tennis world who knew him. Sadly, the camp never achieved its full potential.

South Africa During Apartheid

My experience at Harry Hopman's tennis camp led to success in high school tennis, a Sectional ranking in the New England Lawn Tennis Association (NELTA) and a National ranking in the ATA. This success on the tennis court played an important role in helping me gain the confidence I needed to do well in school, in life and in human interaction. My confidence in my tennis skills and intellectual abilities played a vitally important part in helping me gain admission to Princeton University (my first-choice college).

At Princeton, I played on the second level of the Men's Tennis Team (which was ranked in the top ten nationally) and later left the team (because the coach consistently placed players that I beat in challenge matches ahead of me) to teach tennis in the Princeton Community Tennis Program that was led by the late legendary community tennis pioneer Eve Kraft. This experience eventually convinced me to become a Certified United States Professional Tennis Association (USPTA) tennis teaching pro in 1985. I really enjoyed teaching tennis and, because I lived in Harrisburg at the time, became an insider in the Central Pennsylvania tennis world.

In 1986, I was selected to participate in a historic Rotary International Group Study Exchange Trip to Malawi, Swaziland, Zimbabwe and the Republic of South Africa at a time when the racial system called Apartheid (where blacks were denied the right to live, eat, go to the bathroom or drink at the same water fountains or go to the same movie theaters as whites) was being enforced.

The trip was sponsored by the Rotary Foundation, which is the charitable arm of the largest service organizations in the world. For decades Rotary International operated "Group Study Exchanges" to increase world understanding. In this unique program, people from one part of the world (where a Rotary chapter is located) visit another part of the world (where one or more Rotary chapters are located) to share life experiences. The visitors learn more about the countries they are visiting because they stay in the homes of Rotarians instead of local hotels. This living arrangement fosters some amazing interaction between residents of two very different countries.

As an African-American, I was very excited about the opportunity to go to Africa and learn about life in Malawi, Swaziland and Zimbabwe. However, it was 1985, and the inhuman system of legalized segregation that the South African Government called "Apartheid" was the law of the land. If the trip had been anywhere else in the world, I would have instantaneously decided to go on the trip. However, because the trip included a visit to racially stratified South Africa (and I was the only African-American selected for the trip), I was very concerned about going to a place filled with such prejudice for six very intense weeks.

Black Tennis History Reflection

Unfortunately, many people are not aware of the significant role that Arthur Ashe played in helping to eliminate legalized segregation in South Africa. As the son of parents who grew up in the segregated South and marched with Dr. King, I was very conscious of the racial struggle in America and around the world. I remembered hearing the stories of Arthur Ashe's first visit to South Africa. After trying for many years, Arthur Ashe was able to get an invitation to play in the South African Open tennis tournament in 1973. He decided to go to South

Africa to see how his presence could force the government to change their laws of racial segregation. Ashe felt that if the white leaders saw a black man competing on an equal playing field in an elite sport with white athletes they might realize the potential of black citizens and consider revising some of their policies. However, he was confronted by some black Africans and African Americans during his visit who said that by playing in a tournament in South Africa he was "legitimizing" the government's racist policies.

I am convinced that Ashe's visit helped to chip away at racism in the country. However, the comments of some of the black Anti-Apartheid leaders influenced him to rethink his original assumptions and in 1983 form, with Harry Belafonte (the famous actor and singer), "Artists and Athletes Against Apartheid." This organization was founded to encourage the embargo of all artistic and athletic contact with South Africa. Ashe's efforts helped to inspire others to support the boycott of South Africa which was eventually (once major corporations significantly increased their financial pressure on the country) the primary catalyst in dismantling Apartheid.

Since Arthur Ashe was my favorite public figure, I thought long and hard about his experiences and perspective about visiting South Africa in 1986. I therefore asked myself and my family some very difficult questions? Would I be supporting this horrible system if I went? Or, would I be missing an opportunity to educate the racists in Africa and inform the people at home if I did not go? I decided to go on the trip because I felt that I would be a more effective change agent (in both South Africa and America) if I participated in this trip. One of the main reasons that I decided to go was that I was the only African-American going (out of six participants). I therefore felt that I had a responsibility to share my perspective as a black American with the people in the country and in the USA when I returned. In hindsight, I can say with full confidence that going to the country was the right decision.

* * *

I could not sleep on the 17-hour plane ride to Jan Smuts Airport in Johannesburg because I was trying to anticipate what I would experience during my stay in South Africa. Was it a mistake going to South Africa? How would I be treated? Would I be discriminated against? Was my life in danger? Would I stay in the homes of black or white families? Would the black Africans be happy or disappointed to see me? Will I learn the real reason that Apartheid is so important to the government? What will life be like in Malawi, Swaziland and Zimbabwe? The only thing that I remember about my plane ride was that tears came to my eyes when I first saw African land. It was as if I was returning home after a very long time away. I cannot explain the feeling of connectedness that I experienced as I looked down on this foreign land. I remember that very feeling even today. I am convinced that this experience helped to influence me to want to learn and write about black history.

The History of the Breaking the Barriers Exhibit

As the only African-American on the trip, it was a life-changing experience for me because visiting southern Africa gave me an opportunity to experience first-hand the systematic racism that was experienced by blacks in the United States during legalized segregation.

It was as if I had jumped into a time machine and gone back to the early 20th Century in the Southern part of the US. I was not allowed to eat in certain places or drink from some water fountains in South Africa because I was black. I was denied admission to two movie theatres in Johannesburg because I was black (One of the movies was *Out of Africa* and, surprisingly, the other was *White Nights* starring the black actor Gregory Hines). I was viewed as a second class human being because I was black. These experiences gave me insight into the emotional, psychological and physiological toll that prejudice has on human beings. This racism forced me to question my value as a human being. Even though I was a recent Princeton graduate, who was accomplished professionally, it made me (both consciously and subconsciously) feel like I was not as good as the South African whites. One of the challenges in society is that people who have never experienced racism firsthand do not understand the impact that being treated because of what you look like has on their sense of self-worth.

Breaking The Barriers

Words cannot describe how painful it is to experience institutionalized racism. In many ways the pain is even greater when you have been successful in a more open white environment. I will never forget the internal pain and anger that I experienced in South Africa.

Incredibly, even in the short time I experienced Apartheid, this racism stifled my drive for success. As a 25 year-old who experienced this type of deep prejudice for the first time, I temporarily lost some of the faith that I had in my ability to do and be all that I wanted to be. Fortunately, tennis came to the rescue once again. I gained much of my confidence back when I played tennis with a young white man who was one of the best squash players in South Africa. He was obviously much better at squash than tennis. However, by beating him 6-0, 6-0, I regained a belief that I was a very capable and talented a person. This victory reminded me that I was as accomplished as white people my age in South Africa or anywhere else.

I will never forget my experience in South Africa. As someone who has an interest in history, this six-week transformative experience helped me understand, first-hand, the incredible difficulty of breaking through barriers of racial discrimination. I understood the pain that my parents experienced growing up in the segregated South. For the first time, I realized (in a very personal way) how truly incredible black pioneers who fought the racial status quo were. These individuals had to overcome an entrenched system of discrimination that was the formal law of the land. In addition, they had to beat back feelings of insecurity and low self-worth to achieve some incredible things. The accomplishments of legends like Dr. Martin Luther King, Jr., Nelson Mandela, Paul Robeson, Jackie Robinson, Ralph Bunch, and tennis's own Althea Gibson and Arthur Ashe are even more incredible when considered in the context of fighting a nation where racism was the rule not the exception. This trip got me thinking about ways to honor those individuals who broke through barriers of discrimination but were in danger of being overlooked by the history books.

I began this chapter by briefly describing how the Breaking the Barriers Exhibit was approved by the ITHF. However, I will share the story now in the context of my personal experiences and beliefs related to black tennis history. I invite you, my reader, to empathize with my reasons for introducing people of all races and backgrounds to black tennis history. Twenty years after my trip to Southern Africa, I had the opportunity to honor individuals who were pioneers in tennis. After, returning from Southern Africa I became very active in tennis by running monthly tennis events and volunteering for the USTA. In 2006, with the support of many wonderful people (including the legendary 2008 ITHF Inductee Gene Scott) I broke through a tennis barrier myself by becoming the first black president and chief executive officer (CEO) of the United States Tennis Association (USTA) Eastern Section.

In this role, I was the individual ultimately responsible for leading the section board of directors, overseeing the daily activities of the executive director and ensuring that our mission of "promoting and developing the growth of tennis in New York State, Northern New Jersey and Southern Connecticut" was realized. Serving as the first black leader of this section of the USTA (and the third black section president in USTA history) was particularly significant because the association's major tournament (the US Open) and policies of segregation all originated in New York City (which is an important part of the Section that I led).

My trip to South Africa inspired me (over the subsequent 20 years) to research the stories of talented black tennis players, who, because of racism, could not compete in "White Only" tournaments. My research uncovered many fascinating stories about the perseverance of black tennis players through incredible obstacles. I was afraid that the world would not know these stories. I therefore used my influence as the first black president of the USTA Eastern Section to write a letter to legendary player and International Tennis Hall of Fame (ITHF) president (and 1970 Inductee) Tony Trabert suggesting that the ITHF create an exhibit to honor black tennis history.

I was attempting to use my newly acquired status in the tennis world to convince the Hall of Fame to develop an exhibit honoring black players that could not play in USLTA tournaments because of their race. In the letter, I mentioned that Major League Baseball has had tremendous success honoring players who, because of institutionalized racism, were restricted to playing in baseball's Negro Leagues. It would therefore make sense to do the same thing by honoring the American Tennis Association (ATA) and the players that starred in their tournaments.

Breaking The Barriers

I emailed a famous friend of my dad's named Bud Collins (the legendary tennis historian and commentator who was inducted into the ITHF in 1994 for his broadcast work and incredible books on tennis history) to get his support for this idea. In my opinion, the late Bud Collins was one of the two most entertaining personalities in tennis (the late Vic Braden was the other). I will never forget Bud's comment when I emailed him about this idea. He said, "Why didn't I think of it?" I am convinced that he was very helpful in lobbying behind the scenes for the creation of the exhibit on black tennis history.

I was pleasantly surprised that the ITHF liked the idea and agreed to develop an exhibit on black tennis history that would be displayed during the 2007 US Open in Flushing Meadows, New York. Since the exhibit was my idea, I was asked by Ken Yellis, the ITHF Museum director when the project was approved by the board, to become the curator of this exhibit and play a critical role in the design of the exhibit and black tennis history research. Unfortunately, Ken left the organization before the project got off of the ground. The project was given to the new ITHF Museum Director Gary Cogar. He agreed to keep me on as curator and we got the project started immediately.

Gary was a former dentist who developed a love for leading museums. He decided to leave his practice and pursue museum leadership. The ITHF was fortunate to hire someone with his knowledge about museum leadership, passion for history and exceptional human interaction skills. When I first talked to him about black tennis history it was clear that Gary was born to lead this project. He was a white dentist with museum experience who knew nothing about black tennis history when this project started. However, he developed as deep a passion as any human being could possibly have for this exhibit. Gary went above and beyond the call of duty to ensure that this exhibit was as comprehensive, accurate and informative as possible. It was clear that he fell in love with black tennis history. I will always be indebted to him for being the person principally responsible for making my vision a reality. Gary and I wanted to involve as many black tennis leaders as possible to ensure the accuracy of the exhibit, so we formed a very diverse exhibit committee comprised primarily of black leaders, tennis players, administrators and writers.

The original committee consisted of the following individuals in alphabetical order: D.A. Abrams; Katrina Adams; Jefferson T. Barnes (representing the ITHF board); Martin Blackman; Dale Caldwell; Arthur

Carrington; Gary Cogar; Bill Davis; Bob Davis; Marvin Dent; The Honorable David Dinkins; Marcus Freeman; Virginia Glass; Arveliea Myers; Iris Rivera; Bob Ryland; and, Willis Thomas, Jr. In addition, I asked one of my heroes of the ATA circuit, Art Carrington (Winner of the 1973 ATA Men's Singles Championship), who is one of the most accomplished black tennis historians in the world, to join me as the co-curator of the exhibit.

After a great deal of debate and thought, Gary, Art and I decided to name the exhibit *"Breaking the Barriers"* to honor those individuals who opened doors of opportunity for others by breaking through barriers of race and class in America. The completed exhibit has become the most popular touring exhibit in the history of the ITHF. A record 26,000 people visited this exhibit when it was first shown for the full two weeks of the 2007 US Open. Since that inaugural exhibit, *Breaking the Barriers* has toured the country and been seen by tens of thousands of people. This exhibit proved, beyond a shadow of a doubt, that there is widespread interest in black tennis history among people of all races, backgrounds and nationalities.

Thanks to Gary Cogar's extraordinary leadership, the exhibit and the accompanying documentary film of the same name were developed in just a few months. It therefore could not be as comprehensive as we would have wanted it to be if we had two years to develop it. We would have included many additional people and organizations if we had more time. The success of this exhibit and the fact that it was incomplete led me to found the Black Tennis Hall of Fame, Inc. (BTHOF) on November 30, 2007 to *"Celebrate tennis players and contributors who have broken through barriers of race and to use tennis to help young people break through barriers of poverty."* The organization has been a tremendous success since its founding and has honored many of the individuals (some of whom were not included in the exhibit) who overcame tremendous odds to be successful in tennis as either players, administrators or contributors. We provided additional information and biographies of all of the individuals inducted into the BTHOF in Chapter 14.

CHAPTER 2: How Tennis Got its Scoring

Uncertain Beginnings

No one really knows for sure where or why human beings first decided to hit a ball back and forth with sticks. Clearly, the entertainment derived by hitting a round object with a long wooden stick thousands of years ago eventually led to the creation of sports like baseball and cricket. The temptation for another person with a stick to hit the round object back to the person who first hit the object eventually led to the creation of the sport of tennis that we know today.

For more than a century, historians have attempted to chronicle with precision the evolution of the major sports using the modern equivalent of sticks and balls with little success. Incredibly, there appears to be the same level of confusion about the origins of baseball, cricket and tennis. The combination of poor record keeping, rapid innovations and the widespread appeal of these and similar activities prevents the accurate determination of a birth date and birth location for these sports.

Researchers have discovered sports similar to baseball as early as the 14th Century. Germans played a sport called *"Schlagball"*; Romanians played a sport called *"Oina"*; and, Russians played a sport called *"Lapta."* Many baseball experts believe that American baseball is a derivation of the English sport of *"Rounders"* or *"Town Ball."*

Historians believe that cricket either started as a children's game in England or an adult activity in the Netherlands in the 15th Century. Early versions of the sport were called *"Bowls"* and *"Creckett."* The one definitive thing that we know about baseball and cricket is that no one knows specifically how or where these sports were first played.

Tennis suffers from the same level of historical uncertainty as baseball and cricket. Some tennis historians believe that tennis began in early Egypt in or near the town of Tinnis. However, there is no written evidence of the sport being played in Egypt in ancient times. Most researchers feel that tennis has origins in the monasteries of the Catholic Church.

The Grandparent of Modern Tennis

For hundreds of years the church was the only place that provided "non-royalty" with a good education. Many of the most educated people in society were therefore monks or nuns. Consequently, monks, who had both discipline and time, played an extremely important role in society. In addition to making many scholarly contributions to society, Italian monks are credited with inventing the pretzel while French monks are credited with inventing both champagne and a sport that I consider the most famous "ancestor" of tennis.

France can be considered the first "Tennis Capital of the World" because most experts on tennis history believe that the likely origins of the sport of tennis were monastery cloisters in France in the 11th century. In these serene environments, French monks in the Catholic Church, seeking entertainment and exercise, played a sport called *"Jeu de Paume"* or *"game of the hand."* If one considers the "family history" of tennis, this new sport was to become the "Grandparent" of modern tennis.

The monks who created jeu de paume were individuals who practiced religious asceticism by living with other monks and separating themselves from those people who did not share the same belief or commitment. They spent a great deal of time distancing themselves from society and dedicated their lives to praying, thinking and exercise.

These monks lived in a monastery under vows of obedience, chastity and poverty. They pledged to obey the Catholic Church; sacrifice the love between men and woman (and therefore not marry); and renounce ownership of property and share what little they had with the poor. However, in spite of these restrictions on their lifestyle they were able to actively engage in other forms of entertainment. To stay in shape they developed the sport of jeu de paume where they used their bare hands to hit balls (likely made of cork, wool or hair wrapped in leather, cloth or string) off of outdoor walls or over a rope strung across a courtyard.

The earliest rules of jeu de paume were very similar to those of modern tennis. There is a clear "family" resemblance between the two sports. Jeu de paume (like modern tennis) was originally played by two people standing on opposite sides of a net or rope in a walled courtyard. One person (the server) would start the point by hitting the ball off of the wall to a specific area on the other person's (the receiver's) side of the court. The receiver would attempt to return the ball. The two players would hit the ball back and forth until one person won the point by hitting a winner or the other lost the point by hitting the ball out of bounds, below the rope (or into the net). The first person to win four points and was ahead by two points won the game. In the event that the score was 3 points all they would continue playing until one player was ahead by two points. The player that won 6 games won the set. The player that won two out of three sets won the match.

Jeu de paume in the 17th century.

Jeu de paume became very popular as a way for the monks to exercise and have fun. The sport was also gaining interest outside of the church. Word spread outside of the monasteries about this fun game. This led to private courts being built by wealthy citizens as early as 1230 A.D. The growing interest in jeu de paume among the wealthy led to the development of indoor courts throughout France where weather could not limit play. The increase in the number of courts increased the popularity of the sport so rapidly that it became a distraction for many citizens (especially the monks).

To prevent sore hands and increase the pace with which they could hit the ball players began to use webbed gloves to play the game. Over the years, innovators in the sport convinced players to transition from gloves to paddles to racquets (which were originally called "battoirs") with sheep gut strings to hit the ball back and forth with maximum pace and control.

This recreational activity became so popular and time consuming that many leaders of the church neglected their duties so that they would have more time to play the sport they were addicted to. Jeu de paume became such a distraction that in 1245 the Archbishop of Rouen prohibited his priests from playing the sport. The development of indoor courts led to the rapid spread of jeu de paume (which at this time was most frequently referred to as simply "paume") to local towns. The growing popularity of the sport among citizens motivated King Louis IX of France to impose a ban on the sport because he considered it too much of a distraction for citizens. These restrictions did not prevent wealthy and influential citizens from playing this popular sport. Jeu de paume therefore continued to grow in popularity in spite of the King's restrictions.

The sport became one of the most popular pastimes of the rich and influential. This led to some fascinating stories about the sport. It is even believed that in the early years of paume, one French King lost his life because of his passion for the sport. King Louis X of France, who ruled from 1314 to 1316, died of an illness related to a chill (probably pneumonia) from playing an intense game of paume on a cold rainy day at Chateau de Vincennes in 1316. Clearly the ailment that we know today as the "tennis bug" (where people become so addicted to playing tennis they neglect their family, work and even health) existed in the early days of the sport.

The early paume courts differed somewhat in size and shape from place to place. The very first courts made full use of existing courtyards. However, the later courts were enclosed on all four sides with a slopping roof on three of the four sides of the court. Some courts had galleries under the sloping roofs for spectators. The courts were between 30 and 40 feet wide and 90 and 100 feet long. They were unique in design because the dimensions on either side of the net were not uniform. Each court had a net stretched across the middle that was approximately 5 feet high at the ends and 3 feet high in the middle.

The original French scoring used in paume most likely was based on the face of a clock. Since customized score boards did not exist at the time players used clock faces to score each game which started at "l'Oeuf" (which meant egg and symbolized zero). The first point was "15" or "Quinze." The second point was "30" or "Trente." The third point was "45" or "Quarante-cinq." Over time the third point was reduced simply to "Quarante" or "40" because Quarante was easier and quicker off of the tongue than Quarante-cinq. The winner of four points won the "game" or "Jeu."

Over the years slightly different rules were applied to the sport. However, the game always began with one person hitting (or "serving") the ball off of the roof to their opponent on the other side of the net. The players could utilize different obstacles (i.e. windows, corners, etc.) to prevent a player from returning the ball. The first player to reach six games won the set (there was no tie-breaker or requirement to win by two games). The first player to win two sets won the match.

It is believed that the Italians created the first paume racquets which had a handle and oval or tear drop shaped head. These racquets were generally between 25" and 28" long. The racquet strings were made of sheep gut which allowed players to utilize different spins when hitting the ball. The paume ball was between 2" and 3" in diameter and weighed about 2 ½ ounces. The ball had a cork core and was wrapped with a strong wool cloth. It was therefore hard and did not bounce very well. The game was great exercise and favored athletes with quick reflexes and the ability to control precisely where they hit the ball. Paume was a game of leisure at that time so there were no organizations developing structured competitions.

The Obsession with the Sport

Paume continued to grow rapidly in popularity throughout France. By some accounts there were over 1,800 courts throughout France, Bavaria and Italy in the 14th century. The rapid spread of the sport continued to concern many of the most powerful people in Europe's royal and religious communities. More and more leaders were convinced that this fun recreational activity impacted the ability of average people to be productive citizens and committed Christians.

After the death of the Holy Roman Emperor Henry VII in 1314, the electors who determined the next emperor selected Louis IV over Henry's young and inexperienced son John of Luxemburg. However, the Pope Clement V and his successor John XXII refused to approve Louis IV's election and claimed that the throne was under Papal rule.

For many years the conflict between Louis IV and Pope John XXII consumed Europe. This conflict was so intense that Pope John XXII excommunicated. Louis IV kicked him out of the church in 1324. However, the one thing that they both had in common was the desire to minimize the distractions of the masses. Even though most of their political and religious views were diametrically opposed they both called for a ban on Jeu de Paume because it had become too much of a distraction among the people.

Once again, this ban did not last long. The development of indoor courts helped the sport maintain its popularity among the upper class of society. King Charles V of France helped to increase interest in indoor courts when he built one in the Palace of the Louvre in 1368. At that time in France there was a clear distinction between indoor courts and outdoor courts. The indoor courts were called "Jeu de Courte Paume" or "Game of the Court Hand" and the outdoor courts were called "Jeu de Longue Paume" or "Game of the Long Hand."

The prohibition on playing paume was not limited to the beginning of the 14th century. Ironically, Charles V (who had one of the most celebrated indoor courts built) was forced to restrict play in 1369 because the popularity of the sport led to widespread gambling.

Breaking The Barriers

Laws (that were limited to the lower classes), were passed prohibiting people from playing paume in England in 1388 because it distracted soldiers from practicing archery (an important skill in warfare).

In Paris, an ordinance making the playing of paume illegal was passed in 1397 because politicians thought that the popularity of the sport motivated large numbers of people to neglect both their families and their jobs. These prohibitions had the opposite effect. They focused attention on the sport and helped to increase interest in the sport in more and more places around the world. Many people became obsessed with this fascinating sport. What we call the "tennis bug" today was alive and well in the 14th century.

CHAPTER 3: How Tennis Got its Name

Tennis and Shakespeare

Henry V was the first King of England to develop a passionate personal interest in paume. This fascinating person is remembered as one of the most influential and powerful Kings in history because of his success in making England the greatest power in Europe. He became King after his father Henry IV's death in 1413. He was an exceptional military strategist who in 1598 was immortalized by William Shakespeare in his play *"The Life of King Henry the Fifth"* because of his surprising victory at Agincourt over superior French forces.

In Act I Scene II of Shakespeare's famous play (which today is known simply as *Henry V*), the Ambassador of France tells Henry V that the Dauphin (a French Prince) *"Says that you savour too much of your youth."* The Ambassador goes on to indicate that the Dauphin has (in jest) given Henry paume balls to encourage him to use his energies in some way other than fighting France.

In response King Henry says *"We are glad the Dauphin is so pleasant with us; His present and your pains we thank you for. When we have match'd our rackets to these balls, we will in France by God's grace, play a set, shall strike his father's crown into the hazard. Tell him he hath made a match with such a wrangler that all the courts of France will be disturb'd with chaces... And tell the pleasant Prince this mock of his hath turned his balls to gun-stones."*[4] King Henry is saying that the gift of paume balls insulted him so much that he now plans to fight France.

Henry V conquered most of Northern France from French King Charles IV and was named heir to the French throne and regent of France in 1420. He married Charles's daughter Catherine in 1421 and

[4] *The Chronicle History of Henry the Fifth* by William Shakespeare (Published: 1600)

they had a son Henry on December 6, 1421. Henry V's new role as King of England and France and his union with Catherine were very significant developments in the growth of the early version of modern tennis.

In Shakespeare's play Henry V is depicted as someone who was so concerned about the perspective of average people that he wandered around military camps in disguise at night to find out how his troops really felt about him. This curiosity likely played a role in Henry V developing a love for the sport that will later be known as "tennis."

Henry V died suddenly in 1422 at the age of 34 because of an acute case of dysentery that even the best physicians of the time could not cure. Consequently, his son Henry VI became King of England and France when he was just 8 months old. The ascension of a baby to the throne led to incredible political infighting and chaos which eventually led to Henry VI's two separate reigns as King of England and his murder in 1471. However, during this chaotic time in history the sport of paume not only survived, it was being transformed into "Tennis" in England.

How Tennis Got To England

King Henry V most probably was introduced to paume by his French wife Catherine. His natural curiosity about the perspectives of non-royalty led to his discovery of the wide-spread popularity of paume among the people of France. He fell in love with the game and played it regularly. As the newly recognized King of England and France, he played an important role in introducing the sport to Royal English society where it became very popular as a sport of the wealthy and well-heeled. Most importantly, the English influenced the renaming of the sport. As described below, the popularity of the sport in England and the transition of its commonly accepted name from paume to "Royal Tennis" can be considered the birth of the parent of modern tennis.

The Renaming of the Sport

Before the start of each point in paume the server would shout the French word "tenez" (an imperative meaning to "hold" or "take heed") to alert his or her opponent that he or she was about to serve the ball. The term was uttered as a simple way of saying, "Get ready; I am about to serve the ball." The growing popularity of the sport among the English speaking led to the reworking of the French term "tenez" to "tenetz" to "tennes" to "tennys" and eventually to "tennis." Since the term was uttered before each point it eventually became the commonly used name of the sport. As a result, Jeu de Paume was renamed "Tennis" in England. The name was expanded to become "Tenys Playe" and then "Royal Tennis" because of the sport's popularity among royalty in England.

The adoption of the name "Royal Tennis" can be considered the point in history when the sport became the "Parent" of modern tennis. If one were listing the genealogy of the sport they might list "Jeu de Paume" as the "Grandparent" of modern tennis and "Royal Tennis" the "Parent" of modern tennis. I am pleased to report that modern tennis's "parent" is still alive today and goes by the name "Court Tennis." This sport mirrors jeu de paume and is played in exclusive venues throughout the world. One of the best known court tennis facilities is at the International Tennis Hall of Fame in Newport, Rhode Island.

Cataclysmic Global Change

Royal Tennis remained popular in both England and France from the Time of Henry V's death through the reign of Henry VII. However, political in-fighting in England led to five Kings and six different reigns over a relatively brief of 14 years. Unfortunately, the chaos in royal leadership from Henry V's death in 1471 to Henry VII's reign in 1485 limited the growth of "Royal Tennis" in England. France remained the "Tennis Capital of the World" during this period of history because of the popularity of the sport and the stability of its political leadership.

The sport was extremely popular among both royalty and commoners in France. The popularity of the sport among the wealthy eventually spread to the middle and even to the lower classes. People at all levels of society caught the "tennis bug" and played regularly. It is said that the royal obsession for this sport even led to the death of one French King during this time period. King Charles VIII of France, who ruled from 1483-1498 and was a passionate player of this popular sport, died of a head injury after striking his head on a piece of wood in the entryway leading to his paume court in 1498.

Henry VII was the King of England from 1485 to 1509. He was the last King of England to win his throne on the battlefield after having defeated Richard III at the Battle of Bosworth Field. Henry VII was a powerful, well-respected leader whose reign of 23 years brought political stability to the country. His interest in royal tennis and role as a "tennis parent" significantly increased the popularity of the sport among both English royal society and the masses.

His son, Henry VIII, was born on June 28, 1491 and served as King of England from 1509 until his death in 1547. Henry VIII is often remembered as a morbidly obese man who led the separation of the Church of England from the Roman Catholic Church and had his wife Anne Boleyn beheaded. However, few people know that when he was young he was a handsome and athletic boy who was a talented royal tennis player. More importantly, he played an important leadership role in the growth of royal tennis in England.

Henry VII, like most tennis parents, introduced his son to the sport of tennis early in his life. Young Henry VIII became an excellent junior player and fell in love with the sport. He was a fantastic athlete who was considered one of the better players in the country. He became King of England on April 21, 1509 at the age of 17 and over time developed complete control of the government and eventually over the church as well.

Henry VIII was an intense ruler whose bitter fight with Rome led to the separation of the Church of England from the Roman Catholic Church. His hunger for power led to his appointment as the Supreme Head of the Church of England. His obsessive desire for a male heir led to his six marriages and continual conflict in his personal life. Henry VIII's complete control of the church in England, multiple marriages and execution of two wives (Anne Boleyn and Catherine Howard) helped to make him one of the most colorful and controversial figures in history.

However, one of the positive aspects of his legacy is the role he played in increasing interest in royal tennis in England. Throughout most of his reign, Henry VIII played royal tennis regularly and helped

Breaking The Barriers

to increase the sport's popularity among the upper class men and women of England. Most competitions were between people of the same gender. However, there were some "mixed" competitions between men and women. Henry VIII's love of the game motivated him to order the building of spectacular royal tennis courts in England. One of which, the Royal Tennis Court, Hampton Court Palace, where Henry VIII played in 1528 is still in use today.

Tennis was such a consistent part of his daily life it is believed that he was playing tennis when he got the official word that his wife Anne Boleyn was beheaded. Unfortunately, late in his life, he was prevented from exercising regularly because of illness and compulsive eating. He therefore did not play royal tennis regularly in the last years of his life and grew to be an immobile obese man with a waist of 54 inches. The incredible popularity of royal tennis with the upper echelons of the English and French society led to an expansion among the rich and influential in Germany, Italy and Spain.

Tennis Begone—But Not for Long

For more than 100 years after Henry VIII's death in 1547, the English Monarchy experienced great chaos. Interest in royal tennis waned because of the instability of the country's leadership and the growing influence of the Puritans who did not believe in entertainment of any kind. It was King Charles II's return to the throne after his exile that reignited interest in royal tennis in English society. The King had a passion for royal tennis. Consequently, one of his very first official actions when he was restored to the throne in 1660 was to order the restoration of the royal tennis court at Hampton Court Palace.

After a chaotic reign of King James II (1685-1688), interest in royal tennis continued to grow under the reign of King William III and Queen Mary II. Their equal joint reign (the first and only one in English history) began in 1689. They were successful in establishing "An Act Declaring the Rights and Liberties of the Subject and Settling the Succession of the Crown" (which is commonly called the "English Bill of Rights") in that same year. This important document helped to unify the country by easing long-standing tensions between Parliament and the monarchs. The Bill of Rights gave more power to common people by requiring the Crown to seek the consent of citizens through their representatives in Parliament.

The English Bill of Rights was an extremely important document in world history because it inspired citizens to demand power from their political leaders. This important document not only helped to motivate French citizens to revolt, it inspired individuals in the Americas to rebel against the oppressive rules of King James II which were still in place at the time.

In 1693, King William and Queen Mary also signed the charter for a "Perpetual College of Divinity, Philosophy, Languages, and other good Arts and Sciences" to be founded in the colony of Virginia. This school was named William and Mary and it was the second college founded in America (Harvard was the first). This school played an important role in the founding of the United States.

George Washington received his surveyor's license from William and Mary and future Presidents Thomas Jefferson, John Tyler and James Monroe received their undergraduate education from the college. In addition, one hundred years later the English Bill of Rights inspired the development of the United States Bill of Rights (which is the name given to the first ten amendments to the US Constitution as presented by James Madison) in 1789.

King William III and Queen Mary II were fans of royal tennis and were committed to ensuring that the royal tennis court at Hampton Court Palace was in pristine condition. They were so proud that the facility was in perfect shape they had their royal initials placed above the net on the wall opposite the corridors leading to the court. Their passion for royal tennis combined with the increasing influence of average citizens provided opportunities for non-royalty to play royal tennis.

The English Bill of Rights played an important role in inspiring people over the next one hundred years to fight for individual liberty and personal prosperity. Many important historical events took place over this time period. In 1694, the Bank of England, the world's first central bank was formed. The global Industrial Revolution began in1700 and enabled many common citizens (those not born of titled nobility) to acquire great wealth.

Breaking The Barriers

The growing influence of the English language was symbolized by Samuel Johnson's *Dictionary of the English Language* published in 1718. In the early part of the 18th century, Royal Tennis remained very popular in Europe during this time of cataclysmic change. The sport was introduced to more people in more places than ever before. However, the growing focus on achieving quick wealth increased interest in gambling on the sport. Widespread wagering tarnished the reputation of the sport. The waning influence of royalty combined with corruption in the sport led to its limited popularity in France in the second half of the century.

Although little is written about it, the sport of tennis had reached the Americas by the mid-1600s and was played regularly by members of the upper class in the 1700s. It is believed that in October of 1656 and September of 1659 Peter Stuyvesant, the 7th and last Dutch Director-General of the colony of New Netherland (which is now New York City) from 1647 to 1664 issued proclamations banning all exercise and "Games of tennis, ball-playing, hunting, plowing and sowing..." during holy days.[5] This proclamation was the first written mention of the "parent" of modern tennis (royal tennis) in the Americas. It signified that the playing of tennis was widespread enough in the mid-1600s to be banned on Christian holy days.

Esther Singleton, in her book *Social New York Under the Georges*[6], mentions that Governor William Burnet, the British civil servant and

---

[5] In October 1656 Director-General Peter Stuyvesant announced a stricter Sabbath Law in New Netherlands, including a fine of one pound Flemish for "playing ball," cricket, tennis, ninepins, dancing, drinking, etc. Source: 13: Doc Hist., Volume iv, pages.13-15, and Father Jogues' papers in NY Hist. Soc. Coll., 1857, pp. 161-229, as cited in *Manual of the Reformed Church in America* (Formerly Ref. Prot. Dutch Church), 1628-1902, E. T. Corwin, D.D., Fourth Edition (Reformed Church in America, New York, 1902.) and "We shall interdict and forbid, during divine service on the [fasting] day aforesaid, all exercise and games of tennis, ball-playing, hunting, plowing and sowing, and moreover all unlawful practice such as dice, drunkenness . . ." proclaimed Peter Stuyvesant. Manchester, Herbert, *Four Centuries of Sport in America* [Published: 1931]. The proclamation is on display in Stad Huys (City Hall) in Amsterdam, Holland.

[6] *Social New York under the Georges*, 1714-1776: Houses, Streets, and Country Homes, with Chapters on Fashions, Furniture, China, Plate, and Manners by Esther Singleton (New York: D. Appleton and Com-

colonial administrator who served as Governor of New York and New Jersey from 1720-1728, was an avid sportsman and royal tennis player who listed tennis equipment including "Seven dozen tennis balls" in his personal inventory upon his death in 1729. The book also mentions that in 1766, one of the leading importers of the times, James Rivington, "Imported battledores and shuttlecocks, cricket-balls, pillets, best racquets for tennis and fives, backgammon tables with men boxes and dice."[7] Royal tennis was clearly an important sport in America even during the politically chaotic times of the mid 1600s and 1700s.

In the latter half of the century, major social and political upheaval led to some of the most important events in world history. The Declaration of Independence of the United States was ratified in 1776 while, in 1781, John Hanson was elected the president of the Continental Congress and is considered by some the first president of the United States prior to the ratification of the United States Constitution. Clearly, 1789 was an exceptionally important year in world history. That year, the United States Constitution was ratified and George Washington was elected the first president under the new Constitution. In addition, the French Revolution "Court Tennis Oath" took place.

The Court Tennis Oath

Between 1787 and 1799 there was great unrest in France stimulated by a deep desire of citizens for the same rights of commoners in other countries; crop failures; a peasant revolt against the feudal system (which denied independent land ownership to average citizens); a growing middle class that was denied real political power; a fiscal crisis (intensified by support for the American Revolution); and, the attempt of the regime to increase taxes. In an effort to solve the crisis, French King Louis XVI convened a group called the "Estates-General" comprised of clergy, the nobility and common citizens (who were referred to as the "Third Estate") in 1789.

---

pany, 1902)
[7] Ibid.

Breaking The Barriers

The Estates-General was an antiquated aspect of the French governing system that had not been invoked for 150 years. It was typically used when the monarchy sought input from others (usually in a crisis). The body had no clearly defined powers. However, it was divided into three distinct groups. The first group consisted of the clergy and was called the "First Estate." The second group consisted of the nobility and was called the "Second Estate." The third group consisted of all others and was called the "Third Estate."

Holding Court on the Tennis Court

This Estates-General of 1789 was the impetus for the famous "serment" du jeu de paume" ("oath of the game of hand") which today is referred to as the "Tennis Court Oath." Convinced that they would be attacked by King Louis XVI, a group of 577 members of the "Tiers Etat" (Third Estate), led by French revolutionary Honore Gabriel Riqueti, gathered in the court tennis court at Versailles on June 20, 1789 during the Estates-General.

This influential group of people collectively pledged "Not to separate, and to reassemble wherever circumstances required, until the constitution of the kingdom is established." This formal pledge was signed by all but one of the Third Estate members. It signified the first time that French citizens stood in opposition to Louis XVI and forced him to make major concessions that benefited the people.

The meeting at the tennis court is considered one of the most important events during the first days of the French Revolution. It is particularly significant because the individuals who took that historic pledge put their lives and the lives of their family at great risk. The Tennis Court Oath was considered a revolutionary act and a demand that the monarch relinquish political authority to the people and their representatives. It led to the famous "Storming of the Bastille" on July 14, 1789 which inspired additional rioting throughout France. This simple oath in a time of chaos led to the establishment of a representative National Assembly and eventually a French constitution.

Jacques-Louis David's sketch le Serment du jeu de paume which is currently hanging in the court of the Palace of Versailles

The storming of the Bastille was perhaps the most significant event following the administering of the Tennis Court Oath. The Bastille was a medieval prison and fortress in Paris that in the minds of citizens symbolized control by the monarchy over the people. Estimates of 600 to 1,000 angry people descended on this building and engaged in a bloody battle. This battle was considered an important first military victory of common citizens over the tyranny of the monarch.

This victory inspired the National Assembly to draft a constitution called, "The Declaration of the Rights of Man" on August 26, 1789 which eventually became the preamble to the French constitution adopted on September 3, 1791. The storming of the

Breaking The Barriers

Bastille has such great historical significance that "Bastille Day" or "La Fete National" (The National Celebration) is celebrated on July 14th every year as one of France's major holidays. The Tennis Court Oath will go down in history as one of the most important things to happen on a tennis court not involving tennis racquets and tennis balls.

CHAPTER 4: The Birth of Lawn Tennis

The Birth of Modern Tennis

Napoleon Bonaparte served as the Emperor of France from 1804 to 1815 and the King of Italy from 1805 to 1814. He is remembered as a brilliant military strategist who was a major threat to the nobility of Europe. The stress on Europe's royal society generated by Napoleon's dominant presence and unpredictable military strategy lead to a lull in the popularity of jeu de paume in high society. However, "commoners" continued to enjoy the sport.

Napoleon III was the nephew of Napoleon I and the president of the French Republic from 1848 to 1852 and Emperor of France from 1852 to 1870. There was a major period of industrialization and building renovation in Paris during his reign. In 1862 Napoleon III gave permission to build a jeu de paume court in the Tuileries Gardens near the Place de la Concorde. A second court was added in 1880 and the two courts were the headquarters of jeu de paume in Paris. The popularity of the sport continued to grow given the influence of the country's leaders. The stage was set for the emergence of a new version of the sport to flourish.

The sport of tennis that we know today was created largely because of an invention that has not received the recognition that it deserves in the world of sports. Charles Goodyear was an American inventor who discovered the process of vulcanizing rubber in 1839 and patented it in 1844. This new process led to the development of the game of tennis that we know today.

Dale G. Caldwell

Charles Goodyear
The Most Important Inventor in Sports History

Charles Goodyear was born in New Haven, Connecticut on December 29, 1800. At the age of 14 he went to Philadelphia to learn the hardware business. At the age of 25, two years after he got married, he opened a hardware business in Philadelphia where he specialized in selling agricultural tools. His business was doing quite well until he became ill in the early 1830s and his hardware business was closed.

He became so fascinated with improving the rubber that life preservers were made of that he spent hours experimenting on developing stronger forms of rubber. He moved to New York and had some success in his initial attempts to improve rubber. However, the rubber still was not durable. In 1839 he discovered the vulcanization process for rubber.

Vulcanization is a chemical process (named after "Vulcan" the Roman God of fire) that turns rubber into a more durable product through the addition of sulfur and other chemical elements. Prior to his invention rubber products were extremely sensitive to temperature, not durable, very sticky and had little elasticity.

We take for granted the impact that vulcanized rubber has had on the world of sports. This process is used to create shoe soles, tires, hoses, bowling balls, basketballs, hockey pucks and most importantly tennis balls. No sport benefitted more than tennis from the vulcanization of rubber. Rubber tennis balls bounced higher and lasted longer, therefore enabling players to hit balls back and forth on open grass spaces for extended periods of time fairly easily.

Goodyear patented the vulcanization process in 1844. However, he had to fight patent infringements and never fully benefited financially from his

> *"Rubber tennis balls bounced higher and lasted longer, enabling players to hit balls back and forth on open grass spaces for extended periods of time."*

discovery. Tragically, he died on July 1, 1860 a poor man. In 1898, Franklin Augustus Sieberling honored Charles Goodyear by naming his new company the Goodyear Tire and Rubber Company.

Charles Goodyear spent most of his life in poverty because of health problems and his many failed attempts at improving rubber. His name is legendary because the Goodyear corporation was successful from the start. Sieberling founded the company at the perfect time. In the late 1800s, there was great demand for rubber tires for carriages and bicycles. The company became an industrial icon when the automobile became popular just a few years later. The Charles Goodyear story sadly epitomizes the popular saying "timing is everything."

In the early 1860s in Birmingham, England Augurio Perara and Harry Gem created a game that was a combination of Spanish "Pelota" and English "Rackets" on a local lawn. Pelota and Rackets are two sports where individuals or two teams of two people either facing a wall or each other (separated by a line on the ground or a net) hit a ball back and forth with a racket. The vulcanized rubber balls enabled Perara and Gem to play a game like modern tennis on a croquet lawn in the wealthy Edgbaston section of Birmingham, England. They moved to Learnington Spa in Warwickshire, England and founded what is considered the first lawn tennis club in the world.

In December of 1873, Major Walter Clopton Wingfield (a retired British cavalry officer who spent 10 years of active duty in India and China) created a game similar to the one developed by Perara and Gem to provide a form of entertainment and recreation for guests at a garden party he was holding at this estate Nantclwyd in Llanelidan, Wales. He based the game on an outdoor version of jeu de paume (then known as court tennis) and at the suggestion of his friend Arthur Balfour he called it "Lawn Tennis."

At the age of 41, Wingfield applied for, and received, a patent for Lawn Tennis based on his eight-page rule book entitled "Sphairistike or Lawn Ten-nis." This important patent was the "birth" of modern tennis. He published two books, *The Major's Game of Lawn Tennis* and *The Book of the Game* as well as the very first rules of Lawn Tennis. The sport was played on croquet lawns and cricket fields and quickly caught on in England. It rapidly spread to other major countries and has become the second most popular participation sport in the world.

It took more than 500 years to develop the sport of tennis that we know today. The story of the transition of tennis from a sport played in French monastery courtyards to one played on the lawns of English royalty is amazing. The sport of tennis clearly has a life of its own. The sport called jeu de paume can be considered the "parent" of modern tennis while Major Wingfield's patent represents the birth of the sport we know today. The story of modern tennis's birth has been fascinating. However, the story of its childhood is even more incredible.

The Birthday of Tennis

There is some disagreement among historians as to the date and location of the very first lawn tennis match. This debate will likely never be settled. However, there is little doubt that the "birth certificate" of tennis is the provisional letters of patent (Number 685) for a "Portable Court of Playing Tennis" issued by the British patent office to Major Walter Wingfield on February 23, 1874. This formal recognition of the existence of "Lawn Tennis" is similar to the formal recognition of citizenship that a newborn child is given by a birth certificate. I am convinced that, in spite of the disagreements as to the exact date of the first lawn tennis match, every February 23rd tennis fans around the world should celebrate the "birth" of tennis. Unfortunately, there is currently no official holiday or celebration commemorating this momentous date in the sport.

The Rapid Spread of the Sport

This new and exciting recreational activity spread well beyond London in the first year of its patent. Since the game of croquet was very popular at the time, there were many croquet lawns (typically 90 feet by 60 feet) in the wealthier communities of the world in the late 1800s. These well-manicured accessible open grass spaces were perfect for lawn tennis and helped to accelerate the growth of the sport among the wealthy in its early years.

Some of the publications of the day, popular with common citizens and members of the military, wrote about this new athletic activity. This publicity helped to increase interest in lawn tennis around the world. Word therefore spread rapidly about this fun and entertaining recreational sport which led to lawn tennis courts being set up in the United States as early as 1874. In addition, thanks to the global reach of the British Empire, courts were built in Canada, China, India and Russia in 1875.

Major Harry Gem is considered by many to have been the first to play the sport of lawn tennis. However, he is not credited with inventing the sport because he and his tennis playing partner Augurio Perera were content playing with friends and family on the Gem estate in Edgbaston, England. They therefore did not attempt to market the sport of lawn tennis to others. Major Wingfield on the other hand, understood the value of patenting, packaging and marketing a product. He is therefore considered the founder of modern tennis because of his ability to market tennis as a product—not because he created the sport.

Packaging the Sport

Once the Major received the provisional patent for *Sphairistike or Lawn Ten-nis"* he began mass marketing a "Lawn Tennis Kit." His first priority was to create a marketable package that would make setting up a tennis court and playing the game fun and easy. He therefore developed a box that was 36 inches long by 12 inches wide and 6 inches deep and easy to transport. His lawn tennis kit made it relatively easy to play the sport on any good sized manicured lawn anywhere in the world. His product was also very popular because the original packaging, depicted in the picture below, was considered to be very attractive for the time. At that time, the Major did not have to secure patents from the countries in which he marketed his kit. This made it easy for him to get these kits around the world with little government interference.

Dale G. Caldwell

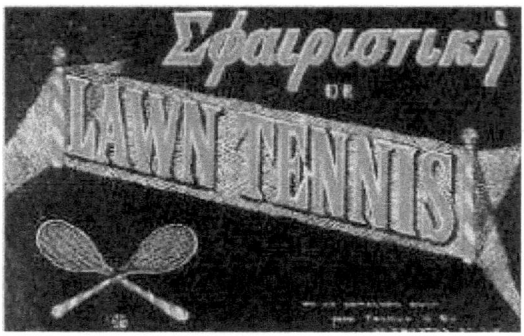

The Lawn Tennis Box Developed By Major Wingfield

Major Wingfield's lawn tennis kit cost five guineas and contained instructions, a bag of rubber balls, four oval tennis bats (or racquets), a net with pegs and ribbons to draw the court and the instructions entitled *The Book of the Game* by Major Walter Wingfield. The dimensions of the court outlined in the directions were very different than the dimensions of today's tennis courts. The court design listed in this kit was significantly shorter than the 78-foot courts used today. Major Wingfield's lawn tennis court was in the shape of an hourglass instead of the rectangular shape of modern tennis courts. The court was 21 feet wide at the net and 30 feet wide at the baseline. There is no official record of the number of kits sold. However, it is estimated that thousands of these kits were sold around the world.

The rapid spread of this new recreational activity was made possible because Major Wingfield's eight-page rule book entitled *Sphairistike or Lawn Ten-nis* was very well circulated throughout the Western world (especially among his fellow military members). In spite of the fact that some of the instructions were confusing, the ease with which to lay out a court made lawn tennis an instant hit with the people who purchased the kit. This kit enabled them to set up a court relatively quickly and participate in a fun activity on any large open grass area anywhere in the world.

The products were appealing to a wide range of consumers because they did not have to buy the full kit to play the game. Each of the items needed to play the game were sold separately. In the late 1800s *The Book of the Game* was 6 pence, 12 balls could be purchased for five shillings, and bats could be purchased for 15 shillings. However, consumers could save money because rackets from other sports like jeu de paume could be used to play the sport instead of the official lawn tennis rackets.

Fun for Men and Women

One of the often overlooked reasons for the success of the sport was that it was one of the few recreational activities that could be enjoyed by both men and women at the same time. Even today, the primary reason for the incredible influence of tennis in the world is that it is an activity that is fun for men and women to watch and play (both together and separately).

Amazingly, the "coed" benefits of tennis are frequently taken for granted. However, there are no other sports in the world with a comparable level of popularity that appeal equally to both genders. The coed nature of lawn tennis quickly made it the most popular way for men and women to get exercise, socialize and (in some cases) flirt at the same time. In addition, it provided a great vehicle for men and women to establish gender based recreational social groups.

Major Wingfield published the rules of lawn tennis in 1874. Unfortunately, they received widespread criticism because they were not very comprehensive or clear. As the sport became more popular, several influential individuals made a concerted effort to control the development of the sport. The most notable of which were Henry Jones and John Walsh.

Henry Jones was a Member of the Royal College of Surgeons (MRCS) and practiced surgery from 1852 to 1869 when he retired and started reporting on games and sport in a publication called *The Field*. He wrote extensively about card games, billiards, croquet and lawn tennis and was well-known by individuals interested in recreational activities. Jones joined the All England Croquet Club at Wimbledon in 1869.

In 1862 Jones published *The Laws and Principles of Whist: Stated and Explained and its Practice Illustrated on an Original System by Means of Hands Played Completely Through by "Cavendish."* This book was recognized as the definitive rules of one of the most popular games at the time. Jones therefore developed an international reputation as an expert on the rules of games. He used his influence as a writer to challenge and rewrite the rules developed by Major Wingfield. In response to the criticism of Jones and other influential individuals, Wingfield developed a second edition of *The Book of the Game* in 1874 which added rules and changed the dimensions of the lawn tennis court.

A battle over lawn tennis rules ensued that threatened to hinder the growth of this new sport. Consequently, a consensus was reached that the development of a common set of rules should be led by the Marylebone Cricket Club (MCC) which at the time had great influence in the world of racket sports. MCC was founded in 1787 in St John's Wood, London and was one of the first clubs to add lawn tennis courts. At the time it was the sole copyright holder and international governing body of the popular sport of Cricket. It therefore had an impeccable reputation for developing comprehensive sports rules and regulations.

It was also recognized as the organization with the most expertise on racket sports (having recently developed rules for royal tennis). Experts at MCC worked with the leaders of the sport of lawn tennis and refined the rules of lawn tennis. The group came up with 25 rules which were published in the next edition of Major Wingfield's *The Book of the Game*. The rules were first announced in *The Field* magazine's May 1875 issue and were well received by the lawn tennis playing public.

This agreement about rules helped to accelerate interest in the sport. In 1875, people throughout England started playing lawn tennis so frequently that interest in playing croquet at the prestigious All-England Croquet Club at Wimbledon dropped precipitously. Therefore, Jones, as Club secretary in 1875, proposed that one of the club's croquet lawns be converted into a lawn tennis court so that the club could compete with other clubs that had already added lawn tennis courts. The Hurlingham Club, the Princes Club and MCC had grown in popularity because of the addition of lawn tennis to their offerings.

Breaking The Barriers

England Leads the Way to Competitive Play

In 1876, the board of the All England Club added Spairistike courts (which had the nickname "Sticky courts" at the time) to accommodate those people who wanted to play the new sport of lawn tennis. The popularity of this recreational activity also led to a rapidly growing interest in competition, especially among men. Consequently, informal tournaments were established to determine who the best player at a club or in an area was at the time. These casual tournaments were the start of the billion dollar global professional tennis tour that we know today.

CHAPTER 5: Tennis Becomes a Global Sport

The First Major Tennis Tournament

In 1877, the All-England Croquet Club's new secretary John Walsh (who was the publisher of *The Field* magazine and a retired physician) proposed that a lawn tennis championship be held at the club. The purpose of this event was to increase interest in lawn tennis and raise money for a horse drawn roller for the club's croquet lawns. Club members Henry Jones, Julian Marshall and Charles G. Heathcote were asked to lead a committee that was charged with developing the rules for this tournament. Henry Jones maintained strong involvement in the tournament and became its referee for several years.

One of the reasons that the club decided to establish this major tournament was to increase the influence of the club in the lawn tennis world. Interest in tennis grew so rapidly that in 1877 the club changed its name from the "All-England Croquet Club" to the "All-England Croquet and Lawn Tennis Club." The club was one of the last major clubs to include a lawn tennis court. By being the first club to establish a major tournament the newly named All-England Croquet and Lawn Tennis Club could establish itself as the premier lawn tennis club in England.

The very first All-England Croquet and Lawn Tennis Club Championships in 1877 consisted only of Men's Singles. Women were not allowed to play in the tournament until 1884. In this inaugural event, there were 22 male tennis players of varying abilities vying for the title of champion. They each paid one guinea to participate in the tournament which was very modest in every way by today's standards. Even though the sport was in its infant stages, the tournament matches had many similarities to today's modern game. However, two of the biggest differences between tennis at this time and the sport we know today were that every competitor served underhand and the net used for this tournament was 4 feet 9 inches tall at the posts. The tournament organizers felt that the net was too high, so in 1878 the net posts were lowered to 3 feet 6 inches at the posts (the same height as the nets used today in professional and amateur tournaments).

Tennis had already become a very popular spectator sport. Consequently, there was a lot of interest in the tournament by club members. However, in spite of tennis's growing popularity, the tournament schedule was built around some of the more popular sporting events in the area. The matches were spread over five days and the finals were not scheduled for the weekend to prevent it from competing with the popular yearly Eton versus Harrow cricket match that weekend at Lord's Cricket Ground. It is interesting to note that weather delayed this tournament in the same way that it delays the multi-million dollar tournaments of today. Because of rain, the singles final was delayed by four full days.

Spencer Gore and William C. Marshall reach the first Men's Singles Final of what later became the Wimbledon Championships. Gore was an accomplished soccer and cricket player who had a natural gift for tennis. He was an aggressive tennis player who grew up within a mile of the All-England Croquet Club. Marshall was a defensive player who focused on not making errors and getting every ball back to his opponent.

A crowd of approximately 200 well-dressed spectators stood to watch the finals between these two men of contrasting styles. It is fascinating that the first "Wimbledon" men's final featured a rivalry of an aggressive player versus a defensive specialist that mirrors rivalries like Laver-Rosewall, McEnroe-Borg, Sampras-Agassi, Federer-Nadal, etc. They each paid 1 shilling to watch Mr. Gore win the match in less than an hour by the score of 6-1, 6-2, 6-4. The final was not as competitive as spectators might have hoped. However, the tournament was a big success. Spencer Gore received 12 guineas and a silver cup presented by a representative of *The Field* sports publication. It is hard to believe that this modest no-frills tennis tournament has become the spectacular Wimbledon Championships which today captivate millions of sports fans from around the world.

Breaking The Barriers

The Tournament's Second Year

The success of the tournament in the first year led to great interest in the tournament in its second year. Spectators in 1878 were anxious to answer the question: "Would Spencer Gore be able to repeat his dominating performance or would a new star emerge?"

The second tournament was even more successful than the first. As the past champion, Spencer Gore reached the finals once again. However, this time he faced a different opponent with a very different strategy than William Marshall. Patrick Francis (Frank) Hadow was a fascinating individual. His father was an Oxford graduate who became the chairman of the P&O Shipping Company. Frank Hadow was an outstanding cricketer and a natural athlete who later became a legendary big game hunter.

Hadow decided to enter the Wimbledon tournament while he was on vacation from his coffee plantation in Ceylon (which is now known as SriLanka). He was a crafty player who did not lose a set on his way to the Men's Final. Spencer Gore's aggressive game enabled him to dominate other opponents on his way to reaching the final. However, Frank Hadow surprised Gore by varying the speed and direction of his shots. He frustrated Gore by not giving him the pace he needed to enhance the effectiveness of his powerful strokes. Hadow's most memorable shot was his lob, which successfully thwarted Gore's aggressive game. His lob forced Gore to spend more time on the baseline. This strategy prevented him from taking full advantage of his power. These brilliant tactics were successful. Hadow surprised the crowd by winning the match by a score of 7-5, 6-1, 9-7. He did not defend his title and, to this day, is the only Wimbledon Champion who never lost a set in the tournament.

A Truly Global Sport

In 1879 and 1880, John Hartley became the first Wimbledon Champion to successfully defend his title. In 1881 William Renshaw won his first of six consecutive Wimbledons. The Gentleman's Championships at Wimbledon helped to make tennis the most popular activity at the club. It therefore changed its name in 1882 from the "All-England Croquet and Lawn Tennis Club" to the "All-England Lawn Tennis Club." However, in 1889 the name, as a tribute to the club's founding as a place to play croquet, was changed to the "All-England Lawn Tennis and Croquet Club."

The popularity of Gentlemen's Singles tournaments inspired the club to expand the tournament. Ladies Singles and Gentlemen's Doubles was added to the list of events in 1884. There were only 13 entrants in the first year of the tournament, which was won by Maud Watson over Lillian Watson by a score of 6-8, 6-3, 6-3. The Gentlemen's Doubles was won by William and Ernest Renshaw over E.W. Lewis and E.L. Williams by a score of 6-3, 6-1, 1-6, 6-4.

Thanks to the success of Wimbledon and the international distribution of Major Wingfield's Lawn Tennis Kit through military bases, the new sport of lawn tennis was spreading rapidly throughout the world. One of the most significant developments in the world of tennis at that time was the spread of the sport to the United States. The growth of tennis in the United States combined with the establishment of the US National Championships in 1881 signified the transition of tennis from "Infancy" to "Childhood."

Tennis in America

The strategic placement of British military bases around the world played an important role in the rapid spread of lawn tennis. As an experienced British military officer, Major Wingfield knew how to take full advantage of what was probably the best distribution network in the world at the time. He used his connections to get as many of his lawn tennis kits on military bases as possible. His strategy worked. Within a year of receiving the provisional letters of patent, lawn tennis was being played on British military bases in Asia, Europe and even the United States of America.

There is significant debate about the roots of lawn tennis in America. However, tennis was being played in America as early as 1874. The first written record of the game being played came from the papers of an officer's wife stationed in Camp Apache Arizona named Martha Summerhayes. In October of 1874, she wrote that she observed another officer's wife named Mrs. Ella Wilkins Bailey playing lawn tennis.

Breaking The Barriers

Apparently, Mrs. Bailey and her husband had just arrived from San Francisco where they were stationed at Camp Reynolds. Presumably Mrs. Bailey learned to play lawn tennis earlier in the year in San Francisco.

Some historians claim that Dr. James Dwight of Nahant, Massachusetts was the first to play lawn tennis in America. Still others believe that Mary Ewing Outerbridge brought tennis to America after purchasing a lawn tennis kit on a British military base in Bermuda. It is likely that lawn tennis was brought to many different parts of America by British military and merchants around the same time in 1874. That was a good

Early Tennis Tournament at Nahant
From the International Tennis Hall of Fame Collection

time to introduce a new sport to the United States because it was a relatively peaceful and prosperous time under the leadership of President Ulysses S. Grant and Vice President Henry Wilson.

Regardless of where it was first played, the sport grew rapidly throughout the United States. Mary Outerbridge's history is extremely important because it indirectly led to the founding of the tournament that would eventually be known as the US Open. In 1874, Outerbridge returned from a very pleasant visit to Bermuda on a ship named the S.S. Camina. She returned with one of Major Wingfield's lawn tennis kits and used it to play one of the first lawn tennis matches in the country at her local club, the Staten Island Cricket and Baseball Club. It is believed that the first tennis tournament was established by Dr. James Dwight. In Massachusetts, Dr. James Dwight organized a local round robin lawn tennis tournament with 15 entries in 1876 with his cousin Fred Sears. In the first final Dwight beat Sears. That same year, the New Orleans Lawn Tennis Club became the first lawn tennis only club in America.

Lawn tennis clubs spread rapidly throughout the country with the most successful clubs being established in the northeastern United States. The clubs in New York, Philadelphia and Boston were among the most powerful because they contained the wealthiest and most influential people in business and tennis. These clubs were very independent. As a result, they each used different rules and equipment for lawn tennis competitions.

The diversity of rules and equipment was not a problem until the best players from these clubs participated in the very first national championship tournament held in Staten Island, New York. This tournament led to a heated debate about rules and equipment that led to the formation of the United States National Lawn Tennis Association (USNLTA) and the creation of the US National Championships, which is known as the US Open today.

The establishment of first national tennis championships in America was in many ways a family affair. One of Mary Outerbridge's six brothers, August Emilio Outerbridge (an older brother who was an officer on the board of directors of the Staten Island Cricket and Baseball Club), was so intrigued by the sport she brought back from Bermuda that he convinced the board to approve the placement of permanent lawn tennis courts at the club in 1874.

However, it was another of her brothers, her younger brother Eugenius Harvey Outerbridge who had the idea of establishing a national lawn tennis championship at the club, which at the time was located on waterfront grounds called Camp Washington (which is under what is now the Staten Island Ferry Terminal).

Breaking The Barriers

Richard Sears, USNLTA Singles Champion
From the International Tennis Hall of Fame Collection

The growing prestige of the "Championships" at Wimbledon helped to increase interest in lawn tennis around the world. Twenty year-old Eugenius suggested that the club hold something that he called "the tournament for the championship of America." Thanks to his influence, the club agreed to hold this national championship beginning on September 1, 1880. The prize was a silver cup valued at $100. Several of the best male players in the country at the time decided to play in the tournament, thereby making it the first "national" tennis championship in America.

From a spectator standpoint, the tournament was extremely successful. Large numbers of spectators came out to view this unique new competition on beautifully manicured lawns by the water. Unfortunately, players had a very different view of the tournament. They considered the tournament a failure because the rules and equipment used in the tournament differed from those used in the club in which they were a member.

This dispute was the official start of the frequent disagreements between players and administrators that continues even in today's highly successful professional tennis events. Many of the top players coming from New England and Philadelphia had used different regulations and equipment. They therefore questioned the fairness of the tournament and caused the first major controversy in American major tournament history. The three aspects of the tournament that caused the most controversy were the method of scoring, the height of the net and the type of balls used.

The men's singles tournament was won by an accomplished player from England named O.E. Woodhouse. He had been a finalist in the Wimbledon All-Comers tournament (the equivalent of the semi-finals in today's tournaments). Woodhouse lost to Herbert Lawford who lost in the finals to John Hartley (the first Wimbledon Champion to defend his title) in the 1880 Wimbledon Championships. At Wimbledon, Lawford beat Woodhouse by a score of 6-3, 6-2, 2-6, 6-3. In the Staten Island tournament, Woodhouse beat Canadian, J. F. Helmuth in the final. The men's doubles competition was won by two local residents. However, the enduring legacy of this tournament was that it drew attention to the fact that there was little consistency of the rules and equipment used by the major tennis clubs in the United States.

The increasing amount of inter-club play between clubs using balls of different weights and nets of different heights increased interest in standardizing rules and equipment. The dissatisfaction of the players with the Staten Island tournament and the inability of the clubs to come to some agreement on regulations and equipment led to several meetings of the most influential people in lawn tennis at the time. The primary purpose of these meetings was to develop consistent regulations for lawn tennis. For several months after the tournament, many formal and informal meetings were held throughout the country (mostly in the Northeast). It was as if tennis was a very sick patient and the most influential "doctors" in the country were debating how they could make their patient healthier.

Eugenius Harvey Outerbridge
The First Chairman of the New York Port Authority

In the beginning of the 20th century the ports of New York and New Jersey were extremely active and served, in many ways, as the foundation of the economic strength of the region. The saying "success brings disagreement" seems to apply to the ports in this area of the country at that time. The maritime success of the two states led to constant disagreement on the fair use of the Hudson River. After a great deal of discussion, bartering and negotiation between some of the most powerful business and political leaders in both states, it was agreed that a joint agency would be established.

One of the individuals who played an important role in the discussions of creating a port authority was the "founder" of the first national tennis tournament in America and one of the three founders of the United States National Lawn Tennis Association (which is now the United States Tennis Association), Eugenius Harvey Outerbridge. He was born in 1860 in Philadelphia to Alexander and Laura Outerbridge. He was one of seven children. His sister was Mary Outerbridge, who was, as was described earlier, one of the first people to bring lawn tennis to America. Eugenius's success in business led to his position as one of the most important leaders in the country.

He founded what is today called the "Homasote Company" as the Agasote Millboard Company in 1909 when he was 49. The company initially sold sanded panels for the sides of railroad carriages. However, in 1915 he brought the company's secret manufacturing process for "fiberboard" from England and made a fortune selling the product to manufacturers of automobile and railroad car roofs. His product was used extensively in the manufacturing of tops for Buick, Dodge, Ford and Studebaker cars. It was also used for the exterior of field houses and military housing in France in World War I.

Outerbridge was one of the first business leaders to develop environmentally friendly products in America. His business legacy lives on today. The Homasote Company is the oldest manufacturer of building products made from recycled materials in the United States. The current global focus on environmentally friendly building products has significantly increased the demand for Homasote's products. The company estimates that their unique production process saves 1.5 million trees every year and eliminates over 65 million tons of solid waste. They continue to be successful and operate out of a 750,000 square foot facility in West Trenton, New Jersey.

The incredible success of the Homasote Company, combined with his prominence in the tennis community, gave Outerbridge great influence in the New York business community. He was so well respected that in 1916 he was elected president of the very powerful New York Chamber of Commerce.

As the chamber president, he followed distinguished national leaders like Alonzo Barton Hepburn, the former United States Comptroller of the Currency (1892-1893) and president of Chase National Bank (1898) who was the chamber president from 1910 to 1912 and Seth Low, the legendary president of Columbia University (1890-1901) and former Mayor of New York City (1902-1903) who served as chamber president from 1914 to 1916.

As a major supplier of products to companies in the transportation industry, Outerbridge developed a passionate interest in issues involving regional transportation. His success as the chamber president, prominence in the tennis community and concern about transportation issues led to his being selected as the first chairman of the Port of New York Authority in 1921. He held this position from 1921 – 1924.

Thanks to the leadership of Outerbridge and other powerful businessmen, on April 30, 1921 a 1,500 square mile district known as the Port of New York Authority (it is now the Port Authority of New York and New Jersey) was created to foster collaboration between New York and New Jersey in regional transportation activity. This organization has the distinction of being the first interstate agency created under a US Constitution clause that allowed Congressionally approved agreements between states.

Breaking The Barriers

In addition to bringing maritime harmony between the two states, the Port of New York Authority was charged with the construction of critical interstate crossings which we now know as the Hudson River span, which became the George Washington Bridge (started in 1927 and completed in 1931), the Goethels Bridge (1928), the Bayonne Bridge (1931), the Lincoln Tunnel (1934). The Port of New York did not build the Holland Tunnel. However, it took management control of the tunnel in 1930.

Eugenius Outerbridge was so well respected for his leadership in the founding of the Port of New York that in 1928 (prior to his death in 1932), the bridge connecting Staten Island, New York to Perth Amboy, New Jersey was named the "Outerbridge Crossing." This bridge was given his name to recognize him for both his Port Authority work, his legendary tennis leadership at the nearby Staten Island Cricket Club and his role in founding the influential United States Lawn Tennis Association.

The agency that Outerbridge helped to establish is now called the Port Authority of New York and New Jersey (PANYNJ) and is one of the most influential government organizations in the world. The Authority currently operates the Port Newark-Elizabeth Marine Terminal; the Holland and Lincoln Tunnels; the Bayonne and Goethels Bridge; the Outerbridge Crossing; the George Washington Bridge; the Port Authority Bus Terminal, the Hudson and Manhattan Railroad (now called the PATH rail system); LaGuardia, JFK, Newark Liberty, Teterboro and Stewart International Airports. The organization has an annual budget of more than $4 billion and oversees the transportation of millions of people every year. The PANYNJ has more than 7,000 employees including a 1,600 person police force.

PANYNJ's first major building construction project was the building of the World Trade Center (WTC) towers in 1973. This 110 story tall two building structure contained more than 10 million square feet of office space and were the tallest buildings in Manhattan at the time. In the tragic September 11, 2001 terrorist attacks that destroyed these massive structures and killed 2,752 people, the WTC lost 84 employees including its executive Director Neil Levin and Police Superintendent Fred Morrone.

Outerbridge will be recognized in the tennis world both for his vision of establishing a national tennis tournament and his role in founding the USNLTA. However, his legacy outside of tennis is equally impressive. He will be remembered for being one of the first businessmen to create environmentally friendly products; for his early leadership of the powerful Port Authority of New York and New Jersey; and, for the bridge that bears his name.

* * *

CHAPTER 6: United States National Lawn Tennis Association

The United States National Lawn Tennis Association (USNLTA)

The frequent (and often contentious) meetings of the most influential people in the sport of lawn tennis eventually proved to be successful. The leaders of the major lawn tennis clubs finally agreed that a governing body should be established to regulate tennis in America. They were convinced that the establishment of a governing body was the medicine that their sick patient needed.

On May 5, 1881 a notice appeared in one of the most popular sports publications of the time, the *American Cricketer*, indicating that the inaugural meeting of the United States National Lawn Tennis Association (USNLTA) will be taking place on May 21, 1881 at the Fifth Avenue Hotel in New York City.

The notice was signed by Clarence M. Clark, the president of the All Philadelphia Lawn Tennis Committee; James Dwight of the Beacon Park Athletic Association of Boston and Eugenius Harvey Outerbridge of the Staten Island Cricket and Baseball Club of New York. The fact that this notice came from the leaders of three of the most influential lawn tennis clubs in the country gave it significant weight in the lawn tennis community.

Modern tennis is currently run by accomplished professionals in their 50s and 60s who play the game recreationally. It is interesting to note that Clark, Dwight and Outerbridge were active and accomplished players who were in their 20s when they led in the development of the USNLTA. At the time of the May 21st meeting Clark was twenty-two, Dwight was twenty-nine and Outerbridge was twenty-one. Not only were they were respected as players, they had the energy and entrepreneurial spirit to create a powerful governing body for the sport. This is in sharp contrast to the ages of most of the leaders of the United States Tennis Association (USTA) today. The majority of leaders of the organization over the last century been in their 50s and 60s. A notable exception to this was the first black president of the USTA, Katrina Adams. In 2015, Adams became the youngest president in modern times at age 47.

There was a great deal of excitement about the potential of a unified approach to lawn tennis at the May 21st meeting in New York City. At the meeting there were 36 delegates representing 19 clubs (with proxy votes for another 15 clubs). Each club represented had only one vote. Some of the clubs in attendance included legendary organizations such as the Albany Tennis Club, Germantown Cricket Club, Longwood Cricket Club, Orange Lawn Tennis Club, University of Pennsylvania and Yale University.

After a great deal of discussion and debate, the leaders of American lawn tennis came to a consensus about the formation of the USNLTA, its leadership, the development of the rules and regulations of the sport, and the structure and location of the national lawn tennis championships.

As a result of this meeting, the first national governing body in the sport of tennis was formed on May 21, 1881. The formation of this organization led to the establishment of similar organizations in hundreds of other countries that has helped the sport of tennis to grow rapidly. The Lawn Tennis Association (LTA), the national governing body of tennis in Great Britain, the Channel Islands and the Isle of Man, was founded in 1888. Tennis Australia, the governing body for the sport of tennis in Australia, was founded in 1904. The International Tennis Federation (ITF), the governing body of world tennis, wheelchair tennis and beach tennis, was founded in 1913. The American Tennis Association (ATA), the governing body of tennis in the black community in the United States, was founded in 1916. The French Tennis Federation, the governing body for the sport of tennis in France, was founded in 1920. May 21, 1881 is therefore a very important day in tennis history that should be celebrated every year as the start of organized tennis in the world.

Breaking The Barriers

The lawn tennis leaders attending this meeting felt that each of their respective clubs should have voting rights in the USNLTA to ensure that their interests would be well-represented by the organization. They also felt that it was important that the first president of the organization be someone with a stellar reputation and impeccable credentials. They therefore named General Robert S. Oliver of the Albany Lawn Tennis Club the first president of the USNLTA. Samuel Campbell was named the vice president of the organization and Clarence M. Clark was named secretary-treasurer.

General Robert Oliver Shaw
The First President of the USTA

At the time that General Robert Shaw Oliver was elected as the first president of the USNLTA he was well known in military circles because of his role as the Inspector General of the New York State Militia. As the founding president of the Albany Lawn Tennis Club he was also very well known in tennis circles. General Oliver was an ideal choice for president of the association because he commanded great respect in both the military and the American tennis community.

Many believe that he was chosen as the first president of the USNLTA because the powerful clubs in Boston, Philadelphia and New York wanted it to appear that the association was not controlled by the three founding tennis leaders from the three most influential tennis clubs in the three biggest cities in America.

In spite of the appearance of complete independence, Oliver was close to his friends and USNLTA founders Clarence Clark, Eugenius Outerbridge and James Dwight. He was a cousin to Dwight's best friends and doubles partners Jim and Dick Sears. His appointment ensured that influence in American tennis remained in the hands of the three most powerful people in the sport. Oliver only served as president for 1 year and resigned from the USNLTA (because of his work schedule and the difficulty of traveling from Albany to New York City regularly) enabling Dwight to become the second president of the association.

Robert Shaw Oliver was born in Boston in 1845 and moved to Albany, New York in 1870 at the age of 25. According to a brief

biography in a "New York Times" article published on July 14, 1903[8]:
"He was born in Boston about sixty years ago, and was a boy at school at the beginning of the civil war. He wanted to enlist among the first, but owing to his youth his family succeeded in persuading him to postpone his enlistment for a time. In 1862, however, he obtained a commission as Second Lieutenant, and joined the Fifth Massachusetts Calvary.

Despite his youth, his service was such as to attract the attention of his superiors, and he was made Adjutant of his regiment and later an aide on the staff of the Twenty-fifth Army Corps.

After the surrender of Gen. (Robert E.) Lee (April 9, 1865), General Oliver went to the Rio Grande, where he was mustered out of the service (discharged). He remained out of active service but a short time, however, rejoining the regular establishment in 1866, when he was assigned as a Second Lieutenant to duty in the District of Arizona. He was promoted to a First Lieutenancy and then a Captaincy. In 1870 he resigned his commission, and in November of that year he married Miss Marion Rathbone of Albany, and went to Albany to live. He was made a partner in the stove manufacturing firm of John F. Rathbone & Son, now known as Rathbone, Sard & Co.

In 1880 Gen. Oliver was appointed by (New York) Gov. (Alonzo B.) Cornell Inspector General of his staff, and, with Adjt. Gen. Frederick Townsend, was instrumental in securing for the State the State camp at Peekskill. When Gen. T. Ellery Lord resigned Gen. Oliver succeeded him as Brigadier General, commanding the Fifth Brigade.

Gen. Oliver is a member of several Albany Clubs. His second daughter, Cora, recently married Joseph H. Choate, Jr., the son of Ambassador to the Court of St. James. He has two other daughters, and one son, who is a graduate of Yale."

General Oliver will always be known as the first president of what is today one of the most powerful organizations in sports. However, his accomplishments outside of tennis were even more impressive. He was well-known in the tennis community because of his role in establishing and leading the prestigious Albany Lawn Tennis Club in Albany, New York in 1878. As the state capital of New York, Albany was a very influential political region of the country at that time. Oliver was politically active and developed a strong relationship with New York residents Theodore Roosevelt and Secretary of War Elihu Root.

---

[8] "The New York Times", July 14, 1903

Breaking The Barriers

In addition to being a successful military officer, Oliver was a successful businessman. He became an owner (with his father-in-law) of the famous Rathbone, Sard & Co. which manufactured the very popular Acorn Stoves and Ranges. Rathbone became one of the most successful appliance manufacturing companies in the country with locations in Albany, New York; Chicago, Illinois; and, Detroit, Michigan. An indication of their success was a Rathbone, Sard & Co. advertisement from 1886 indicating that more than 1,000,000 Acorn ranges made by the company were in use at the time.

General Shaw was appointed Brigadier General of the Third Brigade by New York Governor David Bennett Hill in 1890. This appointment, combined with his prominence in the tennis community increased his visibility in political circles. President Theodore Roosevelt was an avid tennis player who loved the game so much he became the first president to have a tennis court installed at the White House. Roosevelt organized a group of senior level officials in his administration that came to be known as Roosevelt's "Tennis Cabinet." This group of approximately 30 very competitive men would play tennis regularly on the White House court.

General Oliver was selected to be assistant secretary of war for the United States succeeding William Cary Sanger who was appointed by the president in 1901 (under Secretary of War Root). Given Roosevelt's passion for tennis, it is likely that General Robert Shaw Oliver was appointed assistant secretary of war in 1903 by the president because of his prominence in both the military and the tennis community.

In this powerful position, General Oliver had a chance to report to legendary Secretary of War Elihu Root. Secretary Root reformed the War Department, established the U.S. Army war college and enlarged West Point. He was so well respected by Roosevelt that he was named US secretary of state after the death of John Hay (and later became a US senator from New York).

When Secretary Root left his position in 1904, General Oliver (who remained as assistant secretary of state) served as the "right hand man" to the new secretary of war (and future US president and chief justice of the Supreme Court) William Howard Taft. As president of the United States from 1909 to 1913 Taft developed a reputation as a strong delegator. He allowed the people who worked for him to have extraordinary power. At the time of his selection as secretary of war, Taft was Roosevelt's mentee and chosen Presidential successor. It is therefore quite likely that given his long tenure in the assistant secretary of war position (as well as Taft's visibility and leadership style), General Oliver had extraordinary political power in the Roosevelt Administration.

William Howard Taft left his position as secretary of war in 1904 to successfully run for president of the United States in 1908. General Oliver remained as assistant secretary of war from 1903 to 1913 working for Taft's successor Luke Edward Wright from Tennessee, who served as secretary of war until March 4, 1909, and Jacob McGavock Dickinson from Illinois who served as secretary of war from March 12, 1909 until March 4, 1913.

General Oliver's long tenure in his role as assistant secretary of state enabled him to serve with four different secretaries of war (including a future president of the United States and chief justice of the Supreme Court); have the opportunity to serve as acting secretary of war on several occasions; and, enabled him to shape US military policy on the eve of World War I.

Amazingly, General Robert Shaw Oliver's role as a leader in the tennis community helped him secure a powerful role in the Roosevelt administration that enabled him to play a vitally important part in developing the United States's military policy. This was especially significant because he retired from this position slightly more than a year before the start of World War I (and four years before the US entered the war).

* * *

It is fitting that the USNLTA was founded in New York and the first president came from what would eventually be called the Eastern Tennis Association (ETA) because of the tremendous influence of New York, Northern New Jersey and Southern Connecticut in the country at that time. New York, even in 1881, was laying the groundwork for its future role as the Tennis Capital of the World. The extraordinary success of the US Nationals, which became the US Open in 1968, have enabled the US to supplant England as the center of the tennis universe.

Breaking The Barriers

The club delegates at this first meeting believed that, given the success of the Wimbledon Championships, the rules and regulations used for this world-renowned sporting event would likely work well in the United States. They therefore decided to form a committee to develop lawn tennis rules and regulations based on those used by the All-England Club and the Marylebone Cricket Club.

It was also agreed that the USNLTA would govern the national championships. After a great deal of debate, the majority of the members of the USNLTA agreed that the first national championships of the United States (governed by the association) would be held at the newly built Newport Casino in Newport, Rhode Island in August of 1881. The group chose this fabulous club because it was considered by many to be one of the nicest lawn tennis facilities in the country.

The History of the Newport Casino

Newport is located 23 miles south of Providence and 61 miles south of Boston in Newport County, Rhode Island. It was incorporated as a town in 1639 and as a city in 1784. The City was founded by a group of people who left Portsmouth, Rhode Island because of religious disagreements with the leaders in that community. Rhode Island received its Royal Charter in 1663 and, in that year, Benedict Arnold was elected as the state's first Governor based in Newport. This was no surprise because, in 1657 and 1662 respectively, he was the 10th and 12th president of the Colony of Rhode Island and Providence Plantations. The City's Old Colony House was the center of state government until the state capital was relocated to Providence in 1904.

Newport became a financial hub and a place of great wealth in the mid to late 1700's because it was home to some of the largest slave traders and exporters of oil, candles, furniture, silver and fish. The City became home to the most active commercial slave trade in New England and one of the most active in North America. It is believed that more than half of the slave trade voyages in this region of the US started in Newport and other ports in Rhode Island. According to research published by Brown University, sugar and molasses that was produced by slaves in the Caribbean was brought to Rhode Island and distilled into rum. This rum was carried to West Africa and exchanged for captives who would become slaves in America. Newport had 22 rum distilleries which led to great slave trade wealth for many residents of the community.

The Washington Square section of Newport was the center of commercial and social activity in Newport. The financial strength of the community led to the first newspaper (the "Rhode Island Gazette") published by Benjamin Franklin's brother James. Newport benefitted by its relatively close proximity to Boston, New York City and Philadelphia (the three centers of wealth in the United States). Many of the most successful individuals in and around these communities made Newport their summer vacation paradise. The resulting growth in wealth in Newport made it one of the most influential cities in the world and led to the construction of fabulous mansions and the creation of social clubs for the upper classes in Newport.

One of the most prestigious clubs in town was the Newport Reading Room. As legend has it, in the summer of 1879, to win a bet with James Gordon Bennett, Captain Henry Augustus Candy rode his polo horse onto the Reading Room's front porch and then into the club. As a result, his guest privileges were taken away from him for his inappropriate behavior. Bennett was angered by the club's treatment of his friend, so he decided to build a competing social club. That same year he purchased land on Bellevue Avenue to build a club that would be called "the Club of the Newport Casino."

The Casino was designed by the firm McKim, Mead & White and construction was overseen by Nathan Barker. The beautiful complex that was completed in July of 1880 included a three-story clubhouse with commercial stores on the ground floor; space for club members on the second and third floors; and, lawn tennis courts, a royal tennis (now known by the more modern name of "court tennis") court and a theatre with a ballroom. In its opening year, the club made history by becoming the first American social club to allow both men and women to become members. When the club first opened it had one tennis court for the gentlemen, one tennis court for the ladies and one tennis court for doubles. The Casino held many events open to the public and therefore became the first public-private resort in the country.

The USNLTA selected the Newport Casino as the host of the first US National Championships because of its beauty, location in a wealthy community and new construction. However, since tennis was popular among both men and women, it is very likely that the accommodations the club had for both men and women was also a factor in its site selection. The first year was such a success that the club hosted the championships at that location from 1881 to 1914.

In addition, the club has been the home of the Tennis Hall of Fame since 1954. In the next chapter we provide the history of the US National Championships. In Chapter 8, we share the fascinating history of the International Tennis Hall of Fame (ITHF) which, under the name of the National Lawn Tennis Hall of Fame, was opened to the public in 1954. This organization gained global prominence when, in 1986, the International Tennis Federation (ITF) recognized the ITHF as the official hall of fame for the sport of tennis.

CHAPTER 7: The US National Championships

The US National Championships

The very first United States National Lawn Tennis Championships (US Championships) were open only to men who were members of clubs that were official members of the (USNLTA). However, in subsequent years the tournament was open to men (and later women) who were not from USNLTA member clubs. However, the tournament was not open to black players until the legendary Althea Gibson broke through the color line by becoming the first black person to participate in the 1950 US National Tournament.

The old saying "First impressions are lasting" is very true. The success of the first US National Championships in 1881 helped to pave the way for more than a century of incredible tennis success in America. The rules that were adopted by the USNLTA were accepted by both the players and the fans. The many spectators enjoyed the beautiful grounds of the Newport Casino and the tennis skills of many of the men in the tournament. However, one of the main highlights of the tournament was the exceptional play of a young graduate of Harvard named Richard "Dick" Sears.

At this tournament, Sears began his amazing streak of 18 consecutive match wins at the US Championships by beating William Glyn from the Staten Island Cricket Club 6-0, 6-3, 6-2 in the final. This was the very first of Richard Sears's incredible seven championships. He eventually became one of the most dominant tennis players in American history.

The men's doubles tournament featured the first major upset of US Nationals history. Clarence Clark and Frederick Winslow Taylor (see his brief biography below) from Philadelphia beat the heavily

Early Tennis Tournament in Newport
From the International Tennis Hall of Fame Collection

favored Dick Sears and James Dwight in the semi-finals and went on to beat Alexander Van Renssalaer and A.E. Newbold 6-5, 6-4, 6-5 in the finals. The incredible popularity of this tournament, which was run by the USNLTA, helped to increase the influence of both the organization and the sport of lawn tennis in the United States.

Frederick W. Taylor
The Father Of Management Consulting

Clarence Clark was the first of the three USNLTA founders to win a US Nationals Championship. However, it is fascinating to note that his doubles partner made an equally significant mark on the business world. Frederick Taylor was an exceptional doubles player who was best known for his role in creating one of the most influential professions in the world.

Taylor was not only an accomplished tennis player he was a mechanical engineer who had a passion for improving the operational efficiency of businesses. He was born in 1856 to a wealthy family in the Germantown section of Philadelphia. He earned a degree in mechanical engineering from Stevens Institute of Technology and eventually became an engineer at Midvale Steel Works. He became famous when, in the early 1890s, he left this position to perform studies of business operations to determine strategies of maximum efficiency.

The management consulting profession that the world knows today is the practice of helping organizations improve their performance by analyzing their operations and making recommendations on ways they can enhance their productivity and profitability. Taylor was one of the first people to study business operations and recommend improvements. In his well-respected monograph published in 1911 entitled *The Principles of Scientific Management*, he described the principles of effective business operations. This book is considered to be one of the most influential business books ever written because it was the first to recommend comprehensive ways to analyze and improve the operational efficiency of business. Taylor, because of his book and extraordinary work studying and improving business operations, is considered by many to be the "Father" of the management consulting profession.

His work eventually led to the development of powerful management consulting firms like Accenture, Boston Consulting Group, Booz Allen, Deloitte and McKinsey, which provide strategic and operational consulting advice to the leaders of the largest corporations in the world.

* * *

At roughly the same time that Sears was becoming America's first tennis star, James Dwight was becoming tennis's first administrative star. USNLTA President Oliver chose to serve in this role for only one year (1881-1882) most likely because of his political aspirations. However, the reason given for his leaving after only one year was that the distance from Albany to New York made it difficult for him to be as effective a president as he wanted to be. Consequently, James Dwight, one of the three major organization founders, was named as the second president of the USNLTA in 1882. He completed his first term as president in 1884. Dwight played a more important role than any other person in the early development of the association.

Dwight was born on July 14, 1852 in France and died on July 14, 1917. He graduated from Harvard University in 1874 and, after graduation, traveled to Europe where he saw lawn tennis being played for the first time. He bought one of Major Wingfield's lawn tennis kits brought it home and set it up on his uncle's front lawn in Nahant, Massachusetts so he could play this new game with his cousin Fred Sears.

Dwight and Sears fell in love with the game and taught it to a number of people (including their cousin and seven-time US Nationals champion Richard Sears). Many believe that they organized the first tennis tournament in America on his Uncle William Appleton's property in Nahant, Massachusetts in 1876. Dwight beat Fred Sears in the final. His passion for the sport grew from that point on. In fact, he is considered by many to be the "Father" of American Lawn Tennis.

Dwight not only loved playing lawn tennis, he enjoyed teaching others to play the sport. He was one of the first people in America to formalize tennis instruction and publish books on tennis instruction that included pictures. His first book was entitled *Lawn-Tennis* and was published in 1883. His second book *Practical Lawn-Tennis* was published in 1893.

Dwight was only 5 feet 5 inches tall, but he was one of the best tennis players in America. He lost in the singles finals of the 1883 US Championships to Dick Sears and was ranked number 2 in the US in 1885 and 1886. However, he and Dick Sears won 5 doubles titles (1882, 1883, 1884, 1886 and 1887) at the US Championships.

Dwight was an exceptional player. However, he is best remembered as an outstanding administrator. He was a graduate of Harvard Medical School and member of a wealthy family with descendants who came to America on the Mayflower. He did such a good job as president from 1882-1884 that he was reelected president for an unprecedented 19 years (from 1894-1911). As described later in the book, he helped to guide the USNLTA during a vitally important time in its history.

In Dwight's second year as president, Dick Sears won his second US National Championship by defeating Clarence Clark (the first secretary of USNLTA board in 1881) in 1882 by a convincing score of 6-1, 6-4, 6-0. Sears teamed up with Dwight to beat Crawford Nightingale and G.M. Smith in the doubles final 6-0, 6-4, 6-4. In the third US National Championships in 1883, Richard Sears defeated James Dwight 6-2, 6-0, 9-7 in singles. Sears and Dwight teamed up to beat Alexander Van Renssalaer and A.E. Newbold in the Doubles Championships 6-0, 6-2, 6-2.

Dick Sears defeated two of the three founders of the USNLTA in the US Nationals singles finals (Clarence Clark and James Dwight). Amazingly, these two founders were half of the teams that won the first six US Doubles Championships (with different partners). It is hard to imagine the top tennis players of today serving as the top administrators of the sport because of the incredible demands of playing the tour. However, in the early years of the USNLTA, the administrators were some of the best players in the country.

All three of the original USNLTA founders (often referred to as the "Three Musketeers" of American tennis) made history in one way or another. By the second year of the USNLTA Championships two of the three founders had a championship trophy. Clarence Clark won the first US Nationals Doubles Championship and James Dwight won the second US Nationals Doubles Championship (and later became the longest serving president of the USNLTA).

Eugenious Outerbridge (the third Musketeer) never won a US Nationals Singles or Doubles Championship. However, as described earlier in his brief biography, he went on to become president of the Homasote Company, president of the New York Chamber of Commerce and the first chairman of the Port Authority of New York. He was not only one of the most powerful and successful people in the country, he had a bridge named after him.

As the saying goes, "First impressions are lasting." These "Three Musketeers" played an important role in introducing tennis to the American public as the favorite sport of the most influential people in society. This "first impression" of the sport has been "lasting." For good or for bad, tennis has maintained the reputation as the sport of the wealthiest and most influential people in society.

In spite of Dick Sears's domination of the sport from 1881 to 1883, the USNLTA board decided to institute the challenge match system at the US National Championships. In this system, the defending champion was automatically entered in the championship match and only had one match to play to win the championship. The previous year's winner played the winner of the challenge match tournament. It was therefore a lot easier to defend your title because you only had to win one match.

This system was used from 1884 to 1911. It significantly increased the probability of a champion defending his title. This system made it much easier for Richard Sears (who was president of the USNLTA from 1887 to 1888) to win Men's Singles and Doubles US National Championships in 1884, 1885, 1886 and 1887.

In 1884, in the fourth US National Championships, Richard Sears lost his first set in a finals when he defeated Howard Taylor 6-0, 1-6, 6-0, 6-2 in 1884 to win the Singles Championships. Sears and James Dwight beat Alexander Van Renssalaer and A.E. Newbold in the Men's Doubles Championships by a score of 6-4, 6-1, 8-10, 6-4.

T.K. Fraser became the third USNLTA president in 1885 and served in this role for two years. In 1885, in the fifth US National Championships, Sears beat Godfrey Brinley 6-3, 4-6, 6-0, 6-3. Sears and Dwight won their fourth Doubles Championship by beating Henry Slocum (who was USNLTA president from 1892 to 1893) and W.P. Knapp 6-3, 6-0, 6-2.

The Tournament Moves to New York

The U.S. Championships in Newport were extremely successful. Men's singles and doubles debuted in 1881; women's singles debuted in 1887; women's doubles debuted in 1889; and mixed doubles debuted in 1892. Players, spectators and tournament officials considered the tournament a tremendous success. Most USNLTA leaders at the time felt that the tournament site should be the permanent home of the championships.

Breaking The Barriers

However, since its founding, the USNLTA had been controlled by a handful of men residing in the New York, Philadelphia and Boston. That narrow control combined with the success of the U.S. Championships and rapidly growing interest in the sport beyond the northeast corridor triggered significant conflict within the association in the early 20th century. Local communities gained greater influence in the sport. Lawn tennis associations were established around the country to manage the sport in specific geographic areas. New York tournaments were organized by the New York Lawn Tennis Association and tournaments in Northern New Jersey were coordinated by the East Jersey Lawn Tennis Association.

Profitable local tournaments around the country, combined with the sport's growth in the South, the Midwest and in the West led to widespread disagreement about governance of the association, the definition of amateur players and the location of the national tournament. For the first time, people outside the northeastern U.S. exerted significant influence on USNLTA affairs.

Association by-law and constitutional changes were traditionally discussed and voted on at the USNLTA Annual Meeting, typically held in February at the Waldorf-Astoria in New York City. Even though the U.S. National Championships were not contested in New York at the time, American tennis power remained in New York with the leadership and staff of the USNLTA.

The growth of tennis throughout the country, combined with changing world politics and demographics, forced tennis leaders to consider discussing subjects that were previously taboo. Topics included changing the division of power within the association; moving the U.S. Championships from Newport; and, hosting tournaments where amateurs and professionals could compete against each other (which was the most significant area of disagreement until the beginning of the Open era in 1968). Only one of those issues was agreed to at the 1913 annual meeting. For the first time, an organized group of sections was given significant voting privileges in the association.

Each of the then 48 states in the U.S. and the District of Columbia were assigned to a section. According to *American Lawn Tennis*[9] the

---

[9] *American Lawn Tennis (ALT)*, January 15, 1913, Page 398

sections were as follows: Inter-Mountain (Colorado, Idaho, Utah and Wyoming); Middle Atlantic (Delaware, District of Columbia, Maryland and West Virginia); Middle States (New Jersey, New York and Pennsylvania); New England (Connecticut, Maine, Massachusetts, New Hampshire, Rhode Island and Vermont); Northwestern (Minnesota, Montana, North Dakota and South Dakota); Pacific States (California, Oregon and Washington); Southern (Alabama, Florida, Georgia, Louisiana, Mississippi, North Carolina, South Carolina and Tennessee); South Western (Arizona, Arkansas, Nevada, New Mexico, Oklahoma and Texas); and Tri-State (Indiana, Kentucky and Ohio) and Western (Illinois, Iowa, Kansas, Michigan, Missouri, Nebraska and Wisconsin).

This realignment of the association's power base--from complete central control to central leadership with strong regional authority--has defined the organization since 1913. Major national tournaments, among them the National Clay Court Championships, were established in other regions of the country. This unique period of rapid change in U.S. tennis history led to greater sectional power. This increased power led to many more popular tournaments which raised the profile of US tennis around the world and eventually led to greater international influence for both the USNLTA and the U.S. National Championships.

It was clear that the Newport Casino was an elegant place to hold the United States tennis championships. However, the tennis seemed to be less important than the social events and the attention paid to the rich and famous individuals that frequented one of the wealthiest communities in the world. Many of the USNLTA officials who travelled from New York to Newport for the Championships were concerned that tennis was not getting top billing during the tournament. In 1911, Karl H. Behr, a former US Nationals Men's Singles finalist and former Wimbledon Men's Doubles finalist who would later survive the Titanic, lead a group interested in moving the US Championships from Newport to New York City. However, in a vote of 95 to 60, the USNLTA leadership decided to keep the tournament in Newport. It is likely that the relative closeness of this vote influenced the leaders of tennis in America to begin to seriously consider moving the country's tennis championships to a place like New York where tennis, not high society socialization, would take center stage.

CHAPTER 8: The West Side Tennis Club

Moving the Championships

The new balance of power between the sections and the national association led to serious discussions at the 1915 USNLTA Annual Meeting about moving the U.S. National Championships from Newport to another location. It was clear that the tournament's great success deserved a larger expanse to accommodate more spectators and to generate maximum revenue for the USNLTA. Not surprisingly, many sectional leaders preferred that the tournament be moved away from the popular northeast corridor of the United States.

However, the revenue issue was important and New York City was at the time the largest and most influential city in the country. Timing is everything, as the saying goes, and most association leaders at the time believed that a club in New York would increase the visibility and profitability of the U.S. Championships. Coincidently, a local New York tennis club was gaining influence in the world of tennis at the same time that the USNLTA was thinking about moving the championships to New York City.

Thirteen passionate tennis lovers in New York City founded the now famous West Side Tennis Club on April 22, 1892. The first organizational meeting was held on that day and the following individuals were elected: Charles B. Collins, president; E.C. Hebbard, vice president; and, Stephen C. Millett, secretary-treasurer. They first rented space on Central Park West between 88th and 89th Streets and built 3 clay tennis courts. The courts were opened on June 11, 1892. At that time, the main club building was a shed that contained two dressing rooms and two showers without heat. The cost of membership in the club was a $10 initiation fee and a $10 annual fee. To ensure that the club included good tennis players, the founders required members to be able to play a "good game of tennis." In its first full year of operation, the West Side Tennis Club grew to 43 members with five tennis courts on site.

In the late 1890s, many country clubs made lawn tennis available to their members as a secondary amenity. However, the quality of play and rapid growth of the West Side Tennis Club helped to increase interest in tennis. Regular players at the West Side Tennis Club included Harold Humphrey Hacket (ranked as high as number 7 in the US in 1906 and the winner of the US Nationals Men's Doubles Championship in 1907, 1908, 1909 and 1910) and his doubles partner Fred Alexander (who in 1909 also had a high ranking of 7 in the US and, in addition to the 1907, 1908, 1909 and 1910 US Nationals Titles, he won the 1917 US Nationals Doubles title with Harold Throckmorton).

The club held its first open tournament in 1894 and attracted 65 of the best players in the country including Jahial "John" Parmley Paret (who eventually was a finalist in the 1899 US National Championships); Edwin P. Fischer (who was later ranked number 5 in the US and won the US Nationals Mixed Doubles Championships in 1894, 1895, 1896 and 1898); and, O.M. Bostwick and Calhoun Cragin who won the US Indoor Championships in 1901. A very large crowd attended the open tournament which provided refreshments for spectators and very attractive and valuable trophies for the winners. The USNLTA took notice of the success of this tournament and, as a result, decided to hold the Metropolitan Championship at the club in 1897. The first Metropolitan Men's Singles Championship at the Club was won by Stephen Milett (one of the Club's founders).

Once again, builders wanted the land where the West Side Tennis Club was located so the club leaders had to find another location for the rapidly growing organization. In 1902, the club identified vacant land on 117th Street between Morningside Drive and Amsterdam Avenue near Columbia University and close to St. Luke's Hospital and the magnificent Cathedral of St. John the Divine. The club started with four dirt courts and added four additional courts later.

The land was owned by Mrs. John Drexel (a descendent of Anthony J. Drexel who was a partner of J.P. Morgan and founded Drexel University in Philadelphia in 1891). Legend has it that active club member John Appleton "Appy" Allen took a train to Philadelphia to meet with Mrs. Drexel to convince her to lease the club the land. She was, apparently, very resistant at first. However, after three hours of Allen trying to make his case, she gave in to leasing the land to the club for an amazingly low $20 per court per year. The officers of the club at this time were Dr. James Ewing as president; Raymond D. Little as vice president; Albert Kent as secretary; Sheppard Homans, Jr. as treasurer. Oviedo M. Bostwick was in charge of the club's grounds. The club renovated an existing house on the property and made it the most extravagant club house the organization utilized up to that point in its history. Most importantly, the West Side Tennis Club grew in membership to 110 members and had a long waiting list.

The club continued to grow and, in June of 1902 it registered as a nonprofit membership organization under the laws of New York State. The leadership of the organization that signed the registration included some of the most influential individuals in the country. The president of the organization at the time, and the first signer of the registration papers, was Dr. James Stephan Ewing. He was the first Professor of pathology at Cornell University and became famous around the world because of his discovery of a specific type of malignant bone tumor that eventually came to be known as "Ewing Sarcoma." In addition, he helped to establish one of the first cancer research foundations, and in 1907, helped to found the American Association for Cancer Research. In 1913, he helped to found an organization called the American Society for the Control of Cancer. This organization later became the now world famous American Cancer Society. In 1913 he became the pathologist at General Memorial Hospital which is now known as the Memorial Sloan Kettering Cancer Center. As the director of cancer research and the president of the medical board, he played an influential role in making "Sloan Kettering" one of the best known hospitals for patients with cancer.

Other signers include Raymond D. Little (a former Princeton student who won the 1900 intercollegiate tennis singles championship; the US Nationals Mixed Doubles title with Marion Jones in 1901; and, the US Nationals Men's Doubles title with Gustave Touchard in 1911). Sheppard "Shep" Homans, Jr. (the former Princeton All-American fullback in 1890 and 1891) also signed the document. In addition, the organization registration was signed by Albert E. Kent, Henry Dolson Betts, Calhoun Cragin, J. Appleton "Appy" Allen, and, Stephen C. Millett.

The City of New York continued to prosper and grow. Once again, there was great demand for the land where the club was located. Consequently, in 1908, the West Side Tennis Club rented a property on 238th street and Broadway which had room for twelve grass courts (the first time the club had courts of this surface) and fifteen clay courts. This property was different than previous properties because it was larger. Most importantly, for the first time in its history, the West Side Tennis Club had the right to purchase the property from its owners (the estate of former merchant and Mayor of New York City Jacobus Van Cortlandt). There was a chance that the club would finally have a permanent home. Maintaining geographic stability was important because the club was considered by many people to be the most influential tennis club in New York City and continued to run the Metropolitan tennis championship.

Worldwide Competition Comes to New York

The rapidly growing club gained such influence in the tennis world that it was selected to host the final round before the Challenge Round of the 1911 International Lawn Tennis Challenge (which became the Davis Cup after Dwight Davis died in 1945). This match was significant because it was a contest between the US and Great Britain. The winner of this match (which is officially called a "tie" instead of a match) would go on to play the reigning champion Australasia in 1912. The Davis Cup is the largest international team competition in the world. It was founded in 1900 by Dwight Davis as the first international team tennis competition between countries. Since its founding, with 130 participating nations, it has grown to become the largest annual international team competition of any sport. More countries participate in the Davis Cup than any other annual international country competition.

The Davis Cup helped the West Side Tennis Club significantly increase its influence in the global tennis world. The matches drew thousands of people, largely because two of the most popular tennis players in the world, William Larned who had won the 1901, '02, '07, '08, '09, '10 and later '11 US National Championships and Maurice McLaughlin, a dynamic tennis player nicknamed the California Comet, who would go on to win the 1912 and '13 US Nationals Singles Championships. These two legends of the game played for the United States team against the British team. Larned beat Charles Dixon in five sets in the opening match. McLaughlin beat Arthur Lowe in the second match to give the US team a 2-0 lead. However, in doubles, Alfred Beamish and Charles Dixon beat Thomus Bundy and Raymond Little in three straight sets. The match was won when Larned beat Lowe in four sets, giving the US an unsurpassable 3-1 lead. McLaughlin beat Dixon in the final match to give the US a 4-1 victory. Unfortunately, they would go on to play Australasia on January 1-3, 2012 and lose 4-0 in New Zealand. However, the West Side Tennis Club was clearly the winner because of the extraordinary success of the 1911 Davis Cup match.

This event was one of the most important events in the club's history because it convinced many influential leaders that tennis in New York at the West Side Tennis Club was extraordinarily popular. This was extremely important because it proved to the passionate tennis fans that an event featuring only tennis (without the celebrity watching, displays of conspicuous wealth and popular non-tennis entertainment found in Newport) could be extremely successful. This competition also made it clear that the current club location could not handle large crowds on a regular basis. The success of the 1911 Davis Cup therefore convinced the leadership of the Club that it should seek an even larger and more permanent location to accommodate more courts and more tennis fans. The club was in an excellent position to purchase a property because it had carefully managed its finances over the years and had saved approximately $13,000 for the potential purchase of a new location.

The club had appointed a special committee to identify a new location for the club. They considered land in Manhattan; Brooklyn; Bronx; Queens; Nassau County, Long Island; and, northern New Jersey. They initially identified 53 potential locations. The committee was able to reduce this to three properties. The first was in Kew Gardens, Queens; the second was at the Morris Park Estates in the Bronx; and, the third was a property being developed by the Russell Sage Foundation in Forest Hills, Queens.

The property that the Sage was developing called "Forest Hills Gardens" was of special interest to the majority of committee members. In 1906, Brooklyn Attorney Cord Meyer purchase 600 acres of land in a section of Queens called Forest Park. Mr. Meyer renamed this property "Forest Hills." In an effort to build what we would call today "middle class" housing, Margaret Sage (the widow of railroad magnate Russell Sage) purchased 142 of these acres in 1909. As soon as she purchased the land she used, the organization she controlled, the Russell Sage Foundation, was to begin building a model community for working families called Forest Hills Gardens. The organization's objective was to build homes similar to the garden-based communities found in England. Under the guidance of legendary architect Grosvenor Atterbury, the architecture was influenced by the "Tudor" style homes found in London. He utilized an unusual construction method where each house was built from 170 to 190 pre-manufactured concrete panels.

It is rumored that when the members of the search committee first saw the 10 acres of land adjacent to the train station they fell in love with the property. After considerable debate, in a meeting in December of 1912, more than 60% of the West Side Tennis Club members voted to purchase the Forest Hills site. The club therefore agreed to pay the $77,000 asking price for the 10.125 acres of property. They made a down payment of $2,000 and secured a mortgage with an interest rate of 5%. The West Side Tennis Club completed the move to the now legendary Forest Hills tennis complex in the summer of 1913. The leaders of the club decided to have 20 dirt courts developed on a portion of four acres of the property. To match the décor of the area, they built a Tudor-style clubhouse for $25,000 in 1914 which firmly established the club as the newest and most beautiful tennis site in New York City.

The grounds committee at the time was headed by Julian S, Myrick, who, in addition to this volunteer responsibility was the vice president of the Club. At the time of this move, the club membership was comprised of exactly 600 members. West Side's membership included 463 men, 123 women, 10 non-resident members and 4 honorary members. The new facility, combined with the influential and active membership, put the club in a great position to bid on the rights to host the 1914 Davis Cup Challenge Round, where the US, as the defending champion, would host the challenging nation for the team championship of the world. The West Side Tennis Club used its influence with the USNLTA to convince the organization's leaders to host the competition at its newly renovated facility.

War and Tennis

Once the club was officially notified by the USNLTA that it was selected as the 1914 Davis Cup host, they focused on creating an entertaining and profitable environment for tennis fans to watch the matches. Even though they were heavily in debt, they built seating for 15,000 spectators around two lawn tennis courts. The West Side Tennis Club did everything it could to ensure that it was prepared for the matches. However, the world was on the brink of war so the battle for the Davis Cup played out with a pending world war in the backdrop.

The Influence of War

The assassination on June 28, 1914 of the heir to the throne of Austria-Hungary, Archduke Franz Ferdinand and his wife Duchess Sophie Chotek of Austria, started a domino effect of international conflict that led to the outbreak of what would eventually be called World War I in Europe in late July of that year. Tragically, this war would involve every major country in the world, would last from 1914 to 1918, and ultimately lead to the death of more than 9 million soldiers and 7 million civilians. It started out as a war between a collaboration of countries called the "Allies" (the United Kingdom, France and the Russian Empire) and a group of countries called the "Central Powers" (Germany and Austria-Hungary). The conflict eventually expanded with Bulgaria and Turkey joining the Central Powers and the United States, Japan and Italy joining the Allies.

Gavrilo Princip was a member of a revolutionary group called "Young Bosnia" which sought to separate Bosnia from Austria-Hungary and unite it with the Kingdom of Serbia. Princip was one of seven conspirators who planned the assassination of the Archduke. Several of his co-conspirators failed in their attempts to murder the couple as they attended the opening of a hospital in Bosnia and Herzegovina. In an attempt to escape the conspirators, the car carrying the couple tragically stopped near the location where Princip was stationed. He walked up to the car and fired two fatal shots from five feet away at the Archduke and Duchess. The war started when, within a month of the assassination, Austria-Hungary declared war on Serbia and invaded the country in an attempt to eliminate future uprisings. Russia began its military support of Serbia while Germany, which supported Austria-Hungary, took advantage of the war to invade Belgium and Luxembourg. This lead Britain and Australia to declare war on Germany. In 1914, Russia had some military success against Austria-Hungary; however. it failed in its attempt to invade the eastern part of Germany. The war continued to escalate from there.

Recreational sports seemed unimportant to much of the world during a time of significant European military strife. It was clear that tennis would take a back seat during the conflict in Europe. The European world of tennis was more focused on war than the sport. As a result, tennis in New York City, especially at the West Side Tennis Club, gained greater international visibility without competition from European tennis. In spite of the global conflict, the Davis Cup competition continued. Amazingly, the teams that were in contention for the cup represented some of the countries at war. The Australasia (Australia, New Zealand and New Guinea), Belgium, British Isles (England, Ireland, Scotland and Wales), France and German teams were in contention for the Cup in spite of the pending conflict in their countries. In addition, Canada and the United States, who would not join the war that year, had a chance to win the competition. Because of the global tension outside of America the final series of Davis Cup matches were held in the US. The German team (which had a bye) and the Australasian team (which beat Canada to advance to the semi-finals) held their Davis Cup match in Pittsburgh from July 30th to August 1st during the period when the world was waiting to hear if a European war was going to start. Rumor has it that word of the war was kept from the players until after the match was completed.

Australasia won the match 5-0 and earned the right to play the British Isles team (who had handily beaten Belgium in the quarterfinals and then France in the semifinals) in the final round. The winner would

Breaking The Barriers

play the United States team which, because it won the previous year, received a bye to the challenge round (championship match). Australasia beat the British Isles team at the Longwood Cricket Club in Boston. The 1914 Davis Cup Championship match was set to be played at the West Side Tennis Club in Forest Hills on August 13, 14 and 15.

The match was notable because it featured two well-known Americans and two extremely accomplished Australians battling each other for the world team championship of tennis. Maurice Evans McLoughlin was a popular, powerful and fast right-handed serve and volley player from the West Coast who won the US Men's Singles and Doubles Championships in 1912 and 1913 and was a finalist in the 1913 Wimbledon Men's Singles Championships. After the Davis Cup match, he would win the 1914 US Nationals Men's Doubles Championships.

R. Norris Williams was an up and coming player from Philadelphia who won the 1912 US Mixed Doubles Championship. Later in his career he would go on to win the 1914 and 1916 US National Singles Championships; the US National Men's Doubles Championships in 1925 and 1926; and the 1920 Wimbledon Men's Doubles Championships. However, he will forever be remembered as one of the best known survivors of the RMS Titanic disaster. Twenty-one year old Williams and his dad, Charles Duane Williams, were in their first class cabin when the ship struck an iceberg and sank. Williams was swept off of the ship by a wave. However, he was able to swim to a lifeboat, climb in and make it to the rescue ship. Tragically, his father lost his life in the disaster.

The members of the Australasia team were even bigger stars of the international tennis world. Tony Wilding won the Wimbledon Men's Singles Championship in 1910, 1911, 1912 and 1913 and the Australian Men's Singles Championship in 1906 and 1909. He was also an accomplished doubles player who won the 1907, 1908, 1910 and 1914 Wimbledon Men's Doubles Championships and the 1906 Men's Australian Doubles Championship. Norman Everard Brookes won the 1907 and 1914 Wimbledon Men's Singles Championships; the 1907 and 1914 Wimbledon Men's Doubles Championships; the 1911 Australian Men's Singles Championship and later the 1924

Australian Men's Doubles Championship; and the 1919 US Men's Doubles Championship. Clearly, this Davis Cup match was between the countries with some of the most accomplished tennis players in the world at that time. It was a dream match-up for spectators.

In the first match, R. Norris Willliams of the US lost to Tony Wilding of Australasia in three straight sets 7-5, 6-2, 6-3. In the second match Maurice McLoughlin of the US beat Norman Brookes of Australasia 17-15, 6-3, 6-3. The Australasian doubles team of Norman Brookes and Tony Wilding beat the US team of Thomas Bundy and Maurice McLoughlin 6-3, 8-6, 9-7 to take a 2 to 1 lead. On the final day of the competition Norman Brookes beat R. Norris Williams 6-1, 6-2, 8-10 and 6-3 to ensure a victory for Australasia. In the final match, Maurice McLoughlin beat Tony Wilding 6-2, 6-3, 2-6, 6-2.

The US may have lost the match 3-2; however, the West Side Tennis Club was clearly the winner. The Davis Cup Championship match was a success for the club in every way imaginable. The club's investment in the additional seating was brilliant because it enabled them to accommodate thousands of additional spectators. The event helped the club make a lot of money and gain tremendous influence in the international tennis community.

The dream US vs. Australasia match-up drew record crowds and made this match one of the most popular tennis events in American history. Most importantly, the tremendous financial and spectator success of the Davis Cup matches in Forest Hills convinced many of the most influential leaders in the USLTA to recommend that the US Championships move from Newport to Forest Hills. These individuals were convinced that this move would attract more spectators and grow interest in the sport.

However, change is never easy. There were some leaders who wanted to keep the tournament in Newport for sentimental reasons. However, it took an influential individual named Julian Myrick to lead the effort to convince the majority of the USNLTA leadership that moving the tournament to Forest Hills was the right thing to do. Myrick, who became president of West Side in 1915, was an entrepreneur and a natural salesman who started a successful insurance company, Ives and Myrick. He later became one of the founders of the American College of Life Underwriters. Myrick was extremely engaging and skilled at selling life insurance and tennis. He effectively developed a team of influential supporters who collectively used the success of the Davis Cup matches to convince the leaders of the USNLTA to move the U.S. Championships in 1915 from the Newport Casino to the West Side Tennis Club in Forest Hills.

Myrick, Karl H. Behr and several other tennis leaders made it seem that making the move was the only rational choice. New York City was easier to get to than Newport and Forest Hills had become the tennis capital of New York City. Holding the tournament at the West Side Tennis Club, the nicest and most influential club in the city, would enable the USNLTA to grow the tournament because the facility could accommodate many more spectators than the Newport Casino. In addition, the club had significantly more spacious grounds than the Newport Casino and an iconic Tudor clubhouse. Moreover, the international visibility that West Side gained by hosting the 1914 Davis Cup would give the US Championships greater visibility around the world. Finally, and perhaps most importantly, the Myrick team made the case that the New York tournament in Forest Hills would generate significantly more revenue for the USNLTA than the Newport tournament.

The governing body of tennis in the United States, the USNLTA, therefore decided (based on a vote on February 5, 1915 of 128 in favor and 119 against) to move the US National Championships to Forest Hills for the 1915 tournament. The people in Newport were obviously disappointed by this move. However, the Casino was able to survive the loss of the tournament by establishing a successful tennis tournament called the Newport Casino Invitational Tournament in 1915 which served as a grass court warm-up for the US Nationals at Forest Hills. This tournament was therefore able to attract many of the top tennis players in the world.

The first US Championships at the West Side Tennis Club in Forest Hills in 1915 were a tremendous success. In the Men's Singles final, Californian Bill Johnston beat Californian Maurice McLoughlin 1-6, 6-0, 7-5, 10-8 to win the Championships. In the Women's Singles Final; Molla Bjurstedt of Norway beat Hazel Hotchkiss Wightman of Massachusetts 4-6, 6-2, 6-0 to win the tournament. In the Men's Doubles final, Clarence Griffin and Bill Johnston beat Maurice

McLoughlin and Tom Bundy in a very close 2-6, 6-3, 6-4, 3-6, 6-3 to win the competition. In the Women's Doubles final, Hazel Hotchkiss Wightman and Elenora Sears beat Helen Homans McLean and G. L. Chapman 10-8, 6-2 to win the Championship. In the Mixed Doubles final, Hazel Hotchkiss Wightman and Harry C. Johnson beat Irving Wright and Molla Bjurstedt 6-0, 6-1. The Club was able to get the spectators it had hoped for and therefore proved that it was the perfect home for the modern US Championships.

The move of the US Championships to New York in 1915 positioned Forest Hills as the "Tennis Capital" of the U.S. By leading the effort to move the tournament Myrick positioned himself to eventually become an influential president of the USNLTA. Unfortunately, the world war was expanding and tennis in other parts of the world was facing tremendous obstacles. Initially called the Great War, the first World War forced the cancellation of the Wimbledon Championships in 1915, 1916, 1917 and 1918; the French Championships in 1915, 1916, 1917, 1918 and 1919; and the Australian Championships in 1916, 1917 and 1918. However, since the United States was not directly involved in the War prior to 1917 (and the war had not touched US soil) the U.S. Championships at Forest Hills were not cancelled.

Tennis Goes Mainstream

The success of the 1915 U.S. Championships at West Side, combined with that year's cancellation of Wimbledon and the French, gave New York a unique status in the tennis world. The popularity of the sport was not limited to the white upper classes. Many middle class white citizens, as they learned more about the sport, fell in love with the game. In addition, many African Americans, who had been excluded from USNLTA events and local "white only" tennis courts, loved the sport as well. Since the late 1800s, they had developed local black tennis clubs where individuals could develop their game in their community. The clubs also grew interest in the sport by establishing popular competitions between clubs that drew many spectators.

It is fascinating to note that the sport, as in the white community, attracted the most successful individuals in the black community. The love of the sport was so deep in the black community that on November 30, 1916, a small group of African-American leaders in Washington, DC formed the American Tennis Association (ATA) to help to govern and grow tennis in the segregated communities of color. These individuals, Dr. Harry S. McCard, Dr. William H. Wright, Dr. B.M. Rhetta, Mr. Ralph Cook, Henry Freeman and Tally Holmes drew up the organization papers and formed this influential association which has become the oldest black sports organization in the US.

The increasing success of the U.S. Championships in 1916, 1917 and 1918, years when Wimbledon, the French and the Australian Championships were still in hiatus, coupled with the growing international power of the New York City-based USNLTA, firmly established New York City as the "Tennis Capital of the World," an unofficial title it has held for more than 100 years.

Woodrow Wilson was the president of the United States on April 6, 1917 when Congress voted to support his declaration of war on Germany. To support this war effort, the U.S. drafted 2.8 million men to defend the country. The USNLTA, at its February 1917 annual meeting, adopted a resolution supporting President Wilson and the Congress in severing diplomatic relations with Germany. A month later, the association supported proposals for the military draft. Even the USNLTA president, George Adee, was assigned to Fort Dix in New Jersey for military training.

This major military conflict not only intensified the focus of society on the World War, it surprisingly influenced people to think about the cultural and recreational needs of local communities. In fact, President Wilson stated publicly, on several occasions, his belief that sports and exercise could help the war effort by ensuring that young men would be healthy enough to fight a war for the United States.

This focus on local communities resulted in the USNLTA's sectional associations playing a more important role in popularizing grassroots tennis. Local leaders could promote the sport in neighborhoods in a way that the USNLTA national office could not. They were familiar with people's local needs and could manage the sport to suit particular locations around the country. This new hyper-local world tennis order increased the influence of sectional associations and paved the way for the establishment of the seventeen powerful sections of the United States Tennis Association (USTA) that exist today.

In 1917, the US National Championship was officially renamed the "National Patriotic Tournament" to honor the country during a time of war. No trophies were handed out to the winners and the fees for entering the tournament were donated to the American Red Cross to support their efforts in the war. It was the only Grand Slam tennis tournament held that year. In the Men's Singles final, Robert Lindley Murray of California beat Nathaniel William Niles of Massachusetts 5-7, 8-6, 6-3, 6-3. In the Women's Singles final Molla Bjurstedt of Norway defeated Marion Wyckoff Vanderhoef of New York 4-6, 6-0, 6-2. In the Men's Doubles final, two former Princeton collegiate tennis players who lived in New Jersey, Fred Alexander and Harold Throckmorton, beat fellow US players Harry Johnson and Irving Wright 11-9, 6-4, 6-4. In the Women's Doubles final, Molla Bjurstedt and Elnora Sears from Boston beat fellow US players Phyllis Walsh and Grace Moore LeRoy 6-2, 6-4. In the Mixed Doubles Molla Bjurstedt and Irving Wright defeated Florence Ballin of New York and future legendary player Bill Tilden of Philadelphia 10-12, 6-1, 6-3.

The first US troops arrived in France on June 25, 1917. The US, like the rest of the western world, focused much of its financial and human resources on global war until one of the main treaties to end the war, the Treaty of Versailles, was signed on January 25, 1919. Because the end of the world war was imminent, the 1918 tournament was renamed the US Nationals and continued to be one of the most popular and successful sporting events not only in the country, but in the world.

The Forest Hills Stadium

To appease tennis leaders from Philadelphia, the USNLTA decided to hold the 1921 Davis Cup matches in Forest Hills and the US Nationals at the Germantown Cricket Club in Philadelphia, Pennsylvania. The Japanese team beat the Australian team and played the US team for the championship on September 2nd to 5th at the West

Breaking The Barriers

Side Tennis Club in Forest Hills. The US team, led by Bill Johnston and Bill Tilden, beat Japan 5-0 to defend its title as world champions.

The US National Championships were moved to the Germantown Cricket Club in Philadelphia from September 9th through 19th. This venue was chosen because it was impossible for the West Side Tennis Club to host both the Davis Cup matches and then four days later host the US National Championships. It is interesting to note that, at that point in tennis history, hosing the Davis Cup was significantly more prestigious than hosting the US Nationals. It is the opposite in today's tennis world.

In the Men's Singles final, two Philadelphians played each other. Bill Tilden beat Wallace F. Johnson 6-1, 6-3, 6-1. In the Women's Singles final, Molla Bjurstedt Mallory from Norway beat Mary Brown from California 4-6, 6-4, 6-2. In the Men's Doubles final, Bill Tilden and Vincent Richards from New York beat Richard Norris Williams of Philadelphia and Watson McLean Washburn of New York 13-11, 12-10, 6-1. In the Women's Doubles final, Mary Browne and Louise Riddell-Williams of the US beat Helen Gilleandeau and Aletta Bailey Morris 6-3, 6-2. In the Mixed Doubles final, Mary Browne and Bill Johnston defeated Molla Bjurstedt Mallory and Bill Tilden 3-6, 6-4, 6-3.

The 1922 Davis Cup was played at the West Side Tennis Club in Forest Hills from September 1st to 5th. In the Challenge Round, the US team of Bill Tilden, Bill Johnston and Vincent Richards beat Australia 4-1 to hold their title. The US Nationals were held for logistical reasons, once again, at the Germantown Cricket Club from September 8th to 16th. The winners were Bill Tilden in Men's Singles; Helen Wills Moody of California in Women's Singles; Bill Tilden and Vincent Richards in Men's Doubles; Marion Zinderstein Jessup and Helen Wills Moody in Women's Doubles; and Molla Bjurstedt Mallory and Bill Tilden in Mixed Doubles.

Everything seemed to be going well for tennis in the US. The American Davis Cup team and top players were the best in the world. However, this domination resulted in a lower attendance at the Davis Cup matches. The audiences were not as interested in the sport when there were no close global tennis rivalries. They were less interested in matches where the outcome was all but certain. Something had to be done to attract the large audiences that the club was used to attracting in previous events. Consequently, the West Side Tennis Club board of Governors decided to build a stadium that would draw large crowds by making tennis matches major sporting events. The board appointed a committee to develop plans to build a stadium on the club's property.

The committee was created when Louis J. Carruthers (who later served as president of the USLTA from 1931-1932) was club president and was led by former club president and professional engineer Charles S. Landers (who became the first president of the USLTA Eastern Section in 1921 and served in this position through 1922). Landers worked closely with club member and well-known architect Kenneth MacKenzie Murchison to develop the design of a stadium that would seat 14,000 people. In order to build the large stadium, the club had to purchase additional property from the Sage Foundation. The cost of the land acquisition and construction of the stadium was to be in excess of $150,000. To ensure that they had the income necessary to pay the debt service on the loan, the club wisely entered into an agreement with the USLTA to hold important events at the stadium.

According to the book *The West Side Tennis Club Story*, published by the club in 1952 to honor its 60th Anniversary (1892-1952), the club entered into an unprecedented agreement with the USLTA that stated that the West Side Tennis Club "Was to have the right to hold the Davis Cup Challenge Round in 1923, the Men's National Singles Championship from 1924 to 1928, and either the Singles, Davis Cup, or Doubles from 1929 to 1932, thus covering a ten year period."[10] This contract enabled the club to sell subscriptions over 10 year period for choice seats to these popular tennis events. The club wisely made 1,500 premium seats available for purchase for 10 years at a cost of $110 a year. The West Side Tennis Club sold all of the available subscriptions and, in 1923, used this income to take care of a large part of the funding required for the construction of the stadium.

In spite of the success of tennis events at the West Side Tennis Club, the USNLTA still took bids from other clubs to host the US Nationals. The club hoped that the construction of the stadium would ensure that the club retained the tournament for many years.

---

[10] Page 23, *The West Side Tennis Club Story: 60th Anniversary 1892-1952*, Edward C. Potter, 1953

Breaking The Barriers

Construction of the stadium began in April of 1923. President Myrick and the executive committee of the board agreed that the very first event in the stadium would be the first Wightman Cup competition. This event was intended to be an annual women's team tennis competition between the United States and Britain. The trophy to the winning team was donated by Hazel Hotchkiss Wightman who won the US Nationals Women's Singles in 1909, 1910, 1911 and 1919; Women's Doubles in 1909, 1910, 1911 and 1919; and, Mixed Doubles in 1909, 1910, 1911, 1915, 1918 and 1920. In addition, she won the 1924 Wimbledon Women's Doubles Championships; the 1924 Women's Doubles Olympic Gold Medal; and the 1924 Mixed Doubles Olympic Gold Medal.

The competition started on Sunday, August 12, 1923. It was originally supposed to start on Friday, August 10th. However, it was delayed until Sunday in honor of President Warren G. Harding who died suddenly of a heart attack in a San Francisco hotel room on August 2, 1923. Approximately 5,000 people came to the grand opening of the partially completed stadium. The facility was in the shape of a semicircle large enough to accommodate three courts (the Wimbledon Stadium only had one court). There were 39 rows of seats divided among ten entrances. The stadium started the opening match in grand style. Four trumpeters played "The Star-Spangled Banner" while the American, British and West Side Tennis Club flags were each raised in order.

The Stadium Opens with a Rising Star

The very first match was between the American Helen Wills and the British star Kathleen McKane. Helen Wills (who later became Helen Wills Moody) had not yet become a major global tennis star when she played this match. However, she would go on to win her first US Nationals Women's Singles Championship in 1923. Starting with that victory she went on to win 7 US National Singles Championships; 8 Wimbledon Woman's Singles Championships; 4 French Women's Singles Championships; the 1924 Olympic Gold Medal in Women's Singles; 4 US Nationals Women's Doubles Championships; 3 Wimbledon Women's Doubles Championships; 2 French Women's

Doubles Championships; 2 US Nationals Mixed Doubles Championships; 1 Wimbledon Mixed Doubles Championships; and, 3 French Mixed Doubles Championships. However, prior to this first Wightman Cup she was a 17 year-old who had won no championships.

Kathleen McKane, was older. However, she was a 26 year-old up-and-comer as well. McKane was a finalist in the 1922 Wimbledon Women's Singles Championship. However, her most significant accomplishments followed the inaugural Wightman Cup match. McKane went on to win the Women's Singles Championship at Wimbledon in 1924 and 1926. She was a Women's Singles finalist in the 1925 US Nationals and the 1923 and 1925 French Championships. She won the 1923 and 1927 Women's Doubles Championship at the US Nationals and the Olympic Gold Medal in Women's Doubles in 1920. She won the Mixed Doubles US Nationals Championship in 1925 and the Wimbledon Mixed Doubles Championship in 1924 and 1926.

In the first match Helen Wills beat Kathleen McKane 6-2, 7-5. The United States, behind the strength of a team that included a relatively new American citizen and former Norwegian star Molla Bjurstedt Mallory, Eleanor Goss and Hazel Hotchkiss Wightman, won the competition 7-0. However, the most important thing about this match is that it was the event that introduced the tennis stadium that played a critical role in making tennis the sport it is today. The Forest Hills Stadium demonstrated to Americans that tennis is a powerful spectator sport that can enthrall thousands of fans in the same way that baseball, football, soccer and basketball had for many years. This stadium helped to create a tennis fan base that has played a vitally important role in helping to make today's US Open the largest (in terms of attendance) annual sporting event in the world.

> *"The Forest Hills Stadium proved interest in tennis rivaled other spectator sports"*

CHAPTER 9: The International Tennis Hall of Fame

Newport Casino Invitational Tournament

Fortunately, the success of the West Side Tennis Club did not mean failure for the Newport Casino. The Newport Casino Invitational Tournament, which started when the US Nationals were moved to the West Side Tennis Cub in 1915, became a very popular event because it attracted extraordinary tennis players and served the entertainment and social needs of the wealthy fan base.

The tournament invited 50 of the best male tennis players in the world to compete in a grass tennis tournament that served as a warm up for the US Nationals tournament at the West Side Tennis Club (and the Germantown Cricket Club for two years). The inaugural tournament was won by Richard Norris Williams who beat Maurice McLoughlin in an entertaining four set match (5-7, 6-4, 6-3, 6-3). In 1916, Japanese player Ichiya Kumagae stunned the largely American field by beating Bill Johnston in an amazing five set match (6-1, 9-7, 5-7, 2-6, 9-7). The tournament was not held because of the war in 1917 and 1918. However, in 1919, Bill Tilden beat Bill Johnston in the finals 7-5, 8-6, 6-1.

The tournament continued uninterrupted until 1942. Unfortunately, because of the Second World War it was not held from 1943 to 1945. However, it resumed in 1946 with American tennis legend Gardnar Mulloy beating Ted Schroeder 6-1, 2-6, 14-12, 6-3. The tournament once again continued uninterrupted until 1967 when professional tennis changed the sports world forever.

The National Tennis Hall of Fame

The Newport Casino Invitational ensured that tennis was a major focus of the Casino even after the US National tournament moved to New York City. The tournament became a major stop in the East Coast grass court amateur circuit that culminated with the US National Championships at the West Side Tennis Club.

The president of the Casino, James H. Van Allen, led a team of people that lobbied the United States Lawn Tennis Association to establish a Hall of Fame at the Newport Casino. Their argument was that since tournament tennis in America was founded and made popular at the beautiful Newport Casino, it was logical that a hall of fame for the sport be established on the historic grounds of the place where the US Nationals started. In 1954, the USLTA leadership agreed to establish the "National Tennis Hall of Fame" at the Newport Casino. On September 13, 1954, this legendary museum was founded to preserve the history of American tennis and enshrine tennis heroes and heroines. On July 9, 1955 the first official National Tennis Hall of Fame Induction Ceremony was held. Since that day some extraordinary tennis players and individuals have been inducted into the Hall of Fame. The complete list of inductees can be found on the organization's website - www.tennisfame.com.

The Open Era of Tennis

Tennis was undergoing explosive change in the early 1900s. The sport continued to expand throughout the world. This expansion influenced players who were not from wealthy families to play the sport. This access to the sport by players from the middle class led to the establishment of "under-the-table" payments for players, paid exhibitions and eventually a pro circuit. When some of the best players in the world joined the pro circuit so they could make a living playing tennis, support for professional tennis grew rapidly. The first professional tennis tour was started by promoter Charles C. "C.C." Pyle in 1926. Pyle was a sports agent who represented iconic American football star Red Grange. He organized a professional tennis exhibition

Breaking The Barriers

tour starring legendary players Suzanne Lenglen and Vinnie Richards. By joining the tour they gave up their amateur status and could not compete in the major amateur tournaments. This restriction prevented other tennis stars from joining the pro tour and limited its growth. The tour therefore did not gain widespread popularity until the 1950s.

The growing pro circuit in the 1950s and 1960s led to the biggest divide in tennis history. A deep conflict developed between those individuals who felt the major tournaments should only be open to amateurs and those who believed that these major events should be open to all players (including professionals). The supporters of the status quo of amateur tennis felt that it was a "gentleman's" and "ladies'" sport and it was "unbecoming" to earn a salary for playing the sport. The supporters of pro tennis felt that it was time to change to a sport that is "open" to all people (whether or not they were wealthy). The major tennis governing bodies around the world therefore faced intense internal conflict as the supporters of both sides clashed. The conflict between the advocates of the status quo and those who wanted open professional tennis became a global public battle between the wealthy tennis elites and the average fans of the sport.

Tennis has always had three very distinct levels of tournaments. The lower level is represented by the regular local tennis tournaments that attract the best players in a region; the middle level is represented by those tournaments that attract many of the best players in the world; and the upper level included world class events that attracted all of the best players. The tournaments classified as lower and middle level have changed significantly over time. The upper level events have remained the four "Major" or "Grand Slam" tournaments. These influential global sporting events dominate the sport and dictate how the lesser tournaments are structured. The four tournaments, when they were amateur events, were named the Australian Championships, the French Championships, Wimbledon and the US Championships.

The growth of tennis internationally significantly increased interest in the sport. This led to extraordinary opportunities to make money from the sport. The pressure from the players (and fans) to allow professional players to compete with amateurs, combined with the opportunity to increase tournament revenue, influenced the leadership of the tennis governing bodies that controlled the four Grand Slam tournaments to transform these amateur championships to "Open" (professional events open to all of the best players in the world) tournaments. Consequently, in 1967, three of the four major tournaments adapted the names that they are now known by: the "Australian Open"; the "French Open"; and "US Open." Wimbledon kept its name but opened its draw to both professionals and amateurs. In 1968 (frequently called the beginning of the "Open Era" of tennis), for the first time in history, both amateurs and professionals could compete against each other in the Grand Slam tournaments. This was the most significant event in the sport since men played tennis in the very first Olympic Games (women were not allowed to compete in tennis in the Olympics until 1900).

The very first Open Era tournament was the 1968 British Hardcourt Championships played at The West Hants Club in Bournemouth, England. The tournament was held from April 22nd through April 27th. Ken Rosewall and Virginia Wade won the Men's and Women's Singles respectively. Rosewall received a check for $2,400. Men's Finalist Rod Laver received a check of $1,200. Virginia Wade would have received a $720 check. However, because she was still an amateur, she could not accept the prize. Winnie Shaw, the woman she beat therefore kept the $720 prize money. Roy Emerson and Rod Laver won the Men's Doubles. Christine Truman Janes and Nell Truman won the Women's Doubles. Virginia Wade and Bob Howe won the Mixed Doubles.

The first Grand Slam tournament of the Open Era in tennis was the 1968 French Open which took place from May 27th through June 9th. In the Men's Singles Final, Ken Rosewall defeated Rod Laver 6-3, 6-1, 2-6, 6-2. In the Women's Singles Final, Nancy Richey defeated Ann Haydon-Jones 5-7, 6-4, 6-1. In the Men's Doubles Final, Ken Rosewall and Fred Stolle defeated Roy Emerson and Rod Laver 6-3, 6-4, 6-3. In the Women's Doubles Final, Francoise Durr and Ann Haydon-Jones defeated Rosemary Casals and Billie Jean King 7-5, 4-6, 6-4. In the Mixed Doubles Final, Francoise Durr and Jean-Claude Barclay defeated Billie Jean King and Owen Davidson 6-1, 6-4.

Unfortunately, opening tournaments to both amateurs and professionals did not solve all of the problems in professional tennis. Many of the best tennis players in the world were under contract to

Breaking The Barriers

promoters and were prohibited from playing in certain tournaments. Many of the best players in the world could not make a living winning the amateur Grand Slam Tournaments like Wimbledon and the US Nationals. They therefore signed binding contracts with tennis promoters who would pay them to play in exhibition matches around the world. The eight players under contract to agent Dan Dixon (Pier Barthes, Earl "Butch" Buchholz, Cliff Drysdale, John Newcombe, Nikki Pilic, Dennis Ralston, Tony Roche and Roger Taylor), who were nicknamed the "Handsome Eight," were not allowed to participate in the 1968 French Open. The growing revenue available in the sport (from ticket sales and sponsorship) led to conflicts between agents and tennis promoters that divided tennis for several years. The National Tennis League (NTL), the World Championship of Tennis (WCT), the Grand Prix Circuit and several other organizations all competed for the top players. This fight over contracts and money led to player boycotts and public disputes that prevented tennis fans from seeing the best players competing in all of the major tennis tournaments all of the time.

Wimbledon became the second Open Grand Slam tournament. Rod Laver beat Tony Roche in the Men's Final, Billie Jean King beat Judy Tegart Dalton in the Women's Singles Final, John Newcombe and Tony Roche beat Ken Rosewall and Fred Stolle in the Men's Doubles Final, Rosemary Casals and Billie Jean King beat Francoise Durr and Ann Haydon-Jones in the Women's Doubles Fina, and, Margaret Court and Ken Fletcher beat Alex Metreveli and Olga Morozova in the Mixed Doubles Final. The Men's Singles Winner received 2,000 pounds and the Finalist received 1,300 pounds. The Women's Singles Winner received 750 pounds and the Finalist received 450 pounds. The Men's Doubles Winners received 800 pounds and the Finalists received 500 pounds. The Women's Doubles Winners received 500 pounds and the Finalists received 300 pounds. The Mixed Doubles Winners received 450 pounds and the Finalists received 300 pounds.

The next open Grand Slam tournament was the first United States Open Championships. The global influence of US business and politics made the 1968 US Open one of the most anticipated sporting events in history. For the first time, the professional legends of the game would compete against the amateur legends of the game on the beautiful grass courts of the West Side Tennis Club in Forest Hills.

The tournament ran from August 29th through September 8th. It was the 88th US Nationals tournament and the very first US Open. The number one seed in the tournament was Rod Laver and the number 2 seed was Tony Roche. However, it was 5th seeded Arthur Ashe who stunned the field and won the very first US Open Men's Singles by beating the number 8 seed Tom Okker in a thrilling 14-12, 5-7, 6-3, 3-6, 6-3 finals match. Arthur Ashe was an amateur player so he could not collect the winners $14,000 check so it was given to Tom Okker. Legend has it that an anonymous donor, who to this day remains unknown, donated, on Christmas 1968, 15,000 shares of General Motors stock to Arthur Ashe to make up for the prize money he did not receive as an amateur.

Smokin' Ashe—The Big Breakthrough

Arthur Ashe's victory was extraordinarily significant on many different levels. First, the win was significant because he was the very first person to win the US Open (which has become the largest annually occurring sporting event in the world in terms of attendance). Second, he was an amateur who, in the first year of competition between the supposedly inferior amateurs and superior professionals, made a strong case for the superiority of the amateurs. Third, and perhaps most importantly, he proved that an African-American can be the best competitor in one of the most elite, exclusive and richest sports in the world.

The color barrier was broken when: Fritz Pollard and Bobby Marshall entered into what eventually became the National Football League in 1920; Jackie Robinson entered Major League Baseball in 1947; Chuck Cooper entered the National Basketball League in 1950; Althea Gibson played in the US National Championships in 1950; and, Willie O'Ree entered into the National Hockey League in 1958. These extraordinary accomplishments opened doors of incredible opportunity for people of color throughout the world. However, the thing that made Arthur Ashe's 1968 US Open victory special was the incredible fact that he broke through racial barriers while being the first person of any

Breaking The Barriers

race to accomplish this incredible feat. Jackie Robinson was an amazing baseball player who won the first Rookie of the Year Award in 1947 and the Most Valuable Player (MVP) Award in 1949. Many people ask the question "How significant was Arthur Ashe's US Open victory?" It was one of the most significant barrier breaking moments in professional sports. Arthur Ashe's victory at the inaugural US Open was the equivalent of Jackie Robinson winning the Baseball MVP Award while breaking the color barrier in his first year in the major leagues. Unfortunately, as extraordinary as Jackie Robinson was, he did not win the 1947 National League MVP Award. New York Yankee legend Joe DiMaggio won it in the American League and Boston Braves player Bob Elliott won it in the National League.

In the inaugural US Open Women's Championship, number 6 seed Virginia Wade from England stunned top seed American Billie Jean King by beating her 6-4, 6-2. Virginia Wade received $6,000 for winning the first US Open. In Men's Doubles, Americans Bob Lutz and Stan Smith beat Arthur Ashe and Spaniard Andres Gimeno 11-9, 6-1, 7-5. In Women's Doubles, Brazilian Maria Bueno and Australian Margaret Court defeated Americans Rosemary Casals and Billie Jean King 4-6, 9-7, 8-6. There was no mixed doubles competition at the inaugural US Open.

The US Open has grown to become one of the most influential sporting events in the world. I don't think that the organizers of the 1968 Forest Hills tournament had any idea how incredibly powerful and influential this tournament would become. The attendance at the US Open at Forest Hills continued to grow every year until it outgrew the legendary West Side Tennis Club. The attendance at the US Open in 1968 was 97,294 with an average daily attendance of 8,845. The attendance at the West Side Tennis Club increased every year reaching a high of 218,480 with an average daily attendance of 10,404 in 1978.

The tournament moved to what would become the United States Tennis Association Billie Jean King National Tennis Center in 1978 to accommodate significantly many more tennis fans. In the first year of the US Open in this venue, total attendance reached an all-time high of 275,300 with an average daily attendance of 13,110. It was clear that, from the USTA's standpoint, the controversial move to Flushing Meadows was brilliant. The attendance has increased every year until

2009 when it reached an incredible all-time total attendance high of 721,059 with an average daily attendance of 27,733.

The International Tennis Hall of Fame

The only constant during this chaotic period in tennis was the Tennis Hall of Fame at the Newport Casino. This organization continued to memorialize legends of the game every year (whether or not they played the amateur or professional tennis circuits). The rapid growth of professional tennis around the world influenced the National Tennis Hall of Fame leadership to become more international. On April 13, 1976, the organization changed its name to the International Tennis Hall of Fame (ITHF) to let the world know that it honors the global legends of the sport. The ITHF is not only the premier organization recording and celebrating the history of tennis, it holds the Hall of Fame professional tennis championships on its beautiful grass courts. The museum contains some incredible memorabilia of the sport as well as outstanding interactive exhibits on all aspects of the sport (including the *Breaking the Barriers* exhibit that I helped to create).

CHAPTER 10: ITHF Barrier Breakers

Legends of the Game

Every individual who has been inducted into the Hall of Fame can be considered a "Legend of the Game." However, a few of these many legends broke through some unique barriers to become the first person to accomplish something significant in the history of tennis. This book is not only focused on highlighting those individuals who broke through barriers of race, it shares the amazing stories of people who were "ground breakers" in the sport. To understand the importance of "barrier breakers" to the sport we list, on the pages that follow, many of those Hall of Fame Inductees who were the first to break through some important tennis barriers.

International Tennis Hall of Fame Barrier Breakers

Joseph Clark: In 1883, the Harvard student won titles in both singles and doubles at the first-ever Intercollegiate Championships. In addition, he won the 1885 US Nationals Doubles Championship with Dick Sears. Clark was also the USNLTA president from 1889 through 1891. He was inducted into the Hall of Fame in the Inaugural Class of 1955.

James Dwight: Frequently called the "Father of American Tennis" for being one of the first people to bring tennis to the United States in 1874 in Nahant, Massachusetts and for being the longest serving USNLTA president. He was a Harvard trained physician who played an important leadership role in founding the USNLTA, establishing the US National Championships and creating the

International Lawn Tennis Challenge (which is now called the Davis Cup). He was the president of the USNLTA for a record 21 years (1882-1884 and 1894-1911). In addition, he won the US Nationals Doubles Championship with Dick Sears in 1882, 1883, 1884, 1886 and 1887. He was inducted into the Hall of Fame in the Inaugural Class of 1955.

Richard Sears: Considered to be the first great US tennis player. He won the very first US National Singles Championship in 1881 and went on to win the tournament a record seven times between 1881 and 1887. In addition, he won the US National Doubles title six consecutive times from 1882 to 1887. He also served as the USNLTA president from 1887-1888. He was inducted into the Hall of Fame in the Inaugural Class of 1955.

Malcolm Whitman: Made history in 1900 as a member of the very first International Lawn Tennis Challenge (Davis Cup) Team (with Dwight Davis and Holcombe Ward) that beat the British Isles 3-0. His 1932 book *Tennis Origins and Mysteries* was one of the first and most popular books on tennis history. Whitman was an outstanding tennis player who won three consecutive US Nationals Singles Championships (1898, 1899 and 1900). He was inducted into the Hall of Fame in the Inaugural Class of 1955.

William Clothier: In 1954, he became the first president of the International Tennis Hall of Fame and held that position until 1957. As a student at Harvard, he won the Intercollegiate Singles and Doubles Championships in 1902. In addition, Clothier won the 1906 US Nationals Men's Singles Championship. He later became a spy with the FBI and the CIA and was inducted into the Hall of Fame in 1956.

Dwight Davis: In 1900, Davis founded the International Lawn Tennis Challenge with fellow Harvard students Holcombe Ward and Malcolm Whitman. The purpose of the competition was to "promote goodwill for the sport internationally." Davis designed the format of the competition (two singles matches on the first day, doubles on the second day and two singles matches on the third day). In addition, he spent $1,000 of his own money to purchase a trophy specially designed by the legendary Boston based luxury goods company Shreve, Crump & Low. They commissioned William B. Durgin's of New Hampshire to come up with a trophy design that was worthy of this international event. The beautiful trophy that resulted from this collaboration helped to increase the influence of this event in the tennis world.

The first competition between the US and the British Isles at Longwood Cricket Club in Boston was extremely successful for an inaugural event. The name of the event was changed to the "Davis Cup" as it is known today. He won the Intercollegiate Singles Championship in 1899. He teamed with Holcombe Ward to win the US Nationals Doubles Championship in 1899, 1900 and 1901. Davis was an extraordinary individual who served as the president of the USLTA in 1923 and the secretary of war in the Coolidge Administration from 1925 to 1929. He then served as the Governor General of the Philippines in the Hoover Administration from 1929 to 1932. He was inducted into the Hall of Fame in 1956.

William Larned: In 1922, Larned invented the steel-framed tennis racquet and became the first person to establish a company to market steel frame rackets. Unfortunately, metal racquets did not get widespread acceptance until the Wilson Sporting Goods company introduced the T2000 racquet in 1967. Even though he was an inventor, he was better known for his tremendous success at the US Nationals. Larned was an exceptional singles player who tied Dick Sears' record of 7 US National Singles Championships by winning the tournament in 1901, 1902, 1907, 1908, 1909, 1910 and 1911. He became the first man to win seven US National Men's Singles titles in tournaments without the challenge round. In the second year of the US Nationals Championship, the USNLTA instituted the "challenge round" format where the winner of the tournament the previous year only had to play one match to defend his or her title. Since the champion did not have to play in the main draw of the tournament it was much easier to win multiple championships using that format. The challenge round was used in the tournament from 1882 until 1911. Larned's seven titles therefore stand out as one of the most extraordinary accomplishments in tennis. He was inducted into the Hall of Fame in 1956.

May Sutton Bundy: In 1905, Bundy became the first American to win Wimbledon. She won the Women's Singles Championship at Wimbledon for a second time in 1907. In addition, she won the US Women's Singles and Doubles Championships in 1904. In 1956, she became the first woman inducted into the Hall of Fame.

Holcombe Ward: In 1900, Ward made history as a member of the very first International Lawn Tennis Challenge (Davis Cup) Team (with Dwight Davis and Malcolm Whitman) that beat the British Isles 3-0. He won the US Nationals Men's Singles Championship in 1904 and the US Nationals Men's Doubles titles in 1899, 1900, 1901, 1904, 1905 and 1906. As a Harvard student, he won the 1899 Intercollegiate Men's Doubles title. In addition, he served as the USLTA president from 1937 to 1947. He was inducted into the Hall of Fame in 1956.

Mary K. Browne: In 1926, Browne became the first female professional tennis player. She was an exceptional player who won 13 major titles. She won the US Nationals Singles Championships in 1912, 1913 and 1914; the US Nationals Women's Doubles Championships in 1912, 1913, 1914, 1921 and 1925; the US Nationals Mixed Doubles Championships in 1912, 1913, 1914 and 1921; and, the Wimbledon Doubles Championships in 1926. She was inducted into the Hall of Fame in 1957.

Hazel Hotchkiss Wightman: In 1923, Wightman was one of the founders of the Ladies International Tennis Challenge. The event was later named the Wightman Cup to honor her leadership in the event and donation of the magnificent trophy. In 1911, she became the first woman to win three triples (winning the Singles, Doubles and Mixed Doubles) three years in a row. Wightman won a total of 17 Grand Slam titles (4 singles, 7 women's doubles and 6 mixed doubles). In addition, she won the Olympic Gold Medal in Women's Doubles and Mixed Doubles. She was inducted into the Hall of Fame in 1957.

Breaking The Barriers

Molla Bjurstadt Mallory: In 1926, Bjurstadt Mallory became the first person to win eight US Singles Championships (1915, 1916, 1917, 1918, 1920, 1921, 1922 and 1926). She also captured the US Doubles Championship in 1916 and 1917. She was inducted into the Hall of Fame in 1958.

William Tatum Tilden: In 1929, Tilden became the second man (William Larned was the first) to win seven US National Men's Singles titles in tournaments without the challenge round. He won these Championships in 1920, 1921, 1922, 1923, 1924, 1925 and 1929. In addition, he won the US Nationals Doubles Championship in 1918, 1922 and 1923; the US Nationals Mixed Doubles Championship in 1913, 1914, 1922 and 1923; the Wimbledon Men's Singles Championship in 1920, 1921 and 1930; and, the Wimbledon Men's Doubles Championship in 1927. He was inducted into the Hall of Fame in 1959.

John Donald Budge: In 1938, Budge became the first person to win the "Grand Slam" of tennis (the French, Wimbledon, US and Australian Championships in the same year). The opportunity to win a "Grand Slam" did not come about until the International Lawn Tennis Federation (ILTA) designated the French, Wimbledon, US and Australasian Championships as the four major tournaments. In Singles, the only winners of the Grand Slam were Don Budge in 1938, Maureen Connolly in 1953, Rod Laver in 1962 and 1969, Margaret Court in 1970 and Steffi Graf who made history as the first and only person to win the "Golden Slam" (winning all four major tournaments and a Gold Medal in singles) in 1988. In 1940, Budge made history as the first white global tennis star in the segregated era of tennis to play a challenge match against the black American Tennis Association (ATA) Men's Singles Champion. Budge and Jimmy McDaniels played a historic singles match at the Cosmopolitan Club in the Harlem section of New York City. Budge won the match but said that McDaniels was good enough to be a top player in the world. As the number 1 player in the world in 1940, Budge deserves tremendous credit for putting the reputation of "White Tennis" on the line to break through the unfortunate barriers of segregation and social class. In addition to winning all four majors in singles in 1938, he won the 1937 US Nationals Men's Singles Championship and the 1937 Wimbledon Men's Singles Championship. He also won the 1936 and 1938 US Nationals Men's Doubles Championships; the 1937 and 1938 US Nationals Mixed Doubles Championships; and, the 1937 and 1938 Wimbledon Men's Doubles and Mixed Doubles Championships. He was inducted into the Hall of Fame in 1964.

Alice Marble: On July 1, 1950, Marble became the first global tennis star to openly challenge discrimination in tennis. In the July issue of *American Lawn Tennis Magazine*, Marble wrote an open letter to the United States Lawn Tennis Association challenging them to allow Althea Gibson to play in the US Nationals. This letter from a former champion was one of the primary reasons that Gibson was allowed to break the color barrier in tennis at the US Nationals in 1950. Marble was also the first woman to use serve and volley tactics effectively on court. She successfully used this strategy to win the US National Women's Singles Championships in 1936, 1938, 1939 and 1940; the US National Women's Doubles Championships in 1937, 1938, 1939 and 1940; the US National Mixed Doubles Championships in 1936, 1938, 1939 and 1940. In addition, she won the Wimbledon Women's Singles Championships in 1939; the Wimbledon Women's Doubles Championships in 1938 and 1939; and, the Wimbledon Mixed Doubles Championships in 1937, 1938 and 1939. She was inducted into the Hall of Fame in 1964.

Ellen Forde Hansell: In 1887, Hansel became the first woman to win the US National Women's Singles Championships. The first US Women's Championships were played on the Philadelphia Cricket Club grass courts instead of the Newport Casino where the Men's matches were played. At that time, the women players wore long skirts, long sleeves and hats. Hansel beat Laura Knight 6-1, 6-0 in the finals. She never won another grand slam tournament. However, she made history by breaking through an important gender barrier, becoming the first US Women's champion. She was inducted into the Hall of Fame in 1965.

Breaking The Barriers

Jimmy Van Allen: In 1954, Van Allen and his wife Candy made history by founding the Hall of Fame. This incredible organization has become the global home to the history of tennis. He also invented the first tie-break system used in the US National Championships in 1970. The system is now used in every professional tennis tournament. The current tie-break system, originally called the Van Allen Streamlined Scoring System (VASS), promoted a "sudden-death" tie breaker to end sets and matches if the game score was tied at 6 all. Originally, the tie break was the best of nine points with the requirement that the winner had to reach five (5) points. However, if it is tied at 4 all, the person who wins two points in a row wins the tie break. The tie-break was eventually changed to be the best of twelve points where the winner was the first to score 7 points with a 2 point or more margin of victory. Van Allen also created the "no-ad" scoring where the first player to reach four (4) points won the game. This no-ad scoring streamlined tennis and made matches quicker by eliminating the requirement that players win by two points in each game. The no-ad format was made popular because it is the only scoring used by World Team Tennis (WTT). However, it is not used in most professional tennis tournaments. Van Allen was inducted into the Hall of Fame in 1965.

Richard Alonso "Poncho" Gonzalez: In 1948, Gonzalez broke through barriers of race and class to become the first Latino American to win the US National Singles Championships. He won the 1949 US National Singles title as well and became a professional shortly after that victory. He did extremely well on the pro tour winning eight of the eleven finals between 1951 and 1964. In 1972, at 43, he became the oldest person to win a singles professional tournament title. Gonzalez was inducted into the Hall of Fame in 1968.

Maureen Catherine "Little Mo" Connolly: In 1953, Connolly became the first woman to win four Grand Slam singles championships (French, Wimbledon, US and Australian) in a single year. As mentioned in Don Budge's profile, the only people in the history of tennis who accomplished this "Grand Slam" in a single calendar year were Don Budge in 1938, Maureen Connolly in 1953, Rod Laver in 1962 and 1969, Margaret Court in 1970 and Steffi Graf in 1988. In addition to winning all four championships in 1953, Connolly won the US Women's Singles Championship in 1951; the French Women's Singles Championship in 1954 and the Wimbledon Women's Singles Championship in 1954. Connolly also won the Australian Women's Doubles Championship in 1953 and, the French Women's Doubles, as well as the Mixed Doubles Championship in 1954. Connolly was inducted into the Hall of Fame in 1968.

John Albert "Jack" Kramer: In 1972, Kramer became the first executive director of the Association of Tennis Professionals (ATP). He was one of the leading promoters of the men's professional tennis tour in the 1940s and 1950s. He was one of the leaders that influenced the International Tennis Federation (ITF) to vote on allowing "Open" (professional) tennis in 1960. The proposal lost by five votes. However, thanks to the efforts of Kramer and others, in 1968, the ITF voted to allow open tennis. In 1970, he created the Men's Grand Prix Points System. In 1972, he helped to found the Association of Tennis Professionals (ATP) with Donald Dell and Cliff Drysdale. Kramer won the Men's Singles Championship at the US Nationals in 1946 and 1947; the Men's Singles Championship at Wimbledon in 1947; the Men's Doubles Championship at the US Open in 1940, 1941, 1943 and 1947; the Wimbledon Men's Doubles Championship in 1946 and 1947; and the US Nationals Mixed Doubles Championship in 1941. He became famous to millions of tennis players because of the popularity of the Wilson Jack Kramer signature wood tennis racket. He was inducted into the Hall of Fame in 1969.

Althea Gibson: In 1950, Gibson broke through the barrier of racial discrimination in tennis by becoming the first African-American to play in a grand slam tournament match. In 1956, by winning the French Women's Singles Championship, she became the first African-American to win a Grand Slam title. In 1957, Gibson became the first African-American to win the Women's Singles Championship at Wimbledon and the US Nationals Women's Singles Championship. At Wimbledon, Gibson became the first women's champion to receive the trophy from Queen Elizabeth II. She repeated that feat by winning these two titles in 1958. In addition, she won the Women's Doubles

Championships in France in 1956; in the US in 1957 and 1958; and, Wimbledon in 1956, 1957 and 1958. Gibson also won the US Nationals Mixed Doubles Championship in 1957. Prior to entering the previously white only tennis circuit, Gibson won 10 straight American Tennis Association (ATA) Women's Championships between 1947 and 1956. In 1964, Gibson became the first African-American on the Ladies Professional Golf Association (LPGA) tour. She was inducted into the International Tennis Hall of Fame in 1971 and the Black Tennis Hall of Fame in 2008.

Jean Rene Lacoste: In 1926, at the US National Championships, Lacoste made fashion and tennis history by designing the first "tennis shirt" and wearing it in a major match. This short sleeve cotton shirt was the most comfortable shirt ever designed for tennis players. In 1927, he began putting a crocodile emblem on the left breast of the shirt in recognition of his nickname the "Crocodile." Lacoste got this nickname after he won a bet with the French Davis Cup Captain Pierre Gillou. The wager was that if LaCoste won an important Davis Cup Match Gillou would buy him a crocodile-skin suitcase. He won the match, got the suitcase and became known throughout the world as the "Crocodile." In 1933, Lacoste made history by teaming up with Andre Gillier to form the company La Société Chemise Lacoste and began selling the tennis shirt with the crocodile emblem. He therefore became the first global tennis star to found an international clothing and design company. In 1961, Lacoste created and patented the first tubular steel tennis racquet. Wilson made this technology famous by creating the first internationally popular steel tennis racquet called the Wilson T-2000. This racquet was used to make tennis history by tennis legends Billie Jean King and Jimmy Connors. Lacoste was an extraordinary player who won the 1925, 1927 and 1929 French Men's Singles Championship; the 1925 and 1928 Wimbledon Men's Singles Championship; and, the 1926 and 1927 US Nationals Men's Singles Championship. In addition, he won the 1925 and 1929 French Men's Doubles Championship and the 1925 Wimbledon Men's Doubles Championship. Lacoste was inducted into the Hall of Fame in 1976.

Henry Christian "Harry" Hopman: In 1969, with his final victory, Hopman became the most successful Davis Cup Coach in history by leading Australia to 16 Davis Cup victories. Under his leadership, Australia won the 1939, 1950, 1951, 1952, 1953, 1955, 1956, 1957, 1959, 1960, 1961, 1962, 1964, 1965, 1966 and 1967 Davis Cup Championships. He was one of the first tennis coaches to make physical fitness the foundation of tennis excellence. He was also an accomplished player who won the 1929 and 1930 Australian Men's Doubles Championships; the 1930, 1936, 1937 and 1939 Australian Mixed Doubles Championship; and, the 1939 US National Mixed Doubles Championship with Alice Marble. The Hopman Cup is an international team tournament using the trimatch[11] format (men's singles, women's singles and mixed doubles) named in his honor. Hopman was inducted into the Hall of Fame in 1978.

Margaret Smith Court: In 1975, Court won her last of a world record 64 Grand Slam tennis tournament titles. She has the most Grand Slam titles of any man or woman in history. She is the only player to have won the championships in Women's Singles, Women's Doubles and Mixed Doubles in each of the four Grand Slam tournaments at least three times. Her record includes winning the 1962, 1965, 1969, 1970 and 1973 US Nationals and US Open Women's Singles titles; the 1963, 1965 and 1970 Wimbledon Women's Singles titles; the 1962, 1964, 1969, 1970 and 1973 French Nationals and Open Championships; and, the 1960, 1961, 1962, 1963, 1964, 1965, 1966, 1969, 1970, 1971 and 1973 Australian Nationals and Open Championships. She also won the US Nationals and Open Women's Doubles Championships in 1963, 1968, 1970, 1973 and 1975; the Wimbledon Women's Doubles Championships in 1964 and 1969; the French Women's Double's Championships in 1964, 1965, 1966 and 1973; and the Australian Nationals and Open Women's Doubles Championships in 1961, 1962, 1963, 1965, 1969, 1970, 1971 and 1973. In addition, she won the US Nationals and Open Mixed Doubles Championships in 1961, 1962, 1963, 1964, 1965, 1969, 1970 and 1972; the Wimbledon Mixed Doubles Championships in 1963, 1965,

---

[11] Dale G. Caldwell created the term "TriMatch" in 2003 to refer to a team competition with a two singles match and a doubles match.

1966, 1968 and 1975; the French National and Open Mixed Doubles Championships in 1963, 1964, 1965 and 1969; and the Australian Nationals and Open Championships in 1963, 1964, 1965 and 1969. Court was inducted into the Hall of Fame in 1979.

Frank Sedgman: In 1951, Sedgman and Ken McGregor became the first (and only) Men's Doubles calendar year Grand Slam winners. Sedgman and McGregor won the Australian Men's Doubles Championship in 1951 and 1952; the French Men's Doubles Championship in 1951 and 1952; the Wimbledon Men's Doubles Championship in 1948, 1951 and 1952; and, the US Men's Double's Championship in 1950 and 1951. In addition, Sedgman won the Australian National Championships in Men's Singles in 1949 and 1950; the Wimbledon Men's Singles Championship in 1952; and the US Nationals Men's Singles Championship in 1951 and 1952. He also won the 1949 and 1950 Australian Mixed Doubles Championship; the 1951 and 1952 French Mixed Doubles Championship; the 1951 and 1952 Wimbledon Mixed Doubles Championship; and, the 1951 and 1952 US Mixed Doubles Championship. Sedgman was inducted into the Hall of Fame in 1979.

Gladys Heldman: In 1953, Heldman founded *World Tennis Magazine*. Under her leadership as the owner, publisher and contributing writer, this magazine became the most influential publication in tennis. She made history by teaming up with the CEO of Philip Morris, Joseph F. Cullman III to start the first major women's professional tennis tour in 1970. The "Virginia Slims Women's Professional Tennis Tour" became a powerful force in professional tennis. It played a critical role in influencing the creation of the Women's Tennis Association (WTA) that controls women's professional tennis today. Heldman was inducted into the Hall of Fame in 1979.

William Ewing "Slew" Hester, Jr.: In 1977, as president of the USTA, Hester led the negotiations to move the US Open from Forest Hills, New York to Flushing Meadows, New York. He recognized that the US Open had outgrown the West Side Tennis Club so he was open to identifying a larger venue to hold America's Grand Slam tennis tournament. One day, as he was flying over Louis Armstrong Stadium in Flushing Meadows, Queens, he came up with the brilliant idea of moving this tournament to this underutilized large site not far from Forest Hills. He was able to break through barriers of tradition to convince the USTA board and staff to support the development of a proposal to New York City to move the US Open to this location. The City agreed to the move and the development of the grounds. The USTA made investments of more than $10 million to renovate the property. The first US Open at Flushing Meadows took place in 1978. Attendance grew that first year from 218,480 ticket holders the previous year at the West Side Tennis Club to 275,300 ticket holders in Flushing Meadows. Today, the US Open attracts more than 700,000 spectators to the beautiful grounds of Flushing Meadows. Hester was inducted into the Hall of Fame in 1981.

Rodney "Rod" George Laver: In 1969, Laver became the first (and only) man in history to complete the Calendar Grand Slam twice. He accomplished this incredible feat in 1962 and 1969 (once as an amateur and once as a professional). Laver won the Australian Men's Singles Championship and Open in 1960, 1962 and 1969; the French Men's Singles Championship and Open in 1962 and 1969; the Wimbledon Men's Singles Championship and Open in 1961, 1962, 1968 and 1969; the US Men's Singles Championship and Open in 1962 and 1969. In addition, he won the Australian Men's Doubles Championship and Open in 1959, 1960, 1961 and 1969; the French Men's Doubles Championship in 1961; the Wimbledon Men's Doubles Open in 1970; and, the US Men's Doubles Championship and Open in 1960, 1970 and 1973. He also won the French Mixed Doubles Championship in 1961 and the Wimbledon Mixed Doubles Championship in 1959 and 1960. Laver was inducted into the Hall of Fame in 1981.

Mary Ewing Outerbridge: In 1874, Outerbridge became one of the first people to set up a lawn tennis court in the United States. There is great debate among historians about the origins of lawn tennis in the United States. However, many believe that Mary Outerbridge saw lawn tennis being played at a military base in Bermuda and brought one of the lawn tennis kits developed by Major Walter Clopton Wingfield to New York City. She set up one of the first lawn tennis courts in the country at the Staten Island Cricket and Baseball Club. The game grew in popularity and influenced Outerbridge and her brother Eugenius Outerbridge (who would later become the first chairman of the Port Authority of New York and New Jersey) to establish the first national tennis tournament in the United States in 1880. This event was held at the Staten Island Cricket and Baseball Club and indirectly led to the founding of the United States National Lawn Tennis Association (USNLTA) and the US National Championships in 1881. Outerbridge was inducted into the Hall of Fame in 1981.

Clarence Monroe Clark: On May 5, 1881, Clark, the president of the All-Philadelphia Lawn Tennis Committee; James Dwight, the president of the Beacon Park Athletic Association in Boston; and, Eugenius Outerbridge, representing the Staten Island Cricket and Baseball Club published a notice announcing the formation of the United States National Lawn Tennis Association (USNLTA). These three men led the founding of the USNLTA on May 21, 1881 at the Fifth Avenue Hotel with thirty-six delegates representing nineteen clubs and voting rights from sixteen additional tennis clubs. At that meeting, Clark was chosen to be the first secretary of the USNLTA. In addition to founding the USNLTA, Clark was an accomplished doubles player who won the first United States National Championship in Men's Doubles with partner Frederick Winslow Taylor (a mechanical engineer who is considered one of the founders of the management consulting profession). Clark was inducted into the Hall of Fame in 1983.

Arthur Robert Ashe: On September 8, 1968, Ashe became the first person to win the US Open Men's Singles Championship. This victory made him the first African-American man to win one of the four Grand Slam tennis tournaments. In 1970 and 1975 respectively, Ashe broke through additional barriers by becoming the first (and only) African-American to win the Australian Open and Wimbledon Men's Singles Championships. He was also the first African-American named to the United States Davis Cup team. In addition, he was the first (and only) African-American to be named the coach of the US Davis Cup Team. It is hard to effectively communicate in words the significance of the barriers that Ashe broke in tennis during the American tennis "boom."

Althea Gibson was the first African-American to break through the race and class barrier in tennis. However, her incredible accomplishments took place during a time when tennis had not become popular with much of the world. Ashe had the good fortune to become a tennis star as the sport grew to be the second most popular sport in the world. He was a true gentleman on and off of the court in spite of experiencing racist comments before, during and after matches; being denied entry into South Africa; and, not being able to stay in certain hotel rooms or eat at some restaurants. The class and poise with which he dealt with the challenges of being a black tennis player helped to focus the world's attention on diversity in the sport. He can be considered one of the most influential people in the history of tennis because he was able to break through important barriers of class and race both on and off of the tennis court. Ashe was inducted into the International Tennis Hall of Fame in 1985 and the Black Tennis Hall of Fame in 2008.

Billie Jean King: On September 20, 1973, King made history by beating Bobby Riggs in an exhibition tennis match dubbed "The Battle of the Sexes." It was the first time that a woman had beaten a man in such a public way in a professional sport. King won $100,000 for that victory. An estimated 90 million people around the world watched that televised match. That historic event remains one of the most popular tennis matches in history. The global popularity of this competition and its social significance at a time when women were fighting for equal rights and respect made this match one of the most important sporting events in world history. This global tennis phenomenon is credited with sparking a boom in women's sports and gender equality. King has used her celebrity from this match to be one of the most influential spokespersons for women's equality. In addition, King, with her husband Larry, founded the Women's Tennis Association (WTA) and World Team Tennis (WTT). WTA runs the women's professional tour and WTT is the most successful professional team tennis competition in history. Prior to becoming a global celebrity and founding WTA and WTT, King compiled an amazing record of Grand Slam tournament wins. King won the Australian Open Women's Singles in 1968; the French Open Women's Singles in 1972; the Wimbledon Women's Singles in 1966, 1967, 1968, 1972, 1973 and 1975; and, the US Nationals and Open Women's Singles in 1967, 1971, 1972 and 1974. She won the Australian Open Women's Doubles in 1965 and 1969; the French Open Women's Doubles in 1972; the Wimbledon Women's Doubles in 1961, 1962, 1965, 1967, 1968, 1970, 1971, 1972, 1973 and 1979; and, the US Nationals and Open Women's Doubles in 1964, 1967, 1974. 1978 and 1980. King won the Australian Open Mixed Doubles in 1968 and 1969; the French Championship and Open Mixed Doubles in 1967 and 1970; the Wimbledon Mixed Doubles in 1967, 1971, 1973 and 1974; and, the US Nationals and Open Women's Mixed in 1967, 1971, 1973 and 1976. King was inducted into the Hall of Fame in 1987. HhH

Joseph Cullman III: In 1970, Cullman, as CEO of Phillip Morris Company, helped Gladys Heldman and many of the top women players found the Virginia Slims Women's professional tennis tour. He used the Virginia Slims women's cigarette brand to help to provide financial support to this fledgling circuit, which eventually led to the successful women's professional tennis tour that exists today. Cullman was chairman of the US Open from 1969 to 1970 and played an important role in getting the first US Open in 1968 televised. He also served as president of the International Tennis Hall of Fame (ITHF) from 1982 to 1988, chairman of the ITHF from 1985 until 1988, and chairman *emeritus* and executive committee chairman from 1988 to 1998. Cullman was inducted into the Hall of Fame in 1990.

Phillippe Chatrier: In 1984, Chatrier realized his dream of tennis returning to the Olympics. He was a legend in tennis as a player, journalist and, most notably, the president of both the French Tennis Federation (1973 to 1993) and the president of the International Tennis Federation (ITF) from (1977 to 1991). As a player, in 1945, he was the French junior tennis champion. In 1953, Chartrier created the popular magazine *Tennis de France*. He then became vice president of the French Tennis Federation from 1968 to1973 and the captain of the French Davis Cup team in 1969. As a senior French tennis official, he played an important role in the transition to open professional tennis in 1968. Men's Singles and Doubles were first included as a Summer Olympic sport in the 1896 games in Athens, Greece. Women's Singles and Mixed Doubles were added as an Olympic sport in 1900 in the Games in Paris, France. Women's doubles were added in the 1920 Games in Antwerp, Belgium. Tennis was dropped as an Olympic sport after 1924 because of the controversy between professional and amateur tennis. As the president of the ITF, Chartrier, broke barriers by leading the charge to make tennis an Olympic sport. His efforts led to the reinstatement of tennis as a demonstration sport in 1984 in Los Angeles, USA and a full Olympic sport in 1988 in South Korea. In the Seoul 1988 Games, tennis returned with events in Men's Singles and Doubles, Women's Singles and Doubles and Mixed Doubles. Chartrier was inducted into the Hall of Fame in 1992.

Lamar Hunt: In 1967, Hunt was the largest investor in the World Championship Tennis (WCT) circuit for professional tennis founded by David Dixon. The first players in the circuit, which led to the creation of the current Association of Tennis Professionals (ATP) tour in 1990, were Pierre Barthes, Earl Buchholz, Cliff Drysdale, John Newcombe, Niki Pilic, Tony Roche and Roger Taylor. The first WCT tournament was held in January of 1968 in Sydney, Australia and in August of that year Hunt bought out Dixon to take control of 100% of WCT. Under Hunt's innovative leadership the tour became the most successful professional tennis competition in the world. It broke through barriers of tradition to lead to the creation of the very successful men's professional tennis tour that exists today. Hunt was inducted into the Pro Football Hall of Fame in 1972, the National Soccer Hall of Fame in 1982 and, the International Tennis Hall of Fame in 1993.

Arthur "Bud" Worth Collins, Jr: In 1980, Collins published the *Bud Collins Modern Encyclopedia of Tennis* to capture the global history of the sport. This publication, which was followed by several expanded versions of the encyclopedia, was the most comprehensive record of tennis scores and history ever produced. As a tennis reporter on television, radio and newspapers, he covered virtually every major tennis event in an entertaining and colorful way. His reporting was particularly noteworthy because of the innovative nicknames and terms he used to describe players, matches and tournaments and the bright colorful clothing he wore to tournaments. He was able to break through barriers of conservative spectating and make the sport entertaining for average people. He was also instrumental in helping Dale Caldwell convince the International Tennis Hall of Fame to sponsor a touring exhibit on black tennis history at the 2007 US Open. This exhibit, which became the most popular touring exhibit the museum produced, is called the *Breaking the Barriers* exhibit. This book is based on this powerful exhibit. Collins was inducted into the Hall of Fame in 1994.

Major Walter Clopton Wingfield: In 1874, Major Wingfield, a British Army officer, secured a patent for a "New and Improved Court for Playing the Ancient Game of Tennis" which he called "Sphairistike" (which would later be called "Lawn Tennis"). It is believed that he gave a demonstration of the game in 1869 and submitted his patent application in 1873. To increase the popularity of the game, Wingfield brilliantly developed a tennis box set that included rackets, rubber balls, a net, poles, court markers and an instruction manual. The sets cost between five and ten guineas and were sold through French and Co. around the world, predominantly on British military bases. His efforts helped to make the sport popular, which influenced the All-England Lawn Tennis and Croquet Club to establish the world's first major lawn tennis tournament-- Wimbledon, in 1877. The success of Wimbledon helped the sport to grow rapidly around the world. Wingfield was inducted into the Hall of Fame in 1997.

Herman David: As chairman of the All England Lawn Tennis and Croquet Club for 19 years, David played a critical role in establishing professional "Open" tennis at the Grand Slam tournaments. As an influential international leader in tennis, David advocated including professional and amateur tennis at the Grand Slam tournaments as early as October 1959. As a new chairman of the All

England Club, he led a Special General Meeting where a resolution was passed to ask the Lawn Tennis Association (LTA) to propose to the International Lawn Tennis Federation (ILTF) that the major tennis tournaments be open to both professional and amateur tennis players. However, in July 1960, the resolution (failing by only five votes) did not receive the two-thirds vote required for the vote to pass. In 1964, David attempted to convince the LTA to open Wimbledon to professionals. That vote was defeated by 48 votes. However, in 1967, the LTA approved a resolution that would allow professionals to play at Wimbledon and other major tournaments. In addition, with the support of the British Broadcasting Corporation (which introduced color television), David played a critical role in convincing the All England Lawn Tennis and Croquet Club to allow the Wimbledon World Lawn Tennis Professional Championships of 1967 to take place there. The success of this event, largely orchestrated by David to show the appeal of professional tennis in the most famous tennis venue in the world, influenced the ILTA to approve "open tennis." David was inducted into the Hall of Fame in 1998.

Ken McGregor: In 1951, McGregor and Frank Sedgman became the first (and only) Men's Doubles calendar year Grand Slam winners. McGregor and Sedgman won the Australian Men's Doubles Championship in 1951 and 1952; the French Men's Doubles Championship in 1951 and 1952; the Wimbledon Men's Doubles Championship in 1948, 1951 and 1952; and, the US Men's Double's Championship in 1950 and 1951. In addition, McGregor won the Australian National Championships in 1952 and, the US National Mixed Doubles Championship in 1950. McGregor was inducted into the Hall of Fame in 1999.

Martina Navratilova: Navratilova won more Women's Tennis Association (WTA) singles titles than any other person in history. Her 167 tournament wins in singles is 10 more than Chris Evert who is in second place with 157 titles. Navratilova's 177 doubles tournament wins and 1,438 total matches won is a record among men and women. She was ranked as the world's number 1 player for a total of 332 weeks in singles. Navratilova's 237 weeks as the number 1 doubles player in the world is a record. She won 18 Grand Slam singles titles, 31 Grand Slam women's doubles titles and 10 Grand Slam mixed doubles titles. Navratilova won the 1981, 1983 and 1985 Australian Open Women's Singles title; the 1982 and 1984 French Open Women's Singles title; the 1978, 1979, 1982, 1983, 1984, 1985, 1986, 1987 and 1990 Wimbledon Women's Singles title; and, the 1983, 1984, 1986 and 1987 US Open singles title. She won the 1980, 1982, 1983, 1984, 1985, 1987, 1988 and 1989 Australian Open Women's Doubles title; the 1975, 1982, 1984, 1985, 1986, 1987 and 1988 French Open Women's Doubles title; the 1976, 1979, 1981, 1982, 1983, 1984 and 1986 Wimbledon Women's Doubles title; and, the 1977, 1978, 1980, 1983, 1984, 1986, 1987, 1989 and 1990 US Open Women's Doubles title. Navratilova won the 2003 Australian Open Mixed Doubles title; the 1974 and 1985 French Open Mixed Doubles title; the 1985, 1993, 1995 and 2003 Wimbledon Mixed Doubles title; and, the 1985, 1987 and 2006 US Open Mixed Doubles title. She was inducted into the Hall of Fame in 2000.

Stephanie Marie Graf: In 1988, Graf became the only person in history to win a "Golden Slam" when she won the Women's Singles title at all four Grand Slam Championships and the Women's Singles Gold Medal at the Seoul, South Korea Olympics. Graf won 22 Grand Slam singles titles and is the only player in history to have won each of the Grand Slam Championships at least four times. She won the Women's Singles Championship at: the Australian Open in 1988, 1989, 1990 and 1994; the French Open in 1987, 1988, 1993, 1995, 1996 and 1999; Wimbledon in 1988, 1989, 1991, 1992, 1993, 1995 and 1996; and, the US Open in 1988, 1989, 1993, 1995 and 1996. Graf was ranked as the world's number 1 player for a record 377 total weeks. She is also the only person to have one a calendar year Grand Slam since the hard court surface was introduced at the US Open. Graf was inducted into the Hall of Fame in 2004.

Dorothy "Dodo" Bundy Cheney: In 1938, Cheney became the first American woman to win the Australian Championships. However, she is a recognized as a legendary player because she broke through the barrier of age to become the all-time age group championship winner.

Cheney won an incredible 391 "gold balls" given to the winner of every USTA age group court surface (grass, hard-court, clay and indoor) championship tournament winner. Her last victory took place in May of 2012 when she won the 90-and-over doubles championship at the National Senior Women's Hardcourt Championship at the La Jolla Beach and Tennis Club in La Jolla, California. It is easy to forget that one of the primary benefits of tennis is that it is a sport that one can play throughout his or her entire life. Society celebrates the young champions of the most prestigious tournaments. However, being the best in the world at a particular age group is an extraordinary accomplishment. Cheney's winning tournament championships in virtually every age group make her accomplishments every bit as significant as those of Grand Slam tournament winners. She was inducted into the Hall of Fame in 2004 at the incredible age of 88.

Yannick Noah: In 1983, Noah broke through barriers by becoming the first man of African descent to win the French Open. He will always be famous as the person who completed the men's "Black Player Grand Slam" in singles where a black man won the singles division of the US Open, Australian Open, Wimbledon and the French Open. Arthur Ashe won the US Open in 1968, the Australian Open in 1970 and Wimbledon in 1975. Noah's French Open victory in 1983 broke the men's Grand Slam singles racial barrier. Unfortunately, it was not until 2003 when the women's Black Player Grand Slam in singles was completed. Althea Gibson won the French Championships in 1956, Wimbledon in 1957 and the US Championships in 1957. However, she never won the Australian Championships. Serena Williams's victory over her sister Venus in the 2003 Australian Open completed the women's Black Player Grand Slam in singles. Noah was inducted into the Hall of Fame in 2005.

Robert Walter "Dr. J" Johnson: There is a great coach behind every great player. However, there are just a few coaches who have achieved legendary status in the world of tennis. Dr. Johnson (who was affectionately known as "Dr. J") was one of these extraordinary coaches because of his important role in training of many of the best black players in history. However, he will be remembered as the coach of International Tennis Hall of Fame and Black Tennis Hall of Fame inductees Althea Gibson and Arthur Ashe. Dr. J coached Ashe, Gibson and other extraordinary players at his home in Lynchburg, Virginia. In addition to coaching the two best black tennis players in history, Dr. J taught many of the most promising junior players on the American Tennis Association (ATA) tennis circuit. In addition to teaching players conditioning and strategy, he taught his players how to deal with racism, bad line calls and to always maintain their dignity and composure. Thanks to Dr. J's coaching, Ashe and Gibson combined to win 8 Grand Slam singles titles (Gibson 5, Ashe 3); 7 Grand Slam doubles titles (Gibson 5, Ashe 2), and, 1 Grand Slam Mixed Doubles title (Gibson 1). Dr. Johnson was inducted into the Black Tennis Hall of Fame in 2008 and the International Tennis Hall of Fame in 2009.

Brad Alan Parks: In 1976, Parks and Jeff Minnenbraker broke through barriers of disability by conceptualizing the idea of competitive wheelchair tennis. Parks, a former freestyle skiing prodigy who was paralyzed from the waist down by a skiing accident, partnered with other wheelchair bound athletes to develop competitive events in the late 1970s. He partnered with David Saltz, Jim Worth and Dave Kiley in 1980 to found the National Foundation of Wheelchair Tennis (NFWT) and organized a 10-tournament circuit throughout the US that concluded with a national championship. The tour is now called the NEC Wheelchair Tennis Tour and consists of more than 150 tournaments in 41 countries with $1,500,000 in prize money. In 1998, wheelchair tennis was integrated into the International Tennis Federation (ITF). The USTA established the "Brad Parks Award" to recognize individuals who have made outstanding contributions to wheelchair tennis. Parks was inducted into the International Tennis Hall of Fame in 2010.

Fern Lee "Peachy" Kellmeyer: In 1973, Kellmeyer broke through barriers of gender by initiating a lawsuit to protect the rights of female college athletes. "Peachy" (as she was affectionately known because of her positive demeanor), eleven female students, Marymount College, Broward Community College and the coaches from the two schools sued the National Education Association (NEA), the Association for Intercollegiate Athletics for Women (AIAW) and several other governing bodies of women's sports. This suit was initiated because the AIAW did not allow women with college athletic scholarships to participate in their events. An AIWA rule stated that an institution would be ineligible for membership in the association if it gave scholarships to women in any sports area. This rule prevented women who were collegiate tennis players on scholarship from competing in the USLTA Women's Collegiate Championships. This lawsuit, known as Kellmeyer, et.al. vs. NEA, et al. was one of the most instrumental court cases relating to Title IX of the Civil Rights Act of 1964. It helped to enhance women's college sports and open doors of opportunity for thousands of women. Kellmeyer was also an accomplished player who was the West Virginia State Singles Champion in 1957 and 1958; won the Women's Singles division of the Orange Bowl in 1957; at age 15, became the youngest player to play at the US Nationals Championships in 1959; was the number 1 player at the University of Miami in 1964, 1965 and 1966; and was the first woman to play on a Men's Division I college tennis team when she played on the University of Miami Men's Tennis Team. In 1973, she became the first tour director of the Virginia Slims Women's Tennis Circuit which paved the way for the very successful global Women's Tennis Association (WTA) tour today. Kellmeyer was inducted into the International Tennis Hall of Fame in 2011.

Mike Davies: In 1968, Davies was hired as the first executive director of World Championship Tennis (WCT). As the day-to-day leader of the global men's pro tennis tour, he played an instrumental role in transforming tennis into the major professional sport that it is today. In 1970, Davies played a leadership role in developing the first major global men's tour which consisted of thirty-two players playing twenty tournaments in twenty countries. Each player was guaranteed to receive $50,000. The eight players with the best records in the twenty tournaments would be accepted into the WCT finals in Dallas, Texas. This format successfully increased global interest in professional tennis because it made tennis an entertaining sport to the general population. The WCT tour introduced new concepts like colored clothing and tennis balls, chairs on the court during changeovers, tie-breakers to close out sets and, most importantly, the first tour to sign a contract with a major network (NBC). Davies served as the executive director of the WCT tour for thirteen years. In 1982, he became the executive director of the Association of Tennis Professionals (ATP) and played an instrumental role in helping the organization become the successful governing body of men's tennis that it is today. In 1987, he joined the International Tennis Federation (ITF) and increased sponsorship and television revenue for the organization exponentially. Davies was inducted into the International Tennis Hall of Fame in 2012.

Nicholas "Nick" James Bollettieri: In 1978, Bollettieri opened a tennis boarding school called the Nick Bollettieri Tennis Academy (NBTA) near Bradenton, Florida. The extraordinarily successful training program that he developed at this academy has helped to produce many legends of the game. Bollettieri's tennis program has done for many American tennis players what Harry Hopman's tennis programs did for top Australian tennis players. However, Bollettieri's success was not limited to coaching American players. He has helped players from around the world become top players and, a select few, reach the number 1 ranking. The NBTA (which in 1987 became the IMG Academy) has helped to produce the following tennis players who, after working with Bollettieri, reached the world number 1 ranking: Andre Agassi, Boris Becker, Jim Courier, Martina Hingis, Jelena Jankovic, Marcelo Rios, Monica Seles, Maria Sharapova, Serena Williams and Venus Williams. In addition to coaching these 10 world number one players, he coached other top players including: Jimmy Arias, Sara Errani, Tommy Haas, Daniela Hantuchova, Sabine Lisicki, Mary Pierce, Xavier Malisse, Max Mirnyi, Kei Nishikori and Nicole Vaidisova. He also coached many other players who were able to make a living on the professional tennis circuit. Bollettieri's impact on tennis went well-beyond his work with top players. Bollettieri and Arthur Ashe founded the Ashe-Bollettieri Cities (ABC) tennis program in Newark in 1987. The program was expanded to other cities under the name of the Arthur Ashe Safe Passage Foundation. The program ended in 1993 when Arthur Ashe passed away. These phenomenal programs introduced thousands of urban youth to the sport of tennis. However, the magic of the program was that it helped many of the participants excel in school and graduate from college. Bollettieri was inducted into the International Tennis Hall of Fame in 2014 and the Black Tennis Hall of Fame in 2015.

CHAPTER 11: Tennis in the Black Community

Black Tennis Clubs Emerge

The first two decades of the 20th century are remembered as one of the most remarkable periods of growth for the sport of tennis. This expansion of the sport is not as notable for the number of people who started playing tennis as it is for the wide variety of diverse developing organizations whose leaders focused on increasing participation in the sport.

Tennis growth in the United States' local communities led to the establishment of USNLTA sectional associations. The popularity of tennis among black players, who were not permitted to play on "White-Only" tennis courts in these sections, led to the founding of the American Tennis Association (ATA).

The amazing growth of tennis clubs for black players mirrored the sport of tennis's popularity among other communities around the world in the early 20th century. This was most evident in New York City, which was viewed as a place of opportunity for blacks who had moved from southern communities that practiced legalized segregation. Tennis became the sport of the "Black Elite" in New York. The two most famous black tennis clubs there were the Ideal Tennis Club and the Cosmopolitan Club located in the Harlem section of New York City (which many considered the "Capital of Black America").

On Thanksgiving Day in 1916, leaders of the most influential black tennis clubs founded the American Tennis Association (ATA) at the Washington, D.C. YMCA. This organization was established to promote recreational tennis and coordinate competition among players of all races and backgrounds. It is still the country's oldest, continually active African-American sports organization. The ATA's New York section has, since its founding, been called the New York Tennis Association (which covered the entire state of New York) and is known historically as one the association's most active sections. Throughout its history, the ATA has had different sections including the New England Tennis Association (which covers Connecticut, Maine, Massachusetts, New Hampshire, Rhode Island and Vermont), the New Jersey Tennis Association (which covers Northern New Jersey), the Tri-States Tennis Association (which covers Delaware, Pennsylvania and South Jersey), the Midwestern Tennis Association (which covers Illinois, Indiana, Iowa, Kansas, Kentucky, Michigan, Minnesota, Missouri and Wisconsin), and the Western Tennis Association (which covers Arizona, California, Colorado, Idaho, Montana, North Dakota, Nevada, South Dakota, Washington and Wyoming).

The Ideal Tennis Club was founded in the Harlem section of New York City in 1914 on West 138th Street. It has an important place in history because leaders there organized the first multi-state competitions among black tennis clubs, including traveling teams from Baltimore, Boston, New Haven, Philadelphia, Springfield (Massachusetts) and Washington, D.C. Ideal's founding members had great influence in the ATA because they were among the original founders of the organization. The Ideal Tennis Club therefore became one of the most celebrated tennis organizations in the national black tennis community.

The black club with the richest history was the Colonial Tennis Club (whose name was changed to the Cosmopolitan Club). This club was founded in Harlem in 1915. The Cosmopolitan Club would eventually become the most famous black tennis club in America because of its unique connection to two of the greatest champions in tennis history — Don Budge and Althea Gibson.

"By the 1920's, tennis had become the most popular recreational sport among black professionals."

In the early 1920s, tennis was becoming a very popular pastime among the most successful individuals in both the black and white communities. The powerful "White-Only" clubs were at the peak of their power and greatly influenced USLTA actions. Black tennis clubs in local communities and at Historically Black Colleges and Universities (HBCU) were being formed to increase interest and participation in the sport. Tennis had become the most popular recreational sport for doctors, lawyers, professors and ministers and their families in the black communities.

The growth of the sport among the black community's elite mirrored the growth of the sport among the elite in the white community. In the 1920s, tennis had become the favorite sport of many of the most influential people in both the white and black communities around the United States. This was especially true in Boston, New York, Northern New Jersey and Philadelphia. The growth of clubs in this section of the country (especially New York City and Northern New Jersey) demonstrated both the region's influence in tennis and its economic affluence.

One of the most influential clubs was the Shady Rest Country Club. This black club, founded in 1921 in Scotch Plains, New Jersey, was the country's very first black owned and operated country club. It had beautiful tennis courts and a legendary golf course that rivaled many of the courses at the "White-Only" clubs. Shady Rest, like the most prestigious country clubs in the white community, served some of the wealthiest people in the region.

By 1928, there were 18 ATA tennis clubs in the New York Tennis Association (NYTA)[12]. These clubs were located in Brooklyn, Flushing, Long Island, Manhattan and New Rochelle. The NYTA member clubs in 1928 included the Arrow Tennis Club (Manhattan); Blue Bird Tennis Club (Manhattan); Brooklyn Tennis and Country Club (Brooklyn); Corona Tennis Club (Long Island); Cosmopolitan Tennis Club (Manhattan); Ebenezer Tennis Club (Brooklyn); E & S Tennis Club (Manhattan); Eccles Memorial Tennis Club (New Rochelle); Flushing Tennis Club (Flushing); Greenville Tennis Club (Manhattan); Huguenot Tennis Club (Manhattan); Ideal Tennis Club (Manhattan); Manhattan Tennis Club (Manhattan); Orion Tennis Club (Manhattan); St. Nicholas Tennis Club (Manhattan); St. Thomas Tennis Club (Manhattan); Utopian Tennis Club (Brooklyn); and the Wicoma Tennis Club (Manhattan).

---

[12] *Black Tennis: An Archival Collection: 1890-1962* by Arthur A. Carrington, P.13

There were 15 ATA clubs in the New Jersey Tennis Association (NJTA) by 1928[13]. The clubs were located in Asbury Park, Bordentown, Camden, Elizabeth, Hackensack, Jersey City, Newark, Orange, Plainfield, Trenton and Westfield. In the 1920s, tennis was as popular in New Jersey's black community as it was in New York's black community.

The NJTA member clubs included: Asbury Park Tennis Club (Neptune); Bordentown Tennis Club (Bordentown); Camden YMCA (Camden); Capital City Tennis Club (Trenton); Carlisle Tennis Club (Newark); Douglass Tennis Club (Westfield); Hackensack Tennis Club (Hackensack); Imperial Tennis Club (Newark); Plainfield Tennis Club (Plainfield); Shore Players Tennis Club (Asbury Park); The Bachelor's Tennis Club (Orange); The Musolits Tennis Club (Jersey City); The North End Tennis Club (Elizabeth); The Orioles Tennis Club (Montclair); and the Triune Tennis Club (Newark).

Beginning of the End of Tennis Segregation

The segregation of tennis was tested many times over the years. Reginald Weir and Gerald Norman of New York mounted one of the most notable challenges to tennis segregation when they paid an entry fee to participate in the 1929 USLTA Junior Indoor Championships at the 7th Regiment Armory in New York City. Their entry was initially accepted because the tournament director did not know that they were African Americans. Unfortunately, when they checked into the tournament they were denied spots in the draw because of their race. The National Association for the Advancement of Colored People (NAACP) filed a formal grievance against the USLTA claiming discrimination against the players. The USLTA responded by stating that it did not allow 'colored' players in their championships. Incredibly, they never faced fines or sanctions because of this policy.

Historic Budge-McDaniels Encounter

However, despite the blatant discrimination against Weir and Norman, progress was being made. One of the most important tennis

---

[13] *Black Tennis: An Archival Collection: 1890-1962* by Arthur A. Carrington, P.13

matches in history took place in 1940 at the Cosmopolitan Club. Don Budge proved that he was the best white player in the segregated white tennis world by becoming the first male player to win all four of the Grand Slam Championships (Australian, French, U.S. and Wimbledon) in a single year in 1938. To date, the only male players to have accomplished this incredible feat are Budge and Rod Laver in 1962 and 1969. The only women who accomplished this feat are Maureen Connolly Brinker in 1953, Margaret Court in 1970 and Steffi Graf in 1988.

Budge turned professional in 1939 and dominated his pro matches in the same way he dominated the circuit when he was an amateur. He had proven that he was one of the greatest players of all time because for several years he consistently beat all of the top white players in the world. However, as a true competitor, he wanted to test himself against all of the best players in the world (regardless of their race). He had a desire to prove to himself that he was truly the best in the world by beating the top black players who, because of racial discrimination, were not allowed to compete at the Grand Slam Championships.

In 1940, Budge took the great social risk of playing a talented black player named Jimmy McDaniels on the clay courts of the Cosmopolitan Club in Harlem. Jimmy McDaniels was a left hander with smooth strokes who proved that he was the best player in the black tennis world when he won the 1939 ATA men's singles championships at Hampton University in Hampton, Virginia. He went on to dominate the black tennis world in much the same way that Budge dominated the white tennis world. McDaniels won the ATA Championships in 1940 and 1941, confirming his place as one of the best black male players in history.

The social implications of this match in New York City were enormous. Not only was this a contest between a black and white player six years before Jackie Robinson was allowed to play in baseball's major leagues, it was a symbolic match between the elite of the white and black communities. At that time, many people in white society believed that blacks were not capable of competing with the smarter and more athletic whites in sports like baseball, football or basketball. These racist individuals believed that even if the unthinkable happened and blacks could eventually compete in baseball, football and basketball, they would never be able to compete with whites in the elite and highly intellectual sport of tennis.

However, Budge knew that a person's color had nothing to do with his or her tennis ability or intellect. In the minds of those people who did not understand the passions of an elite athlete, Budge had nothing to win and everything to lose in this match. Historians have not given Budge the credit he deserves for doing the right thing and voluntarily breaking the color barrier in tennis. If Budge had lost that match, the results of "White-Only" tennis championships around the world would have been called into question. Large numbers of people would have challenged the widely held belief that blacks were intellectually and athletically inferior to whites.

The Cosmopolitan Club was filled to capacity for this historic match. Before the first serve the largely African-American audience was filled with anticipation and hope. A good showing by McDaniels would help to legitimize African-American tennis and the ATA. A win would be a historic victory for African Americans the likes of which (because of the implications for upper class white society) had never been seen before in the world of sports. The sports world's color barrier had been broken before this match in sports like boxing and cycling. However, the class- based color barrier in an elite sport like tennis had not been penetrated.

The match was much more competitive than the final score indicates. Don Budge won the match 6-1, 6-2. However, after the match, it is rumored that Budge and some reporters attending the match stated that McDaniels was playing at a level comparable to many of the top ten players in the world. This group felt that if McDaniels had the opportunity to practice against the best white players he could eventually become one of the best tennis players in the world. This historic match helped to pave the way for the integration of the sport by another talented player from the Cosmopolitan Club.

The Color Barrier is Officially Broken

Althea Gibson was born in Silver, South Carolina. However, she moved to New York in 1930 when she was just 3 years old. Gibson was an extraordinarily gifted athlete who won the New York City Police Athletic League (PAL) paddle tennis championship as a teenager. The PAL Director Buddy Walker introduced her to tennis which she picked up quickly. Gibson's obvious talent in tennis enabled her to earn an honorary membership in the Cosmopolitan Club where she got free lessons from the legendary one-armed tennis instructor Fred Johnson.

Gibson became so good that she won the ATA 18 and under national championships in 1944. In 1946, she lost a very close ATA women's singles championship match in Wilberforce, Ohio, to Roumania Peters by the score 6-4, 7-9, 6-3. Gibson was not used to losing and was heartbroken. This extreme disappointment was the catalyst she needed to commit herself to doing whatever was necessary to become a champion. Gibson instinctively knew that she needed focused high- level instruction to take her game to the next level. She therefore willingly moved south to improve her game under the tutelage of Dr. R. Walter Johnson in Lynchburg, Virginia, during the summers and Dr. Hubert Eaton in Wilmington, North Carolina, during the school year. These tennis and life coaches had experience helping to improve the games of some of the best players in the black tennis community. In 1946, they began the very involved process of developing Gibson's mind and body in a way that would enable her to become one of the best female athletes in the world.

This arrangement was exactly what Althea needed. She won the 1947 ATA women's singles title and went on to win 9 other women's singles championships, from 1948-56 and 8 ATA mixed doubles national titles, from 1948-55 with Dr. Johnson. In much the same way that Don Budge wanted to test his skills against all of the best players regardless of race, Althea Gibson wanted to play against the world's best white players.

After more than a half-century of fighting the national governing body of tennis for equal rights on the tennis court, black players were finally allowed to play in some USLTA tournaments in the late 1940s. Gibson made history at the USLTA National Indoor Championships in 1950 by becoming the first black player to be seeded in any USLTA national championship. She lost in the finals and became the first black player to reach a final of a USLTA national championship. However, Gibson longed to become the best player in the world and recommitted herself to working as hard as she possibly could to win a Grand Slam Championship at least once in her life.

In spite of the integration of some tennis tournaments, Gibson was not allowed to play at the U.S. National Championships. The reason given by the USLTA was that her record was not strong enough for entry into the tournament. Even though she had done well in indoor tournaments the USLTA wanted her to prove her skills at the outdoor tune-up events for the championships which were held at "White-Only" tennis clubs that would not allow her to play.

Her success at the indoor tournament proved to many influential people that she had the ability to compete with the women playing the U.S. National Championships. Betram Baker of the ATA and others in the tennis community lobbied the USLTA to allow her to play in the tournament. The pressure on the USLTA to do the right thing intensified when former world champion Alice Marble had a letter published in the most influential tennis publication of the time, *American Lawn Tennis,* that publicly criticized the USLTA for not letting Althea play the national championships.[14]

Alice Marble was a living legend of the sport. She reached the No. 1 ranking in the world in women's tennis, won the 1936, 1938, 1939 and 1940 U.S. National Championships which brought her total Grand Slam titles to 18 (five in singles, six in doubles and seven in mixed doubles). No one in the tennis world could question her credibility in assessing a player's ability to compete in the U.S. National Championships. Portions of her letter read *"Miss Gibson is over a very cunningly wrought barrel, and I can only hope to loosen a few of its staves with one lone opinion. If tennis is a game for ladies and gentlemen, it's also time we acted a little more like gentle-people and less like sanctimonious hypocrites.... If Althea Gibson represents a challenge to the present crop of women players, it's only fair that they should meet that challenge on the courts."* She went on to say that if Gibson were not given the opportunity to compete, *"Then there is an ineradicable mark against a game to which I have devoted most of my life, and I would be bitterly ashamed."*[15]

The influence of her support convinced the USLTA to allow Gibson to compete in the Eastern Grass Court Championships and the

---

[14] *American Lawn Tennis;* July 1950
[15] *American Lawn Tennis;* July 1950

National Clay Court Championships. She performed well in these tournaments and became the first African-American to gain entrée into the U.S. National Championships at Forest Hills, in 1950. On her 23rd birthday, August 25, she beat Barbara Knapp in the first round of the U.S. National Championships 6-2, 6-2. Gibson lost a close three set match in the tournament's second round to three-time Wimbledon Champion Louise Brough.

Gibson proved with certainty, however, that she could compete effectively with the top white players in the world. Her skills grew rapidly in each tournament she entered, helping her become the first black player to grace the winner's circle in a Grand Slam event. Gibson won the Women's Singles and Doubles titles at the 1956 French Championships, and therefore became the first African-American to gain entrée into the Wimbledon draw at the All-England Club. She went on to win five titles at Wimbledon: two in singles in 1957 and 1958, and three in doubles, in 1956, 1957 and 1958; three titles at the U.S. National Championships: two in singles in 1957 and 1958, and one in mixed doubles in 1957; and one Australian doubles trophy, in 1957.

Astonishingly, she earned 11 Grand Slam victories within three years, was the No. 1 ranked player in the world, in 1957 and 1958, and the first African-American to be voted the Associated Press Female Athlete of the Year in 1957 and 1958. She was inducted into the International Tennis Hall of Fame in 1971, the Eastern Tennis Hall of Fame in 1988 and the Black Tennis Hall of Fame in 2008.

Althea Gibson's first Wimbledon victory was so historic, she was honored with the same type of ticker-tape parade in New York that the legendary New York Yankees receive when they win the World Series. She retired from tennis fairly early in her career and became the first African-American woman professional golfer. She will always be a global tennis legend to tennis lovers of all races because she broke virtually every racial tennis barrier in the world.

CHAPTER 12: Breaking the Barriers Timeline

The Black Tennis and History Timeline

Tennis has become an international sport because it is played on a professional level in almost every country in the world. It therefore has the potential to appeal to anyone from anywhere in the world. In recent years, there has been a global effort to increase interest and participation among players 10 years old and younger. As a result, the sport has grown in interest among young people throughout the world. Thanks to the extraordinary work of tennis administrators, the sport also has embraced players with mental and physical handicaps so virtually anyone anywhere can play the sport.

The two major audiences that have made the sport extraordinarily popular are those who love playing tennis (*"Tennis Players"*) and those who enjoy watching it (*"Tennis Fans"*). There is some overlap between these two segments of the tennis society. However, they are very different in many respects. Many of the people who can be categorized as Tennis Players have caught the "Tennis Bug" where playing the sport stimulates their emotions so intensely they have an addiction to playing tennis. They feel the need to get on the tennis court and hit tennis balls as often as possible. These people are usually physically active and in good shape and enjoy the physical, mental, emotional and social aspects of playing tennis.

The segment of the tennis audience called *Tennis Fans* includes many of these frequent players who, in addition to playing the sport, like to watch amateur or professional tennis live or on television. However, there is a sizable segment of the tennis playing community that does not like to watch tennis. It is interesting to note that a significant number of *Tennis Fans* watch tennis but do not play tennis regularly or at all. They are drawn to the sport for two primary reasons. The first reason that some people are drawn to the sport is that they love watching the attractive men and women who play pro tennis for a living hitting the ball as hard as they can back and forth in an effort to win a point. These Tennis Fans do not play tennis or watch it in their neighborhood. However, when the major tournaments are in town or on TV they are watching as many matches as possible. The second reason they watch the sport is because of their interest in knowing as much about the tennis celebrities as possible. They follow Serena Williams or Roger Federer or other tennis stars in much the same way that they follow their favorite musician or actor. They read the gossip pages and are anxious to learn about the lives of the tennis stars.

There is a much smaller third segment of the tennis community that are called "Tennis Lovers." These are people who have a deep passion for watching, playing, reading about the sport, volunteering and learning about the history of the sport. Tennis is their avocation. The *Breaking the Barriers Timeline* in this chapter was developed for this audience. This timeline was included in the *Breaking the Barriers* exhibit to provide a context with which to understand the diversification of the sport in the United States (US). We list a significant event in tennis history by year in a box and an important general or black history fact in italics. Since the focus of the exhibit was on the integration of tennis in the US, many of the general history facts are based on US black history. In addition, we include the election or assassination of US Presidents because they played such a significant role in establishing policies related to race relations. One of the more controversial aspects of the exhibit was the inclusion of the number of lynchings of African Americans in the US each year that statistics were available. We felt that it was important for audiences to know about the brutal aspects of racial discrimination in the US. This knowledge helped many people develop greater empathy with the struggles of black tennis players. Being denied entry to a tournament because they were black paled in comparison to being lynched because you looked at or said hello to a white woman. We have been told that this timeline made the exhibit come "alive" for many people because it helped them understand the

Breaking The Barriers

extent of racial discrimination in the US and enabled them to connect tennis with general history. In addition, *Tennis Lovers* said they learned a lot about general tennis history from the timeline. The timeline ends in 1975 when Arthur Ashe won Wimbledon because this victory marked a very significant moment in black tennis history. Finally, after 98 years (1877 to 1975), a black woman (Althea Gibson) and a black man (Arthur Ashe) had broken through the ultimate tennis barrier and finally won the two biggest singles tennis tournaments in the world.

Breaking the Barriers Timeline

1874 – Queen Victoria grants a patent to Major Walter Clopton Wingfield for the game of Sphairistike or Lawn Tennis.

1875 – *The Civil Rights Act of 1875 guarantees equal rights to black Americans in public accommodations and jury duty.*

1876 – The First tennis tournament in the United States is held in Nahant, Massachusetts

1877 – The First Wimbledon is held at the All England Lawn Tennis and Croquet Club in London, England

1880 – *James Garfield is elected the 20th President of the United States.*

1880 – The first United States National Tennis Championship is held at the Staten Island and Racquet Club in New York City.

1881 – *President Garfield is assassinated.*

1881 – The United States National Lawn Tennis Association (USNLTA) is founded in New York City.

1881 – The first USNLTA National Championship is held at the Newport Casino in Newport, Rhode Island.

1881 – *The Tuskegee Institute is founded on July 4th by tennis player and fan Booker T. Washington.*

1881 – *Spelman College (the first black college for women) is founded.*

1881 – *The Segregation of Public Transportation is upheld when Tennessee enacts a statute that requires separate cars for first-class black passengers.*

1882 – There are 49 lynchings of black Americans. It is important to note that we are reporting information about lynchings to provide a realistic context in which we are chronicling the history of blacks in tennis. The lynching figures are derived from the Tuskegee Institute Archives which kept statistics on reported lynchings from 1882-1968. While approximately one third of the lynching victims were white, only the figures for blacks are reported in this timeline.

1883 – The Civil Rights Act of 1875 is overturned by US Supreme Court. The court determines that the Federal Government cannot bar corporations or individuals from discriminating on the basis of race.

1883 – The are 53 lynchings of black Americans.

1884 – Grover Cleveland is elected the 22nd President of the United States.

1884 – There are 51 lynchings of black Americans.

1885 – There are 74 lynchings of black Americans.

1886 – The Knights of Labor reaches peak membership of 700,000 with approximately 75,000 African-American members. The American Federation of Labor is organized by white individuals disaffected from the Knights of Labor and excludes blacks.

1886 – Slavery is abolished in Cuba.

1886 – There are 74 lynchings of black Americans.

1887 – Blacks are banned from Major League Baseball.

1887 – Two of America's first black owned banks open – The Savings Bank of the Grand Fountain United Order of Reformers in Richmond, Virginia and Capital Savings Bank of Washington, DC.

1887 – There are 70 lynchings of black Americans.

1888 – Benjamin Harrison is elected the 23rd President of the United States.

1888 – There are 69 lynchings of black Americans.

1889 – Florida becomes the first state to use the poll tax to disenfranchise black voters.

1889 – Frederick Douglass is appointed minister to Haiti.

1889 – There are 94 lynchings of black Americans.

Breaking The Barriers

1890 – The Chautauqua Tennis Club in Philadelphia is established with other black clubs forming in Baltimore, New York and Washington, D.C.

1890 – *There are 85 lynchings of black Americans.*

1890 – *In the US Census of 1890, 12% of US population is black.*

1890 – *Under the Mississippi Plan, literacy and "understanding" tests are used to disenfranchise black American citizens. South Carolina, Louisiana, North Carolina, Alabama, Virginia, Georgia and Oklahoma later implement these tests to minimize the number of black voters.*

1891 – The first French Championships (originally called the Championnat de France) is held at IIe de Puteaux in Paris, France.

1892 – *There are 161 lynchings of black Americans.*

1892 – *Grover Cleveland is elected the 24th President of the United States.*

1892 – *The National Medical Association is formed in Atlanta by African-American physicians because they are barred from the American Medical Association.*

1893 – *Dr. Daniel Hale Williams, a black surgeon, performs the first successful operation on a human heart in the United States.*

1893 – *There are 118 lynchings of black Americans.*

1894 – *The Pullman Company strike causes a national transportation crisis. African-American workers are hired as strike breakers.*

1894 – *There are 134 lynchings of black Americans.*

1895 – *African-American leader and statesman Frederick Douglass dies.*

1895 – *The Atlanta Compromise delivered by Booker T. Washington states that the "Negro problem" would be solved by a policy of gradualism and accommodation.*

1895 – *Several Baptist organizations combine to form the National Baptist Convention of the USA – largest black religious denomination in the US.*

1895 – *There are 113 lynchings of black Americans.*

1896 – In Plessy v. Ferguson the Supreme Court decides that separate but equal facilities satisfy the Fourteenth Amendment guarantees, thereby sanctioning Jim Crow segregation laws.

1896 – William McKinley is elected the 25th President of the United States.

1896 – There are 78 lynchings of black Americans.

1897 – The American Negro Academy is established in Washington, DC to encourage African-American participation in art, literature and philosophy.

1897 – Two of America's first black-owned insurance companies are established – The North Carolina Mutual and Provident Insurance Company of Durham, North Carolina and the National Benefit Life Insurance Company of Washington, DC.

1897 – There are 123 lynchings of black Americans.

1898 – The Spanish American War is started.

1898 – There are 101 lynchings of black Americans.

1898 – Rev. W.W. Walker organizes the first interstate tournament for blacks in Philadelphia. Thomas Jefferson of Lincoln University of Pennsylvania is the first champion.

1899 – The African-American Council protests lynchings and massacres with a national day of fasting.

1899 – There are 85 lynchings of black Americans.

1899 – The tournament returns to Philadelphia where Rev. Walker defeats Henry Freeman of Washington DC for the championship.

1900 – James Weldon Johnson and brother John Rosamond Johnson compose "Lift Every Voice and Sing" – song is eventually adopted as the Black National Anthem.

1900 – There are 106 lynchings of black Americans.

1900 – Although the tournament is relocated to Washington D.C., Rev. Walker again emerges victorious, beating Charles Cook of Howard University.

1901 – President McKinley is assassinated. Vice President Theodore Roosevelt succeeds him as the 26th President of the

Breaking The Barriers

United States. He eventually forms a "Tennis Cabinet" of senior leaders in his administration who play tennis together on a weekly basis.

1901 – *Booker T. Washington becomes the first black American to dine at the White House.*

1901 – *African-American Congressman George H. White leaves office – no African-American will serve in Congress for the next 28 years.*

1901 – *There are 105 lynchings of black Americans.*

1902 – *Black Jockey Jimmy Winkfield wins the Kentucky Derby in an era when African-American jockeys dominated the sport.*

1902 – *There are 85 lynchings of black Americans.*

1903 – *W.E.B. DuBois publishes* The Souls of Black Folk, *in which he rejects the gradualism of Booker T. Washington, calling for agitation on behalf of African-American rights.*

1903 – *There are 84 lynchings of black Americans.*

1904 – *Bethune – Cookman College was founded.*

1904 – *There are 76 lynchings of black Americans.*

1905 – *"The Chicago Defender," the first major black newspaper, is founded by Robert Abbot.*

1905 – *There are 56 lynchings of black Americans.*

1905 – The first Australian Championships (originally called the Australasian Championships) is held at the Warehouseman's Cricket Ground in Melbourne, Australia.

1906 – Mrs. C.O. "Mother" Seames of Chicago begins giving tennis lessons to young black players.

1906 – *A major race riot breaks out in Atlanta. The riot results in 10 deaths (8 blacks and 2 whites).*

1906 – *There are 62 lynchings of black Americans.*

1907 – *Madame C.J. Walker of Denver develops and markets her hair straightening method and creates one of the most successful cosmetics and hair care firms in the nation. She becomes the first black millionaire.*

1907 – *There are 58 lynchings of black Americans.*

1908 – *John Baxter "Doc" Taylor from the University of Pennsylvania becomes the 1st African-American to represent the United States in the Olympics and to win an Olympic Gold Medal. He was part of the US 1600 meter medley relay team.*

1908 – *Jack Johnson becomes the 1st African-American to be crowned Heavyweight Champion of the World.*

1908 – *William Howard Taft is elected the 27th President of the United States.*

1908 – *There are 89 lynchings of black Americans.*

1909 – In interstate play, the Crescent Club of Washington DC battled the Monumental Club of Baltimore for the Club Championship.

1909 – *The NAACP is formed to promote the use of the judicial system to restore the legal rights of black Americans.*

1909 – *African-American Mathew Henson and Admiral Robert E. Peary become the first known men to have reached the North Pole.*

1909 – *There are 69 lynchings of black Americans.*

1909 – The first faculty tennis club at Tuskegee Institute is formed by E. Davidson Washington, Booker T. Washington's son, and C.G. Kelly.

1910 – *The first issue of "Crisis," a publication of the NAACP, debuts with W.E.B. DuBois as editor.*

1910 – Black player Edgar Brown popularizes the top spin and baseline game, thereby signaling the end of the prevailing "chop and net game."

1910 – *There are 67 lynchings of black Americans.*

1910 – The black press begins actively reporting on black tennis club activities.

1911 – *The National Urban League is formed to help African Americans secure equal employment.*

1911 – *There are 60 lynchings of black Americans.*

1912 – Believing that "athletic competition and good sportsmanship are prerequisites for building good personalities and character," Mrs. Maude Lawrence,

Breaking The Barriers

Madelyn Baptist McCall, Ruth Shockey and Mrs. C.O. "Mother" Seames form the Chicago Prairie Tennis Club.

1912 – Woodrow Wilson is elected the 28th President of the United States.

1912 – There are 61 lynchings of black Americans.

1913 – Harriet Tubman – former slave and abolitionist – dies.

1913 – The Wilson Administration begins federal segregation of work places, rest rooms and lunch rooms.

1913 – There are 51 lynchings of black Americans.

1913 – The West Side Tennis Club moves for the final time to Forest Hills, Queens, New York.

1914 – World War I begins in Europe.

1914 – There are 51 lynchings of black Americans.

1915 – The US Nationals are held for the first time at the West Side Tennis Club in Forest Hills, Queens, New York.

1915 – The Colonial Tennis Club is founded. It later becomes the famous Cosmopolitan Club in Harlem.

1915 – The Great Migration of African Americans from the South to northern cities begins. Booker T. Washington, renowned African-American spokesman, dies.

1915 – There are 56 lynchings of black Americans.

1916 – Meeting on Thanksgiving Day, 1916 at the YMCA in Washington, DC, members from the major black tennis clubs found the American Tennis Association (ATA), the oldest continually active African-American sports organization. H. Stanton McCard is elected the first president.

1916 – The gas mask invented by African-American Garrett Morgan is used to rescue 32 men trapped in a tunnel 250 feet beneath Lake Erie.

1916 – There are 51 lynchings of black Americans.

1917 – The 1st ATA National Championships are held at Druid Hill Park, Baltimore. Tally Holmes and Lucy Diggs Slowe are the first Men's and Women's Singles Champions respectively. Holmes and Sylvester Smith capture the Doubles title.

1917 – By winning the ATA Women's Singles title, Lucy Diggs Slowe becomes the first female African-American national champion in any sport.

1917 – The New York Tennis Association of the ATA is founded.

1917 – *The United States enters World War I.*

1917 – *Race riots in East St. Louis start when 470 African-American workers are hired to replace striking white workers. The riots lead to the death of over 200 people (some of whom were lynched).*

1917 – *The NAACP organizes a march down Manhattan's Fifth Avenue protesting lynchings, race riots and the denial of basic human rights.*

1917 – *There are 36 lynchings of black Americans.*

1918 – *World War I ends.*

1918 – *Race riots in Pennsylvania claim 9 lives – 6 blacks and 3 whites.*

1918 – *There are 64 lynchings of black Americans.*

1918 – The 2nd National ATA Tournament is held at the Ideal Tennis Club of Harlem, New York. Jamaican May Rae wins the ATA National Women's Singles Championship and Tally Holmes wins the Men's Singles Championship. Percy Richardson and D. Monroe capture the Men's Doubles Championship.

1919 – *The Ku Klux Klan is revived at Stone Mountain, Georgia and operates in 27 states.*

1919 – *Post war social tensions lead to "Red Summer" where race riots take place in 26 locations. The worst violence takes place in Elaine, Arkansas where 5 whites and 240 blacks are killed.*

1919 – *There are 76 lynchings of black Americans.*

1919 – The 3rd ATA National Tournament is held again at the Ideal Tennis Club of Harlem. Sylvester Smith of Washington, DC beats two-time national champion Tally Holmes. May Rae retains her Women's Singles title. Tally Holmes and Ted Thompson win the Men's Doubles Championship.

Breaking The Barriers

1920 – 19th Amendment to the Constitution is ratified, giving all women the right to vote. Nonetheless, African-American women, like African-American men, are denied the right to vote in most southern states.

1920 – The Harlem Renaissance starts. This is a remarkable period of creativity for black writers, poets and artists.

1920 – Andrew "Rube" Foster leads the effort to establish the Negro National (Baseball) League.

1920 – Warren G. Harding is elected 29th President of the United States.

1920 – There are 53 lynchings of black Americans.

1920 – The 4th ATA Nationals are held for 3rd year in a row at the Ideal Tennis Club. Jamaicans May Rae and B.M. Clark win the ATA National Women's and Men's Singles Championships. Clark and Eugene Kinckle Jones win the Men's Doubles.

1920 – "Mother" Seames and her husband purchase property on the South Side of Chicago and build 4 tennis courts—this site becomes the first private grounds for a black tennis club in the United States.

1921 – Bessie Coleman, the first black female pilot, becomes the first woman to receive an international pilot's license.

1921 – There are 59 lynchings of black Americans.

1921 – The 5th ATA Nationals are held at the Suburban Gardens Tennis Courts in Washington, DC. Tally Holmes wins his 3rd National ATA Championship. Lucy Diggs Slowe of Baltimore wins the Women's Singles. Ted Thompson and Tally Holmes regain their Men's Doubles title.

1921 – Dwight Davis, the donor of the Davis Cup, serves as an umpire at the ATA National Semi-Finals.

1922 – A federal anti-lynching bill is killed by filibuster in the United States Senate.

1922 – There are 51 lynchings of black Americans.

1922 – The 6th ATA Nationals are held at the Germantown Tennis Club and at the YWCA in Philadelphia. Edgar Brown of Indianapolis and Isadore Channels from Chicago win the

Singles Championships. Tally Holmes and Ted Thompson win the Men's Doubles title.

1922 – The Springfield Racquet Club of Springfield, Massachusetts is founded.

1922 – The New Jersey Tennis Association (NJTA) of the ATA is formed.

1923 – *President Harding dies. Vice President Calvin Coolidge becomes the 30th President of the United States.*

1923 – *The Cotton Club opens in Harlem.*

1923 – *There are 29 lynchings of black Americans.*

1923 – The 7th ATA Nationals are held at the Prairie View Tennis Club in Chicago. Edgar Brown defeats New Yorker Eyre Saitch 6-3, 6-2, 11-9. Isadore Channels faces Lottie Wade in the finals and is again victorious. McGriff and Downing win the Men's Doubles.

1923 – The earliest integrated tournament sanctioned by the USLTA takes place at Kissena Park in Flushing, Queens. Dwight Davis, the Founder and namesake of the Davis Cup, serves as the head umpire for this tournament.

1924 – *Opera star Roland Hayes becomes the first African-American to perform at Carnegie Hall in New York City.*

1924 – *There are 16 lynchings of black Americans.*

1924 – The 8th ATA Nationals return to Druid Hill Park in Baltimore. Tally Holmes wins his 4th title and Isadore Channels her 3rd. In the Men's Doubles, Tally Holmes and Ted Thompson defeat Saitch and Smith. In the Women's Doubles, Emma Leonard and Channels defeat Radcliff and Seames. In the Mixed Doubles, Dr. Rhetta and Miss Nellie Nicholson defeat Channels and Hudlin. Russell Smith wins the first Boys 18 Singles title.

1925 – *Civil Rights activist Malcolm X is born.*

1925 – *The National Bar Association, the organization of black attorneys, is established.*

1925 – *There are 17 lynchings of black Americans.*

1925 – The 9th ATA Nationals are held at the Manual Training and Industrial School in Bordentown, NJ—this is the first time the event is held at a black school. Increased facilities and accommodations allow the tournament to become a preeminent social event as well as a top-notch athletic competition. Ted Thompson and Lulu Ballard win the Men's and Women's Singles Championship respectively. Tally Holmes and Thompson win the Men's Doubles, Lulu Ballard and Ora Washington win the Women's Doubles, and Mrs. C.O. Seames and Dr. L.C. Downing win the Mixed Doubles. Lenoir Cook wins the Boys 18 Singles title.

1926 – *The Carnegie Corporation purchases Arturo Schomberg's collection of books and artifacts on African-American life. The collection becomes the basis for the Schomberg Center for Research on Black Culture.*

1926 – *Dr. M. Johnson becomes the first African-American president of Howard University.*

1926 – *There are 23 lynchings of black Americans.*

1926 – The 10th ATA Nationals are held in St. Louis, Missouri. Eyre Saitch and Isadore Channels win the singles title. Eyre Saitch and Ted Thompson capture the Men's Doubles title and Lulu Ballard and Ora Washington retain the Women's Doubles title. E. Robinson and E. Cole win the Mixed Doubles Championship. Maceo Hill wins the Boys 18 Singles title.

1926 – In a 1926 survey of 70 back colleges, only 36 have tennis courts and only 4 have tennis coaches.

1927 – *Abe Saperstein forms the Harlem Globetrotters basketball team.*

1927 – *There are 16 lynchings of black Americans.*

1927 – The 11th ATA Nationals are held at the Hampton Institute in Hampton, Virginia — the first ATA National Tournament held in the South. Both Ted Thompson and Lulu Ballard win their second National Singles title. Thompson and Tally Holmes win the Men's Doubles and Lulu Ballard and Ora Washington win the Women's Doubles. Louis Jones and Blanche Winston win the Mixed Doubles title and Douglas Turner wins the Boys 18 Singles title.

1928 – The 12th ATA Nationals return to Bordentown, New Jersey. Edgar Brown captures the Men's Singles title and Lulu Ballard repeats as the Women's Singles Champion. Saitch and Dr. Sylvester Smith win the Men's Doubles Championship. Ora Washington and Lulu Ballard successfully defend their Women's Doubles title. Blanche Winston and W.A. Kean win the Mixed Doubles Championship. Reginald Weir wins the Boys 18 Singles title.

1929 – The 13th ATA Nationals are held once again at Bordentown, NJ. Edgar Brown and Ora Washington win the singles. Saitch and Smith retain their Men's Doubles title and Ballard and Washington repeat as Women's Doubles Champions. Dr. O.B. Williams and Anita Gant win the Mixed Doubles and Nathaniel Jackson wins the Boys 18 Singles title.

1929 – Douglas Turner from the University of Illinois makes history as the runner-up in the "Big Ten" college tennis championships.

1929 – Herbert Clark Hoover is elected the 31st President of the United States of America.

1929 – Dr. Martin Luther King, Junior is born.

1930 – Wallace Fard Muhammed founds the Nation of Islam movement in Detroit.

1930 – There are 20 lynchings of black Americans.

1930 – The 14th ATA Nationals are held in Indianapolis. Douglas Turner and Ora Washington win the singles title. Anita Gant and Dr. O.B. Williams seize the Mixed Doubles trophy. Washington and Winston win the Women's Doubles and John McGriff and Elwood Downing win the Men's Doubles. Nathaniel Jackson repeats as Boys 18 and Under Champion.

1931 – The 15th ATA Nationals are held at the Tuskegee Institute in Alabama. Flood lights allow night play for the first time. Reginald Weir of New York City triumphs in the Men's Singles and Ora Washington wins her third Women's Singles Championship. Nathaniel and Franklyn

Jackson win the Men's Doubles. Ora Washington and Blanche Winston are the winners of the Women's Doubles Championships. Anne Roberts and Ted Thompson capture the Mixed Doubles Championships while Franklin Smith wins the Boys 18 Singles title.

1932 – *The unfortunate Tuskegee Syphilis Experiment begins under the direction of the US Public Health Service. The experiment ends in 1972.*

1932 – *Franklin D. Roosevelt is elected the 32nd President of the United States of America.*

1932 – *There are 6 lynchings of black Americans.*

1932 – The 16th ATA Nationals are held at the Shady Rest Country Club in NJ. Reggie Weir, on a changed line call, goes on to win the Men's Singles title. Ora Washington defeats Francis Gittens for the Women's title. Richard Hudlin and Douglas Turner win the Men's Doubles and Ballard and Washington win the Women's Doubles. Martha Davis and Henry Williams win the Mixed Doubles, while Franklyn Jackson wins the Boys 18 Singles title.

1933 – The 17th ATA Nationals are held at the Hampton Institute. Reginald Weir again faces Nat Jackson in the finals and wins decisively in straight sets. Ora Washington wins her fifth consecutive Women's Singles Championship. Nathaniel and Franklyn Jackson win the Men's Doubles title, and Ora Washington and Anita Gant win the Women's Doubles title. Emma Leonard and Dr. Clarence O. Hilton capture the Mixed Doubles. Hubert Eaton wins the Boys 18 Singles title.

1934 – *The Apollo Theater opens in Harlem.*

1934 – *There are 15 lynchings of black Americans.*

1934 – The 18th ATA Nationals are held at Lincoln University in Lincoln, Pennsylvania. Nathaniel Jackson wins the Men's Championship and Ora Washington repeats yet again in the Women's Championship. Ora Washington and Lulu Ballard win the Women's Doubles title. Nathaniel and Franklyn Jackson capture the Men's Doubles Championship. Emma Leonard and Dr. C.O. Hilton repeat as Mixed Doubles Champions. Theodore Cousins wins the Boy's 18 Singles title.

1935 – *In Norris v. Alabama, the US Supreme Court rules that a defendant has a right, regardless of his or her race, to trial by a jury of his peers.*

1935 – *There are 18 lynchings of black Americans.*

1935 – The 19th ATA Nationals are held at West Virginia State College. Franklyn Jackson and Ora Washington win the Men's and Women's Singles titles respectively — Washington's 7th in a row. The Men's Doubles title is captured by Nathaniel Jackson and Franklyn Jackson and the Women's Doubles title is retained by Ora Washington and Lulu Ballard. The Mixed Doubles event is not held. The Boys 18 Singles Championship is won by Ernest McCampbell. The Girls 18 Singles Championship is added to the ATA National Championships. The first winner of the Girls 18 Singles Championship is Mae Hamlin.

1936 – *Jesse Owens wins four Gold Medals at the 1936 Olympics in Berlin.*

1936 – *Mary McLeod Bethune is the first black woman to receive a presidential appointment. She is appointed a special ambassador to President Roosevelt.*

1936 – The 20th ATA Nationals are held at Wilberforce University. Lloyd C. Scott wins the Men's Singles and Lulu Ballard ends Ora Washington's streak to take the Women's Championship. Nathaniel and Franklyn Jackson retain their Men's Doubles title for another year. Ora Washington and Lulu Ballard successfully defend their Women's Doubles Championship. For the second consecutive year, the Mixed Doubles event is not held. The Boys 18 Singles Champion is Johnson Wells and the Girls 18 Singles Champion is Angelina Spencer.

1937 – *Joe Louis knocks out Jim Braddock to become the World Heavyweight Champion.*

1937 – The 21st ATA Nationals return to Tuskegee Institute. Dr. Reginald Weir wins his 4th singles title and Ora Washington claims her 8th singles title. James Stocks and

Thomas Walker win the Men's Doubles Championship. The Women's Doubles Championship is won by E. Lilyan Spencer and Bertha Isaacs. Flora Lomax and W.H. Hall win the reinstalled Mixed Doubles title. Johnson Wells wins his second Boys 18 Singles title and Mae Hamlin wins her second Girls 18 Singles title. Fred Johnson, the one armed marvel who became one of Althea Gibson's early coaches, win's the Veteran's Singles.

1938 – The 22nd ATA Nationals returns to Lincoln University. Franklyn Jackson wins the Men's Singles title and Flora Lomax wins the Women's Singles title. Nathaniel and Franklyn Jackson regain their Men's Doubles title. Margaret and Roumania Peters win the Women's Doubles and Lulu Ballard and Gerald Norman, Jr. win the Mixed Doubles title. Johnson Wells wins an unprecedented third Boy's 18 Singles Championship and Mayme Stanley wins the Girl's 18 Singles Championship.

1939 – Bill "Bojangles" Robinson organizes the Black Actors Guild.

1939 – The 23rd ATA Nationals are held at Hampton Institute. Jimmie McDaniel from Xavier University beats Dr. Reginald Weir for the Men's Championship and Flora Lomax is victorious over Roumania Peters for the Women's title. McDaniel and Cohen triumph over the Jackson Brothers to win the Men's Doubles title. Roumania and Margaret Peters retain the Women's Doubles title. The Mixed Doubles is won by Ora Washington and Dr. Sylvester Smith. Robert Isaacs wins the Boys 18 Singles Championship and Vivian Murphy wins the Girls 18 Singles Championship.

1940 – Richard Wright publishes his first novel, Native Son.

1940 – Hattie McDaniel is the first black actor to receive an Academy Award – best supporting actress in Gone with the Wind.

1940 – The 24th ATA Nationals returns to Wilberforce University. Jimmie McDaniel retains the Men's title after a 5 set match against Richard Cohen of Denver. Agnes Lawson wins the Women's Championship. Clifford Russell and

Howard Minnis win the Men's Doubles and Margaret and Roumania Peters win the Women's Doubles. Flora Lomax and William Hall capture the Mixed Doubles title. Joseph King wins the Boys 18 Singles title and Helen Hutchinson wins the Girls 18 Singles title.

1940 – The historic Don Budge versus Jimmie McDaniel Match at the Cosmopolitan Club in the Harlem Section of New York City takes place. Budge wins the match 6-1, 6-2.

1941 – *Japan attacks Pearl Harbor.*

1941 – *The United States enters World War II.*

1941 – *The US Army creates the Tuskegee Air Squadron of African-American men.*

1941 – The 25th ATA Nationals are held in Tuskegee, Alabama. Jimmie McDaniel wins the Men's title and Flora Lomax wins her third Women's Singles title. Jimmie McDaniel and Richard Cohen win the Men's Doubles title and Margaret and Roumania Peters win the Women's Doubles title. Eoline Thornton and Harold Mitchell win the Mixed Doubles title. Raymond Jackson wins the Boys 18 Singles title and Thelma Mc Daniel wins the Girls 18 Singles title.

1941 – Holcombe Ward, USLTA president, sends a congratulatory letter to the ATA on the occasion of its Silver Jubilee, stating: "…I extend most cordial greetings and sincere wishes for the success of the American Tennis Association in its further development, work and efforts to maintain the high standards of the game of tennis wherever played." "Wherever played," of course, did not include "White Only" tennis courts or USLTA tournaments.

1942 – *The Congress of Racial Equality (CORE) is founded by James Farmer.*

1942 – *The US Marine Corps accepts African-American men for the first time.*

1942 – The 26th ATA Nationals are held at Lincoln University. Dr. Reginald Weir wins his 5th Singles title and Flora Lomax wins her fourth Women's Singles title. Lomax and Lillian Van Buren take the Women's Doubles and

Howard Minnis and Clifford Russell capture the Men's Doubles. Kathryn Jones and William E. Jones win the Mixed Doubles. Richard Cunningham wins the Boys 18 Singles title and Nana Davis wins the Girls 18 Singles title.

1942 – Fred Johnson enters Althea Gibson in her first tournament — the New York State Open Championship, Girls Division — which she wins.

1943 – The 27th ATA Nationals are cancelled due to WWII.

1944 – Frederick Douglas Patterson establishes the United Negro College Fund.

1944 – The 28th ATA Nationals are held at the Cosmopolitan Club in New York City. Lloyd Scott defeats Robert Ryland for the Men's title and Roumania Peters captures her first Women's Singles title. Margaret and Roumania Peters win the Women's Doubles. Howard Minnis and Ronald Fieulleteau win the Men's Doubles. Lillian Van Buren and Delbert Russell capture the Mixed Doubles title. Carl Williams wins the Boys 18 Singles title and Althea Gibson wins the Girls 18 Singles title.

1944 – Althea Gibson wins the ATA National Girls 18 and Under Championship.

1945 – World War II ends.

1945 – Nat King Cole becomes the first African-American to have a radio variety show, which airs on NBC.

1945 – Ebony Magazine publishes its first issue.

1945 – The 29th ATA Nationals return to the Cosmopolitan Club. Lloyd Scott claims his second Men's title and Kathryn J. Irvis wins the Women's Singles Championship. Lloyd Scott and Louis Graves win the Men's Doubles while Margaret and Roumania Peters repeat as Women's Doubles winners. Delbert Russell and Lillian Van Buren repeat as Mixed Doubles winners. Franklyn Baily wins the Boys 18 Singles title and Althea Gibson wins her second Girls 18 Singles title.

1946 – The US Supreme Court in Morgan v. Virginia rules that segregation in interstate bus travel is unconstitutional.

1946 – The 30th ATA Nationals are held at Wilberforce University. Jimmie McDaniel of Los Angeles wins the Men's Championship. Roumania Peters wins her second Women's title against 17 year-old Althea Gibson from New York City. James Stock and McDaniel defeat Lloyd Scott and Louis Graves for the Men's Doubles title while Margaret and Roumania Peters capture the Women's Doubles. Ora Washington and George Stewart take the Mixed Doubles. Clyde Freeman wins the Boys 18 Singles title and Gwendolyn Whittington wins the Girls 18 Singles title.

1947 – *Jackie Robinson becomes the first African-American to play Major League Baseball in the 20th Century.*

1947 – The 31st ATA Nationals return to the Tuskegee Institute. Panamanian George Stewart wins the National Men's Singles Championship handily, beating Lloyd Scott 6-1, 6-1, 6-2. Young Althea Gibson turns the tables on last year's Champion Roumania Peters and captures her first ATA Women's Singles title. The Peters sisters retain their Women's Doubles title and John Chandler and Harold Mitchell capture the Men's Doubles Championship. The Mixed Doubles Championships were won by Ora Washington and George Stewart. Clyde Freeman wins his second Boys 18 Singles title and Wilma McGhee wins the Girls 18 Singles title.

1948 – *President Truman signs Executive Order 9981 which states: "It is hereby declared to be the policy of the President that there shall be equality of treatment and opportunity for all persons in the armed services without regard to race, color, religion or national origin."*

1948 – *Alice Coachman becomes the first African-American woman to win an Olympic Gold Medal when she captures gold in the high jump.*

1948 – The 32nd ATA Nationals are held at South Carolina State University. George Stewart and Althea Gibson repeat as Singles Champions. Stewart and Hubert Eaton win the Men's Doubles, while the Peters sisters, "Pete and

Repeat," added another Women's Doubles title. Althea Gibson pairs with Dr. R. Walter Johnson to take the Mixed Doubles title. Wilbert Davis wins the Boys 18 Singles title and Helen Mundy wins the Girls 18 Singles title.

1949 – *Businessman Jesse Blanton, Sr. establishes WERD-AM, the first black-owned radio station.*

1949 – The 33rd ATA Nationals are held at Wilberforce University. The Men's Singles final is cancelled due to heavy rain. The Men's Doubles is postponed, with George Stewart and Hubert Eaton winning at a later date. Althea Gibson wins her third Women's Singles crown. Margaret and Roumania Peters capture the Women's Doubles event. Althea Gibson and R. Walter Johnson successfully defend their Mixed Doubles title. Robert Dibble wins the Boys 18 Singles title and Helen Mundy wins her second Girls 18 Singles title.

1950 – *Gwendolyn Brooks becomes the 1st African-American to receive a Pulitzer Prize.*

1950 – *Ralph Bunche becomes the 1st African-American recipient of the Nobel Peace Prize.*

1950 – The 34th ATA Nationals are again held at Wilberforce University. Oscar Johnson from Los Angeles defeats former champion George Stewart for the Men's title. Althea Gibson takes her 4th Women's Singles Championship title. She teams with Dr. R. Walter Johnson to capture the Mixed Doubles title. James Stocks teams with Oscar Johnson to win the Men's Doubles. James Thompkin wins the Boys 18 Singles title and Florence Gibson wins the Girls 18 Singles title.

1950 – Althea Gibson becomes the first African-American to play in the US Nationals. She beats Barbara Knapp 6-2, 6-2 at the West Side Tennis Club in Forest Hills, Queens, New York in this historic first round match. In the second round, Gibson loses to Louise Brough 1-6, 6-3, 6-8. She is leading in the third set 7-6 when a thunderstorm forces the halt of play. The next day Gibson loses three straight games to lose the match.

1951 – *The US Supreme Court rules racial segregation in District of Columbia restaurants is unconstitutional.*

1951 – The 35th ATA Nationals returns to Wilberforce University. George Stewart and Althea Gibson capture the singles titles. Brother and sister Leo and Mary Fine win the Mixed Doubles. Margaret and Roumania Peters win the Women's Doubles. Dr. Hubert Eaton and George Stewart capture the Men's Doubles. Larry Green wins the Boys 18 Singles title and Lorraine Williams wins the Girls Singles 18 title.

1951 – Victor Miller and Roosevelt Megginson become the first blacks to compete in the USLTA Interscholastic Championships in Charlottesville, Virginia.

1952 – *Ralph Ellison publishes the legendary book entitled Invisible Man.*

1952 – *Tuskegee Institute reported no lynchings in the United States for the first time in the 71 years of keeping records.*

1952 – The 36th ATA Nationals continue at Wilberforce University. The Singles Championships is a repeat of the previous year with George Stewart defeating Norman Appel and Althea Gibson vanquishing Mary Etta Fine. The Peters sisters, Margaret and Roumania capture yet another Women's Doubles title. Althea Gibson and Dr. R.W. Johnson capture the Mixed Doubles title. William Winn wins the Boys 18 Singles title and Barbara Pratt wins the Girls 18 Singles title.

1953 – The 37th ATA Nationals are held at Bethune Cookman College. George Stewart and Althea Gibson repeat as Singles Champions. Margaret and Roumania Peters continue their streak in the Women's Doubles. Althea Gibson and Dr. Johnson retain their Mixed Doubles title. The Men's Doubles is cancelled because of rain. William Winn wins his second Boys 18 Singles title and Barbara Pratt wins her second Girls 18 Singles title.

1953 – Lorraine Williams becomes the first African-American to win a USLTA National Championship — the National Girls' 15 Singles.

1954 – *The Supreme Court in Brown v. Board of Education declares segregation in all public schools in the United States unconstitutional, nullifying the earlier doctrine of "separate but equal."*

1954 – *Malcolm X becomes Minister of the Nation of Islam's Harlem Temple 7.*

1954 – The 38th ATA Nationals return to Bethune Cookman College. Earthna Jacquet and Althea Gibson win the singles events. Jacquet teams up with Wilbert Davis to win the Men's Doubles Championship. Ending a decade-long grip on the Women's Doubles title by the Peters sisters, Evelyn George and Ivy C. Ransey capture the title. Althea Gibson and Dr. R. Walter Johnson successfully defend their Mixed Doubles Championship. Donald Archer wins the Boys 18 Singles title and Blancher Bailey wins the Girls 18 Singles title.

1955 - *Rosa Parks refuses to relinquish her seat on the bus to a white man, initiating the Montgomery Bus Boycott.*

1955 - *14 year-old Chicago resident Emmitt Till is murdered in Mississippi for allegedly whistling at a white woman.*

1955 - *Chuck Berry records the hit song "Maybellene."*

1955 – The 39th ATA Nationals return to Wilberforce University. Robert Ryland defeats Howard Minnis for the Men's title and Althea Gibson continues her reign by defeating Nana Davis Vaughn. Walter Thomas and C. Albert Dixon of Syracuse, New York capture the Men's Doubles title. Taking the Women's Doubles title were Mary Etta Fine and Eva Fine Bracey. Willis Fennell wins the Boys 18 Singles title and Emily Wilson wins the Girls 18 Singles title. Arthur Ashe, Jr. wins the Boys 12 Singles title.

1956 – *Nat King Cole becomes the first African-American to host a prime time variety show on national television — the show appears on NBC.*

1956 – Althea Gibson wins the French Championships and becomes the first African-American to win a Grand Slam tennis championship.

1956 – The 40th ATA Nationals return to Wilberforce University. Robert Ryland defeats Vernon Morgan, the New York State ATA Champion, to retain his Singles title. Althea Gibson wins her record 10th consecutive title by beating Nana Davis Vaughn. Angela Imala and Lorraine Williams win the Women's Doubles, while Dr. Hubert Eaton and George Stewart capture the Men's Doubles. Gwendolyn McEvans and Lt Col. W.A. Campbell win the Mixed Doubles title. William Neilson wins the Boys 18 Singles title and Clara Henry wins the Girls 18 Singles title.

1957 – Congress passes Civil Rights Act of 1957 — the first legislation protecting black rights since Reconstruction.

1957 – Martin Luther King, Jr., Charles K. Steele and Fred L. Shuttlesworth establish the Southern Christian Leadership Conference. The SCLC becomes a major force in organizing the civil rights movement and bases its principles on non-violence and civil disobedience.

1957 – President Eisenhower sends federal troops into Little Rock, Arkansas to ensure the enforcement of a federal court order to desegregate Central High School.

1957 – Althea Gibson becomes the first African-American to win Wimbledon.

1957 – The 41st ATA Nationals are once again held at Wilberforce University. George Stewart and Gwen McEvans win the singles titles. Stewart and John Chandler team to win the Men's Doubles title. Fine and Bracey win the Women's Doubles. Doria Harrison and Ernie Ingram capture the Mixed Doubles. Horace Cunningham wins the Boys 18 Singles title and Gwendolyn McEvans wins the Girls 18 Singles title. Arthur Ashe, Jr. wins the Boys 16 Singles title.

1957 – Althea Gibson becomes the first African-American to win the US Nationals.

1957 – Althea Gibson is named the Associated Press Woman Athlete of the Year and winner of the Babe Didrikson Zaharias Trophy as Female Athlete of the Year.

1958 – The Alvin Ailey Dance Theater is formed.

1958 – Althea Gibson wins her Wimbledon Women's Singles Championship.

1958 – The 42nd ATA Nationals are held at Wilberforce University. Wilbert Davis and Mary Etta Fine win the singles titles. Wilbur Jenkins and Tom Calhoun win the Men's Doubles. Miss Fine and her sister, Eva Fine Bracey, capture the Women's Doubles title. Clyde Freeman and Gwen McEvans win the Mixed Doubles Championship. Joe Williams wins the Boys 18 Singles title and Darnella Everson wins the Girls 18 Singles title. Arthur Ashe, Jr. wins his second Boys 16 Singles title.

1958 – Althea Gibson wins her second US Nationals Women's Singles title.

1958 – Once again, Althea Gibson is named the AP Woman Athlete of the Year.

1958 – Althea Gibson announces her retirement from amateur tennis.

1959 – Berry Gordy, Jr. founds Motown Records in Detroit.

1959 – Bob Ryland participates in tennis promoter Jack Marsh's World Pro Championships in Cleveland and becomes the first black male tennis professional.

1959 – The 43rd ATA Nationals are held at Wilberforce University once again. Wilbert Davis retains his title defeating Wilbur Jenkins of Jacksonville, Florida in five sets. Gwen McEvans wins her second Women's Championship by beating Darnella Everson. Joseph Pierce and Shaw Emmons win the Men's Doubles in a one set sudden death match limited because of darkness. Marlene and Darnella Everson capture the Women's Doubles. Charles Brown wins the Boys 18 Singles title and Marlene Everson wins the Girls 18 Singles title.

1960 – *The sit-in protest movement, designed to fight against segregated restaurants, begins at a Woolworth's lunch counter in Greensboro, North Carolina.*

1960 – *The Student Nonviolent Coordinating Committee (SNCC) is founded at Shaw University.*

1960 – *Civil Rights Act of 1960 was passed by Congress, which provided for penalties for obstructing anyone in registering or casting a vote.*

1960 – *Wilma Rudolph wins three track and field gold medals at Rome Olympics.*

1960 – The 44th ATA Nationals return to Hampton Institute. 17 year old Arthur Ashe, Jr. beats 6 time champion George Stewart to capture the Men's Singles Championship. Mimi Kanarek wins the Women's title. The Men's Doubles winners are Wilbur Jenkins and Tom Calhoun. Stockard and Williams capture the Women's Doubles. Elaine Bush and George Stewart capture the Mixed Doubles. Arthur Ashe, Jr. wins the Boys 18 Singles title and Carolyn Williams wins the Girls 18 Singles title.

1960 – Arthur Ashe, Jr. captures the US Boy's 18 Indoor Singles Championship.

1961 – The Congress of Racial Equality (CORE) organizes Freedom Rides through the Deep South.

1961 – The 45th ATA Nationals are held once again at Hampton Institute. Arthur Ashe, Jr. wins the Men's Singles crown, while 16 year-old Carolyn Williams captures the Women's title. Ashe and Ron Charity team-up to win the Men's Doubles. Williams and Marvalene Faggett win the Women's Doubles. Mimi Kanarek and Ernie Ingram win the Mixed Doubles. Bob Davis wins the Boys 18 Singles title and Carolyn Williams wins the Girls 18 Singles title.

1961 – Arthur Ashe, Jr. wins the US Interscholastic Singles Championship and repeats as US Boys Indoor Singles Champion.

1962 – *Ernie Davis from Syracuse University becomes the 1st African-American to receive the Heisman Trophy.*

1962 – James Meredith becomes the first black student to enroll at the University of Mississippi.

1962 – The 46th ATA Nationals return to Wilberforce University. Arthur Ashe, Jr. gains his third consecutive Men's Singles Championship by defeating Wilbur Jenkins in straight sets. Carolyn Liquori, a white player, captures the Women's Singles title. Kanarek and Liquori captured the Women's Doubles while Wilbert and Robert Davis win the Men's Doubles title. Mimi Kanarek and Ernie Ingram repeat as Mixed Doubles winners. William Morton wins the Boys 18 Singles title and Carolyn Williams wins an unprecedented third Girls 18 Singles title.

1963 – Eugene "Bull" Conner, the Commissioner of Public Safety in Birmingham, Alabama, uses fire hoses and police dogs on peaceful African-American marchers. Pictures of children being hosed down and dogs attacking defenseless nonviolent protestors give global credibility to the US Civil Rights movement.

1963 – Medger Evers, Mississippi NAACP field secretary, is assassinated outside his home in Jackson.

1963 – 200,000 people participate in the March on Washington and Martin Luther King, Jr. delivers his "I Have a Dream" speech.

1963 – The 16th Street Baptist Church in Birmingham is bombed, killing four young girls.

1963 – President John F. Kennedy is assassinated.

1963 – The 47th ATA Nationals are held at Wilberforce University. Wilbert Davis captures the Men's Singles title and Ginger Pfiefer wins the Women's Singles title. Howard Minnis and William Monroe capture the Men's Doubles, while Pfiefer and Maimee Frye win the Women's Doubles. Lucy McEvans and Charles Berry win the Mixed Doubles title. The Boys and Girls 18 Singles tournaments are not held.

1963 – Arthur Ashe, Jr. became the first African-American named to the Davis Cup Team.

1963 – Arthur Ashe, Jr. wins the US Hard Court Championship.

1964 – President Lyndon B. Johnson declares war on poverty and signs the Equal Opportunity Act.

1964 – Cassius Clay (later Mohammed Ali) becomes the World Heavyweight Champion.

1964 – President Johnson signs the Civil Rights Act of 1964 which bans discrimination in all public accommodations and by employers.

1964 – James E. Chaney, 21; Andrew Goodman, 21; and, Michael Schwerner, 24 are working to register black voters in Mississippi when they are arrested by the police and released into the custody of the Ku Klux Klan. These three individuals, two black and one white, are killed by Ku Klux Klan members and thrown into a dam.

1964 – Martin Luther King, Jr. receives the Nobel Peace Prize.

1964 – The 48th ATA Nationals are held at Wilberforce. Veteran George Stewart wins the Men's Singles title and Bonnie Logan wins the Women's Singles title. Luis Glass and Lendward Simpson capture the Men's Doubles Championship and Sylvia Hooks and Bonnie Logan win the Women's Doubles Championship. Charles Berry and Bessie Stockard win the Mixed Doubles Championship. The Boys and Girls 18 Singles tournaments are not held.

1964 – At age 15, Lendward Simpson becomes the youngest male to play in the US Nationals at Forest Hills.

1965 – Malcolm X is assassinated in the Harlem section of New York City.

1965 – Dr. Martin Luther King, Jr. leads the Selma Marches. In the initial march blacks and whites begin a march in Mongomery, Alabama across the Edmund Pettus Bridge but are stopped by an angry white mob. During this "Bloody Sunday" march more than fifty marchers are hospitalized after the police use tear gas, whips and clubs against them. This march paves the way for a later march across the bridge and helps to convince Congress to finally pass the Voting Rights Act.

1965 – The Voting Rights Act that makes it easier for Southern black citizens to vote is signed into law. It therefore

Breaking The Barriers

becomes illegal to use literacy tests, poll taxes and other requirements intended to restrict blacks from voting.

1965 – *An uprising in the Watts section of Los Angeles results in thirty four people being killed and a thousand injured.*

1965 – *Edward Brooke of Massachusetts becomes the 1st African-American to be popularly elected to the US Senate.*

1965 – *Constance Baker Motley is the first African-American woman elevated to a Federal judgeship.*

1965 – *Civil Rights Leader Julian Bond wins a seat in the Georgia State Senate.*

1965 – *President Johnson issues Executive Order 11246 which requires government contractors to take "affirmative action" toward the hiring and employment of African Americans.*

1965 – The 49th ATA Nationals return to Wilberforce. Luis Glass wins the Men's Singles Championship. Bonnie Logan retains her Women's Singles title. Luis Glass and Lendward Simpson retain their Men's Doubles title. Jean Richardson and Helen Watanabe win the Women's Doubles title. Sylvia Hooks and William Morton, Jr. win the Mixed Doubles Championship. The Boys and Girls 18 Singles tournaments are not held.

1965 – UCLA student Arthur Ashe, Jr. becomes the first African-American to capture the NCAA Singles Championship. In addition, he becomes the first African-American to win the NCAA Doubles Championship. His partner is Ian Crookenden.

1966 – *The Black Panthers are founded by Huey Newton and Bobby Seale in Oakland, California.*

1966 – The 50th ATA Nationals return for the fifth consecutive year to Wilberforce. Wilbert Davis takes back the Men's Singles trophy, while Bonnie Logan wins her 3rd Women's Singles title in a row. Arthur Carrington and John Mudd win the Men's Doubles Championship. The Women's Doubles title is won by Bonnie Logan and Bessie Stockard. Sylvia Hooks and William Morton, Jr. retain their Mixed Doubles Championship. Donald Ringgold wins the Boys 18 Singles title and Tam O'Shaughnessy wins the Girls 18 Singles title.

1967 – Stokely Carmichael, a leader of the Student Nonviolent Coordinating Committee (SNCC) uses the term "Black Power" in a speech in Seattle. The term becomes very popular among communities around the world.

1967 – US Supreme Court in Loving v. Virginia strikes down interracial marriage bans.

1967 – Devastating race riots take place in July in Newark, New Jersey and Detroit, Michigan.

1967 – Thurgood Marshall takes seat as the first African-American Justice on the United States Supreme Court.

1967 – The 51st ATA Nationals return to Wilberforce. Wilbert Davis wins the Men's Singles title and Bonnie Logan wins the Women's Singles title. Arthur Carrington and John Mudd repeat as Men's Doubles Champions. Bessie Stockard and Sylvia Hooks team up to win the Women's Doubles. Bonnie Logan and Lendward Simpson capture the Mixed Doubles. The Boys and Girls 18 Singles tournaments are not held.

1967 – Arthur Ashe wins the US Clay Courts Championship.

1967 – Arthur Ashe partners with Charlie Pasarell to win the US Indoor Doubles.

1968 – Martin Luther King, Jr., age 39, is assassinated standing on the balcony of the Lorraine Motel in Memphis, Tennessee. In the wake of the assassination, 125 cities in 29 states experience uprising; 46 people killed, 35,000 injured.

1968 – President Johnson signs the Civil Rights Act of 1968 which outlaws discrimination in the sale and rental of housing.

1968 – New York Senator and Presidential candidate Robert F. Kennedy is assassinated in Los Angeles.

1968 – "The Poor People's Campaign" to gain economic justice for poor people in the United States is launched at Lafayette Park and Connecticut Avenue in Washington, DC.

1968 – San Francisco State University establishes the 1st Black Studies Program.

Breaking The Barriers

1968 – Shirley Chisholm of New York is the 1st black woman elected to the US Congress.

1968 – There is black boycott of the Mexico City Olympics.

1968 – The 52nd ATA Nationals are held for the 7th consecutive year at Wilberforce. The Men's Singles Champion is Robert Binns. Bonnie Logan wins her 5th Women's Singles title. Marty Gool and Gregory Morton capture the Men's Doubles title, while Bessie Stockard and Anne Koger take the Women's Doubles Championship. Bonnie Logan and Lendward Simpson repeat as winners of the Mixed Doubles. The Boys and Girls 18 Singles tournaments are not held.

1969 – The Ford Foundation gives $1 million to Morgan State University, Howard University and Yale University to teach courses in African-American Studies.

1969 – The 53rd ATA Nationals move to St. Louis, Missouri. Marty Gool captures the Men's Singles title and Bonnie Logan keeps her streak alive by winning the Women's Singles title for the 6th straight year. Marty Gool and Gregory Morton win the Men's Doubles. Reuter and Beauchamp capture the Women's Doubles. The Mixed Doubles crown is retained by Bonnie Logan and Lendward Simpson. David Williams wins the Boys 18 title and Jackie Holloway wins the Girls 18 Singles.

1970 – Clifton Wharton, Jr. is named the president of Michigan State University, the first African-American to lead a major, predominantly white university.

1970 – Bobby Seale and six other defendants (popularly known as the Chicago Seven) are
acquitted of the charges of conspiring to disrupt the 1968 Democratic Convention.

1970 – Kenneth Gibson becomes the first black mayor in a Northeastern city when he assumes the post in Newark, New Jersey.

1970 – The 54th ATA Nationals return to St. Louis. Gene Fluri captures the Men's Singles and Bonnie Logan wins her 7th consecutive Women's title. Gene and Tom Fluri win the

Men's Doubles Championship. Reuter and Beauchamp successfully defend their Women's Doubles title. Bonnie Logan and Lendward Simpson win the Mixed Doubles. Steve Gilliam wins the Boys 18 Singles title and Jolynn Johnsons wins the Girls 18 Singles title.

1970 – Juan Farrow wins the US Boys 12 Singles Championship and teams with Chip Hooper to win the Boys 12 Doubles title.

1971 – *The Supreme Court upholds busing as a legitimate means of integrating public schools.*

1971 – *The Congressional Black Caucus is formed in Washington, DC.*

1971 – *Prisoners riot at the Attica Correctional Facility.*

1971 – *Rev. Jesse Jackson founds People United to Save Humanity (PUSH).*

1971 – *NY Congresswoman Shirley Chisholm makes an unsuccessful bid for the Democratic presidential nomination. She is the first African-American to campaign for the nomination.*

1971 – The 55th ATA Nationals return to St. Louis. John Wilkerson captures the Men's Singles title and Bessie Stockard wins the Women's Singles title. William Heinbecker and Jerry Johnson win the Men's Doubles Championship. Pamela Steinmetz and Bunny Wall seize the Women's Doubles Championship. The Mixed Doubles is won by Beverly Hussell and Alberto Loney. The Boys and Girls 18 Singles tournaments are not held.

1971 – Arthur Ashe, Jr. and Marty Riessen win the French Open Doubles title.

1971 – Althea Gibson becomes the first African-American elected into the International Tennis Hall of Fame.

1972 – *Barbara Jordan of Houston and Andrew Young of Atlanta become the first black Congressional Representatives elected from the US South since 1898.*

1972 – The 56th ATA Nationals move to Boston. Horace Reid beats Arthur Carrington in an epic five set match televised on the local PBS station to win the Men's Singles title. Lorraine Bryant wins the Women's Singles title. The

Women's Doubles is won by Elaine Busch and Brenda Johnson. Lee Stavins and Chris Scott capture the Mixed Doubles title. The Men's Doubles Final was cancelled. Bruce Foxworth wins the Boys 18 Singles title and Deborah Hunter wins the Girls 18 Singles title.

- 1972 – Juan Farrow captures the US Boys 14 Singles title.
- 1972 – Diane Morrison wins the National Public Parks Girls 16 Singles Championship.
- *1973 – Thomas Bradley is elected the first black mayor of Los Angeles in the modern era and holds the office for 20 years.*
- *1973 – Maynard H. Jackson, Jr. is elected the first black mayor of Atlanta.*
- *1973 – Coleman Young is elected the first black mayor of Detroit.*
- 1973 – The 57th ATA Nationals return to Boston. Arthur Carrington captures the Men's Singles Championship. The Women's Singles is won by Mimi Kanarek. Shri Anadon and Luis Glass win the Men's Doubles Championship. Jean Burnett and Arvelia Meyers win the Women's Doubles Championship. Ann Koger and Tyrone Mapp win the Mixed Doubles Championship. Robert Johnson wins the Boys 18 Singles title and Linda Jones wins the Girls 18 Singles title.
- 1973 – Juan Farrow wins the US Boy's 16 Indoor Singles Championship.
- *1974 – Hank Aaron hits his 715th home run to become the all-time leader in home runs in Major League Baseball.*
- 1974 – The 58th ATA Nationals move to Washington, DC. Roger Guedes wins the Men's Singles title. Jean Burnett captures the Women's Singles title. The Men's Championship is won by Bruce Foxworth and Roger Guedes. Bessie Stockard and Barbara Faulkner win the Women's Doubles Championship. Ann Koger and Tyrone Mapp successfully defend their Mixed Doubles crown. Junius Chatman wins the Boys 18 Singles title and Lisa Hopewell wins the Girls 18 Singles title.
- 1974 – Lendward Simpson becomes the first black player in World Team Tennis when he signs with the Detroit Loves.

1975 – Frank Robinson becomes the first African-American Major League Baseball manager when he takes over the Cleveland Indians.

1975 – The first black owned television station, WGPR, begins broadcasting in Detroit.

1975 – The 59th ATA Nationals are held in San Diego. Benny Sims captures the Men's Singles title and Diane Morrison wins the Women's Singles title. M. Andrews and Lawrence King team up to win the Men's Doubles Championship. The Women's Doubles Championship is claimed by S. Dancy and Lisa Rapfogel. The Mixed Doubles Championship is captured by R. Harris and Dee Stewart. Tony Brock wins the Boys 18 Singles title and Lisa Rapfogel wins the Girls 18 Singles title.

1975 – Arthur Ashe, Jr. becomes the first African-American man to win the Men's Singles Championship at Wimbledon by beating Jimmy Connors in a tactically brilliant match.

We ended the *Breaking the Barriers* exhibit in 1975 because Arthur Ashe's victory at Wimbledon was a seminal event in black tennis history. For many years, people did not believe that African Americans were smart or athletic enough to be the best tennis players in the world. Ashe's victory, in combination with Althea Gibson's Championships, proved that an African-American woman and man could win the two biggest tennis tournaments in the world – Wimbledon and the US Open/Nationals. Althea Gibson and Arthur Ashe also represent the end of the "Golden Age" of the ATA. They are the first and only players to win an ATA 18 Singles title, an ATA Open Singles Championship and a Grand Slam Singles Championship.

CHAPTER 13: Breaking the Barriers Exhibit Panel 1

Tennis has become the world's second most popular sport largely because of the geographic, cultural, stylistic and racial diversity of its professionals. The sport has developed passionate fans of different backgrounds because of this diversity. Unfortunately, diversity was not always encouraged by the sport's leadership. Most people are familiar with the tennis and life successes of Althea Gibson and Arthur Ashe. However, because of racial discrimination in tennis and America, few people know the incredible story of the many talented players who were not allowed to compete in major tennis tournaments because of their race.

For over fifty years prior to Gibson's victories, blacks had been competing in club and regional tournaments. Banned from entering segregated events, African-American tennis enthusiasts in 1916 formed their own organization, the American Tennis Association (ATA), to provide blacks with the opportunity to play competitive tennis on a national level. Their struggle to gain equal access to tennis paralleled the struggle of all blacks to gain equal access to American society. This exhibit tells their fascinating story.

DR. BOOKER T. WASHINGTON
FOUNDER — TUSKEGEE INSTITUTE

Booker T. Washington
Courtesy of the ATA

Panel 1 of the Breaking the Barriers Exhibit starts with the founding of the sport in 1874. The panel presents general black history and black tennis history from that point until 1913.

From the International Tennis Hall of Fame Collection
We included this picture because it presented a positive picture of an early black tennis player.

Breaking The Barriers

The Cover of Major Wingfield's Sphairistike or Lawn Tennis Box
Collection of the International Tennis Hall of Fame

The Cover of Major Wingfield's Sphairistike or Lawn Tennis Book
Collection of the International Tennis Hall of Fame

The Early USNLTA Championships

The first championships were actually contests between individual club champions. As such, the entrants as well as the spectators were drawn from the upper echelons of white society. When an Irishman threatened to defeat the defending champion, the rules were changed to restrict the tournament to American citizens. Unfortunately, racism, xenophobia, religious discrimination and sexism were rampant in organized tennis. The tournament directors seemed to minimize competition for Christian white male players.

Early tennis tournament in Nahant
Collection of the International Tennis Hall of Fame

Breaking The Barriers

Early Tennis Championship at Newport
Collection of the International Tennis Hall of Fame

Richard Sears, The First UNLTA Men's Singles Champion
Collection of the International Tennis Hall of Fame

"I'm sure the black players today don't know much about the history of black tennis...They haven't witnessed the hardships, the dangers, the anguish. The baton has been passed, but they don't know where the baton came from"

—Bill Davis, former ATA president,
5x ATA National Singles Champion

Currrier and Ives Darktown Series

The two deeply offensive prints below, produced by *Currier & Ives* in 1885, graphically illustrate the racial stereotypes commonly portrayed in that era. All appears well in the first print, where blacks mimic their white counterparts in both dress and attitude. Mayhem results, however, when they presume to play. The message is one that

LAWN TENNIS AT DARKTOWN.
A Scientific Player.

Currier & Ives Darktown Series, 1885
Collection of the International Tennis Hall of Fame

Breaking The Barriers

LAWN TENNIS AT DARKTOWN.
A Scientific Stroke.

Currier & Ives Darktown Series, 1885
Collection of the International Tennis Hall of Fame

will be repeated as long as ignorance persists; namely, that blacks possess speed and strength, but lack the fine motor skills, coordination and intelligence to master the "skill" sports. This fallacy based on racist presumptions has created barriers for blacks attempting to excel in such diverse sports as gymnastics, swimming, golf, figure skating, cycling, fencing and tennis, as well as skill positions like quarterback. This is also true in the highly skilled roles in ballet and opera. In spite of the barriers, there have been exceptional black performers and champions in all of these endeavors.

Tuskegee Tennis

In the South, tennis reputedly had its beginnings on the faculty courts of Tuskegee Institute. One of the first such courts was built in front of the Academic Building. Two additional courts were located near the home of Institute president, Booker T. Washington. Early participants were Warren Logan, Emmet J. Scott, S.E. Courtney, and E.T. Atwell.

White Hall, Tuskegee Institute – Courtesy of the ATA

The Early Clubs

Private black tennis clubs played a major role in establishing early inter-city and inter-state tournaments. The Chautauqua Club in Philadelphia, the Ideal Tennis Club in New York, the Monumental Tennis Club in Baltimore, the Chicago Prairie Tennis Club, the Tuskegee Faculty Tennis Club, the Association and Crescent Tennis Clubs in Washington, DC, and the Flushing Tennis Club in Queens were among the earliest. By 1916 there were at least 58 black tennis clubs, mostly in the East. These were soon followed by the West Louisville Tennis Club, the Cosmopolitan Club in Harlem, the Shady Rest Tennis Club in New Jersey, the Springfield Racquet Club in Massachusetts, the Germantown Tennis Club in Philadelphia and the Algonquin Club in Durham, North Carolina. In addition to providing facilities, instruction and tournament play, these clubs frequently became the center of community social life. The combination of tennis

Breaking The Barriers

1925 Springfield Racquet Club
Courtesy of Art Carrington

1945 North End Tennis Club
Courtesy of B. Nesbitt

competition with a rigorous calendar of social events would, in time, become an ATA tradition.

Early Courts

At the close of the 19th Century, tennis appealed to black professionals and businessmen for the same reasons that it appealed to whites – it was a fast paced, physically demanding form of recreation that required minimal investment in time, equipment and real estate. Black elites, like their white counterparts, viewed tennis as an ideal carry-over sport that offered the advantages of social connection as well as athletic competition. The lack of public courts, coupled with restricted access to private facilities, forced those with the desire to play to build their own courts. These humble backyard courts of clay or dirt would, in time, produce some of the greatest players in the history of tennis.

Early Tennis Courts
Collection of the International Tennis Hall of Fame

Breaking The Barriers

Late 19th Century Rural Tennis Court
Collection of the International Tennis Hall of Fame

Private Court of the Privileged Class
Collection of the International Tennis Hall of Fame

Edgar Brown

Westerner Edgar G. Brown, in the first decade of the 20th Century demonstrated a much more aggressive—and athletically demanding—baseline game with the introduction of top-spin. Later in his amateur career he would receive a one year suspension from ATA tournament play for refusing to finish a doubles match that, in his opinion, extended into darkness. The fact that there were no other tournaments available to blacks concentrated considerable power into the hands of a few ATA administrators.

Edgar G. Brown
ATA National Champion
Courtesy of the American Tennis Association (ATA)

Breaking The Barriers

"Mother" Seames

In the Midwest, tennis had an early start in Chicago. Mrs. C.O. Seames, affectionately known as "Mother," began teaching tennis to black youth on clay or dirt courts as early as 1906. In 1912 she was one of a group that formed the Chicago Prairie Tennis Club, still in existence today. "Mother" Seames purchased some property on the South Side of Chicago in 1920 and built four tennis courts, the centerpiece of one of the country's first private black tennis clubs.

Mrs. C.O. "Mother Seames"
Courtesy of the Collection of the International Tennis Hall of Fame

Dale G. Caldwell

The Black Newspapers

Prior to the Open Era, results of local and state ATA tournaments went largely unreported in the white press. The results of the ATA National tournament were published in "American Lawn Tennis" towards the back of the issue in some years, but it was the black newspapers that chronicled the details of the matches. Such newspapers as *The Pittsburgh Courier, The New York Amsterdam News, The Chicago Defender* and the various editions of "Afro-American News" put tournament results on their front pages. Today, these publications remain our primary source of information for the details of these early black tennis tournaments. There was often a fascinating, if not sobering, juxtaposition of articles on the pages of these newspapers. The same page might herald tennis tournament champions, and also provide readers with the sordid details of church bombings, the Klan and lynchings.

Breaking The Barriers

Page Fourteen   Call Vernon 6016   The Afro-American—Baltimore, Md.—South's Biggest and Best Weekly   Saturday, Aug. 27, 1927

TED THOMPSON REGAINS CROWN

Scene At The 11th National Tennis Tourney At Beautiful Hampton Institute Saturday When Five Tennis Titles Changed Hands

HAMPTON—Part of the crowd of 1,000 fans who watched Lula Ballard and Ora Washington of Philadelphia triumph over Isadore Channels and M. Wilson in the National doubles. Miss Ballard, who is left handed, also won the National women's singles championship. Center, Tennis officials from left to right—1. M. Burrell, E. K. Jones, G. F. Norman, W. H. A. Burnett, M. Granger, Miss Laura V. Junior, Dr. H. S. McCard, Dr. D. Y. Hoage, Dr. W. J. Wright, E. D. Downing. Upper left—Tally Holmes, doubles champion; Douglass Turner, junior champion; Ted Thompson, national singles and doubles champion. Turner is also Illinois state champion.

FIVE NATIONAL TENNIS TITLES CHANGE HANDS

Thompson Singles Champion, Lula Ballard Queen of Woman Players

THREE 1925 TITLE HOLDERS COME BACK

Asso. Votes to Hold All Future Tourneys At Bordentown, N.J.

By P. Bernard Young, Jr.

Hampton, Inst., Va.—Some say champions do not come back. But three came back with a vengeance today when Ted Thompson king of the courts in 1925, runner-up in 1926 and champion in 1927 by virtue of his brilliant five-set victory over Eyre Saitch; Miss Lula Ballard, 1925 queen of the courts and 1926 runner-up by defeating Miss Isadora Channels, four time national champion, in straight sets; and Thompson and Tally Holmes swept thru to the heights they held in former years, winning in three sets from Allison Davis and Sterling Brow.

These three comebacks; the victory of Douglass Turner over E. B. Ashe in Junior singles and the winning victory of Louis Jones and Miss Blanche Winston over Dr. L.C. Downing and "Mother" C.O. Seames, former national mixed doubles title-holders, combined to establish new marks in five of the six events fought for in the eleventh national championships of the American Tennis Association of which Dr. Harry S. McCard of Baltimore is president.

WOMEN DOUBLES EXCEPTION

The only event in which the title did not change hands was in women's doubles in which that splendid Pennsylvania team of Misses Lula Ballard and Ora Washington turned back Miss Channels and Mrs. E. Hawkins Wilson.

Brilliancy of weather matches the musical tenor of flashing racket until Thursday afternoon when the courts were flooded in a downpour of rain, but hard work put five of the seven courts of the School By The Sea into playing shape.

"GAS" USED

Muddy courts were sprinkled with saw dust and gasoline and repeatedly burned over until they were dry. Tarpaulins covered the courts during the rain but the heavy rain rendered them useless.

END AT DUSK

Friday and Saturday thru the good work of Dr. Irison Hoage, New York, Dr. W.H. Wright, Baltimore and Dr. W. A. Barrett, St. Louis, referee and alternative referee, respectively, the last championship was decided just as dusk was settling over the beautiful _____ Mecca of Tennis. Between seventy and eighty matches were run officially in the preliminary rounds, and on account of rain Thursday, they regained 31 matches, including the quarter-finals, semi-finals and finals in all events.

Into the rare beauty of Hampton Institute's famous campus with every facility at the disposal of tennis players and followers worked as early as the middle of last week. Cars of New England to Alabama and as far west as Iowa were seen putting along the winding road of the world-famous institution.

BROWN ABSENT

Every player of note, with the exception of Edward Simmons, ranking player of Dayton, Edgar Brown of St. Louis, just married, former champion, and Miss Lillian Hines, ranking star of North Carolina and a few others of lesser note was there.

136 IN MEN'S SINGLES

With a total entry breaking all previous records, and with 136 entries in men's singles, 64 in women's singles, 31 in junior singles, fifty-nine in men's doubles teams established new marks in those four individual events, the eleventh annual championships were destined from the beginning to fulfill the prediction that the 1927 tennis extravaganza would excel any other ever held. The officers and officials of the American Tennis Association, of the Virginia Tennis Association which in co-operation with Hampton staged the tournament, and especially Chas. H. Williams, physical director of the school where championships are a tradition deserve a world of credit.

THOMPSON IN SHAPE

Thompson entered this tournament determined to regain the honor he won in 1926 at Bordentown. When he finished the match against Saitch he was in far better physical shape and almost immediately went into his doubles championship event, giving the veteran Tally the kind of support expected of a partner of a championship combination.

SAITCH HELPLESS

Except as flashed he was helpless against Ted frequently being caught flatfooted against the brilliant shots of the new champion. Ted eased up a bit in the fourth set for although he and the star from New York are bitter rivals on the court, they are good friends. He lost that set, but the final set was only a matter of time. Ted played winning tennis today and before Saitch was hurt was playing shot for shot. His victory was hard won and deserved for it was a fight all the way. Comment heard in the stands indicated how strongly the opinion held that Ted today approached more nearly than any day since Bordentown in 1925, the tennis of which he is capable. And when Ted is right is practically unbeatable.

TO BORDENTOWN

The A.T.A. decided to go to Bordentown next summer and thereafter regularly in the absence and acceptance of other invitations.

1927 "Afro-American Newspaper"
Courtesy of Art Carrington

1930 *Pittsburgh Courier*
Courtesy of Art Carrington

CHAPTER 14: Breaking the Barriers Exhibit Panel 2

Panel 2 of the Breaking the Barriers Exhibit picks up in 1914 at the point where the previous panel ends. The panel presents general black history and black tennis history from that point until 1959.

The First ATA Tournament

The inaugural ATA Tournament was held at Druid Hill Park, Baltimore, Maryland in August 1917. Thirty-nine competitors came from thirty-three different clubs. In all, only three events were contested. Tally Holmes became the first ATA Men's Singles Champion and teamed with Sylvester Smith to win the Men's Doubles title. Miss Lucy Diggs Slowe captured the Women's Singles event, thereby becoming the first African-American woman to hold a national championship in any sport.

The ATA and Black Colleges and Universities

Initially, ATA National Tournaments were comfortably situated at private black clubs or public parks. As the size of the tournament grew, there was a need for a larger site that could serve more players and their families. However, accommodations for blacks, particularly in the segregated South, were limited.

The solution was to use the courts, dorms and dining halls of black colleges and universities that had been vacated for the summer recess. The arrangement worked on many levels. For parents accompanying their children, it presented tennis as a sport that could

Dale G. Caldwell

American Tennis Association
EXECUTIVE BULLETIN

| BULLETIN No. 20 | Issued by the Executive Secretary | JULY, 1957 |

THE A. T. A. IS BORN
THANKSGIVING DAY - THURSDAY, NOVEMBER 30, 1916

Below is a Facsimile of the original "Call" to organize the American Tennis Association

Baltimore, Md.
November 1, 1916.

Dear sir:—

A movement is on foot to organize a "National Tennis Association" among colored men, for the following purposes (1) to bring colored tennis enthusiasts and players into closer and friendlier relations, (2) to improve the standard of existing clubs, (3) to encourage the formation of new clubs, (4) to hold, annually a genuine, recognized, national championship tournament at such time and place as is deemed best by the association, (5) to regulate the time of playing local or regional tournaments in order to prevent conflicting or overlapping dates, (6) to appoint referees, to give official standing to such tournaments, and (7) to promote generally the standard of the game among colored men.

We believe that all the tendencies, experiences, and general conditions of the last few years point to the desirability of forming such an association.

To this end, a temporary organization has been formed by The Association Tennis Club, of Washington D. C., and The Monumental Tennis Club, of Baltimore, Md., which is requesting that each club send a representative, empowered to act for his club, to a meeting to be held at the Y. M. C. A. (12th St. near T St.) Washington, D. C. on Thursday, Nov. 30 th (Thanksgiving Day) 1916, at 10 o'clock, A. M.

The object of this meeting is to effect permanent a organization, elect officers and an executive committee (or board of governors) and draft a constitution for the control of the activities of the association. Your club is therefore most earnestly requested to send such a representative to this very important meeting and help in the organization of such a desirable and necessary body. Will you kindly let us know not later than November 17th, whether or not, your club will send a representative to his meeting? Or if your club approves of this movement and wishes to join the association, but cannot send a representative, will you kindly send a letter to that effect?

A similar letter is being sent to the clubs listed on the inside page.

Please notify any clubs of good standing in your locality (not already named) of this meeting and supply them with one of the inclosed circulars.

For information communicate with R. V. Cook, 406 Presstman St., Balto., Md.

Yours for tennis,

D. O. W. Holmes,
Chairman, Committee on Organization,

R. V. Cook, Secretary.

Please turn to page 9

A limited number of extra copies of this Executive Bulletin may be obtained upon request.
BERTRAM L. BAKER, Executive Secretary   399 JEFFERSON AVENUE, BROOKLYN 21, N. Y.

"ATA Executive Bulletin"
Courtesy of Bill Davis

be part of the college experience. It was also a subtle reminder that education would be important when your tennis career was over.

From their perspective, the colleges gained access to this middle class group of potential donors. The dormitory accommodations fostered an almost communal sense of belonging that made social

1918 - Dr. Wilkinson, E.K. Jones, Lucy Diggs Slowe, J. Kemp, Tally Holmes, May Rae, Dr. Sylvester Smith, W. Reading
Collections of the International Tennis Hall of Fame & Museum

interaction all the easier. Soon, the tournaments were as popular for the social events as for the tennis. Hampton Institute, Tuskegee Institute, Lincoln University and particularly Wilberforce University were favorite college sites for these early tournaments.

Eugene Kinckle Jones and Edgar Brown

Jones was an early administrator of the ATA serving as treasurer, as well as a 1920 Doubles Champion. Edgar Brown, known for incorporating top spin into a baseline game, was the ATA singles champion in 1922-23 and 1928-29.

E.K. Jones and Edgar Brown
Courtesy of the ATA

Isadore Channels and Lulu Ballard

These two gifted athletes each won four ATA Singles titles, dominating the 1920s. Channels, like Eyre Saitch and Ora Washington, was a star basketball player as well as a tennis champion. She anchored the champion Chicago Romas. Eight years after she won her 3rd ATA Singles title, Ballard ended Ora Washington's quest for eight consecutive championships when Washington succumbed to sunstroke.

Members of the Morehouse College tennis team
Courtesy of B. Nesbitt

Weir and Norman: The First Cracks in the Barrier

Reginald Weir, the tennis captain of CCNY, and Gerald Norman, Jr., high school champion, paid an entry fee to enter the 1929 USLTA Junior Indoor Championships in New York City at the 7th Regiment Armory. When they showed up, they were denied spots in the draw. On behalf of the two players, Gerald Norman, Sr. sought help from the NAACP, which led to the filing of a formal grievance against the USLTA. This tactic forced organized tennis into the uncomfortable position of publicly defending its policy of denying blacks the opportunity to compete in its tournaments. In response to the

Lulu Ballard
Courtesy of the ATA

complaint, the USLTA reiterated its stance to "Decline entry of colored players in our championship." Although barred from USLTA tournaments in his prime, Dr. Reginald Weir would come back to make tennis history by being the first black man to win an official USLTA championship, capturing the National Senior Indoor title in 1956.

Dr. Reginald Weir

Former tennis captain at CCNY, Reginald Weir won the ATA National Men's Singles title from 1931-33 before leaving tennis to attend medical school. Following graduation, Dr. Weir promptly

Dr. Reginald Weir
Collections of the International Tennis Hall of Fame and Museum

regained the men's title in 1937 and captured his fifth singles title in 1942. Seventeen years after winning his first championship, Dr. Weir became the 1st black permitted to play in a USLTA Championship – the 1948 US Indoor. In 1952 Dr. Weir, now over 40 years old, and George Stewart, the reigning ATA Champion, became the first black men to play at the National Championships at Forest Hills. Well past their best tennis performances, they both lost in the first round.

Ora Washington

One of the most dominant performers in tennis history, Ora Washington won a total of 23 ATA National Championships: 8 singles, 12 doubles and 3 mixed doubles. A star center for the Philadelphia

Reginald Weir and Gerald Norman
Collections of the International Tennis Hall of Fame and Museum

Tribunes, the premier women's basketball team in the 1930s, her height and reach at the net intimidated opponents. Using an unorthodox grip halfway up the handle, she would chop at the ball with an abbreviated swing. Bob Ryland claims that she was one of the best players who ever lived. "She was nice but she was mean on the courts," Ryland states. Taking on all comers, she was virtually unbeatable for over a decade. She was reported to have challenged Helen Wills Moody—the white world champion—to a match on several occasions, never receiving a reply. Some claim that Ora was quietly persuaded to retire from tennis, as her total dominance was thought to discourage new recruits to the game.

Breaking The Barriers

1931 City College of New York tennis team, Reginald Weir, Captain
Courtesy of CCNY Archives

Jimmie McDaniel

In 1940 Jimmie, the ATA's National Champion, met Don Budge, the world's premier player and recent Grand Slam winner, in an historic exhibition match at Harlem's Cosmopolitan Club in front of a capacity crowd. Whether it was nervousness over facing the unbeatable white champion in front of a black crowd or difficulty in adjusting to the clay courts, McDaniel lost decisively 6-1, 6-2. Nevertheless, due in part to Budge's gracious remarks about Jimmie's skills, the tennis community was shown that interracial matches could be competitive and compelling without being inflammatory. Addressing the crowd after the match, Budge said: "Jimmie is a very good player. I'd say he'd rank in the first 10 of our white players. And with some more practice against players like me, maybe someday he could beat all of them." It would take another decade of pushing against the door before blacks would be given the opportunity to play in the Nationals at Forest Hills. In the meantime, Jimmie McDaniel won four ATA National Men's Singles titles and became one of the legends of black tennis.

Ora Washington
Collections of the International Tennis Hall of Fame & Museum

Althea Gibson – The Journey from Harlem to Lynchburg

"If I made it, it's half because I was game to take a wicked amount of punishment along the way and half because there were an awful lot of people who cared enough to help me."
—Althea Gibson in her autobiography,
I Always Wanted to Be Somebody

Plucked from the streets of New York by her play street director, a street wise and street tough Althea Gibson was turned over to Fred Johnson, the legendary one-armed professional at the Cosmopolitan

Ora Washington with some of her many trophies
Courtesy of the ATA

Tennis Club, for tennis instruction. She was soon winning ATA Girls tournaments. Moving up to the Women's Singles, Althea lost a heartbreaker to Roumania Peters 6-4, 7-9, 6-3. Sitting in the stands were two black physicians, Dr. R. Walter Johnson and Dr. Hubert Eaton, who shared a passion for tennis and a commitment to helping black players reach their potential. Seeing a talented individual who desperately needed structure in her life, they made a generous offer to have her live with Dr. Eaton's family in Wilmington, NC and attend high school during the school year. During the summer, she would live

Jimmie McDaniel, 1943
Courtesy of the Xavier University Archives and Special

with Dr. Johnson and his family in Lynchburg, Virginia where she would receive instruction on his home court and travel to tournaments on weekends. Under Dr. Johnson's tutelage, Althea returned to the ATA Nationals in 1947 and won the Women's Singles Championship, the first of a record 10 consecutive ATA National titles.

1944 Althea Gibson – Courtesy of Bob Davis

George Stewart

Panamanian George Stewart captured 7 ATA Men's Singles Championship titles between 1947 and 1964. This left-handed artist with a racquet was known for his heavy top spin and formidable kick serve. In 1952, he and Dr. Reginald Weir were the first African-American men to play in the USLTA National Championships in Forest Hills.

The First Grand Slam winner, Don Budge
Collections of the International Tennis Hall of Fame & Museum

Oscar Johnson

    Oscar Johnson won the 1946 - 1948 Pacific Coast Junior Championship in singles and doubles. By winning the 1948 National Junior Public Parks Championship at Los Angeles' Griffith Park, he became the first black to win a USLTA-affiliated national event. Later in the year, he entered the USLTA National Junior Indoor Championships at St. Louis. When tournament officials saw that he

George Stewart
Courtesy of Bob Davis

was black, he was refused entry. Acting on his behalf, Richard Hudlin, the former University of Chicago star, and attorney Frank Summers appealed to the USLTA office in New York, insisting that Johnson be admitted because he had won one of their national titles. The USLTA relented and forced local officials to admit the 18 year old Johnson. Oscar reached the quarterfinals before losing to future Hall of Famer Tony Trabert.

Fred Johnson at the Cosmopolitan Club
Courtesy of Bob Davis

Althea's Journey to Forest Hills

Following her success at the 1948 ATA Nationals, Althea longed for the chance to test herself against the world's best at the USLTA Nationals at Forest Hills. Although she had performed admirably in several indoor championships, this was not sufficient for the tournament officials at Forest Hills. Unless she performed well at the outdoor tune-up events for the Nationals, she would be considered

Breaking The Barriers

Bob Ryland in Central Park
Photo by Edward Baker

"unproven." The catch, of course, was that these events were held at private clubs and her applications to play were not likely to be accepted.

Working through the ATA, Bertram Baker and others pressured the USLTA to find a way to let her compete. Additionally, in the July, 1950 issue of "American Lawn Tennis," former world champion Alice Marble condemned the hypocrisy of the USLTA's refusal to let Althea compete.

Oscar Johnson
Courtesy of the Schomburg Center for Research in Black Culture

She correctly concluded that social changes would make eventual minority participation inevitable and boldly confronted the ULSTA with the simple question, "Why not now?"

In response to rising public pressure, the Eastern Grass Court Championships and the National Clay Court Championships accepted Althea's application. She performed well enough to
secure an invitation to the Nationals. In 1950, Althea Gibson became the first black to play in the US Nationals at Forest Hills.

Breaking The Barriers

Bob Ryland – The First Black Professional

Learning tennis at an early age from his father and "Mother" Seames in Chicago, Bob Ryland quickly rose to stardom by winning the Illinois state high school championship in 1939, beating Jimmy Evert, Chris Evert's father. Playing for Wayne State University, Bob was the first black man to play in the NCAA tournament, advancing to the quarterfinals in 1946. In 1954 and 1955 he was the ATA men's singles champion. Arthur Ashe said that at 14 his only dream in tennis was to be good enough to beat Bob Ryland. In 1955 Ryland received a nomination by the ATA to play in the USLTA Nationals at Forest Hills. At the age of 35, with no experience on grass, he lost in straight sets in the first round. Bob became the first black professional tennis player when he joined Jack Marsh's circuit in 1958. In the 1960s Ryland worked briefly at the St. Albans Tennis Club in Washington, DC where he gave tennis lessons to some of Washington's elite. He later coached a young Harold Solomon in the Juniors, touring pro Leslie Allen, and such celebrities as Bill Cosby, Dustin Hoffman, Barbara Streisand and Tony Bennett.

From Forest Hills to World No. 1

After playing at Forest Hills in 1950, Althea's performance on the courts seemed to hit a plateau. For the next several years the major championships eluded her. Teaming up with coach Syd Llewellyn helped get her tennis mechanics straightened out and helped her to focus on her goals. A turning point was her selection to join a 1955 State Department tour of Southeast Asia giving tennis exhibitions. Regular play against seasoned players, without the pressure associated with the major tournaments, allowed Althea to experiment with strokes and strategy until she found the winning combination.

The following year Althea Gibson won the French Singles Championship, becoming the first black to win a Major singles title. She teamed up with Angela Buxton to win both the French Doubles and the Wimbledon Ladies Doubles. However, she was not invited to

Lorraine Williams, 1953 USLTA National Girls Champion
Courtesy of the ATA

play in the US National Doubles held at the Longwood Cricket Club in Boston. In 1957, Althea won the Wimbledon singles and doubles. Her return to New York was celebrated with a ticker tape parade. At Forest Hills she captured the US National Singles title and became the unquestionable No.1 woman player in the world. To prove it wasn't a fluke, she repeated as Champion at Wimbledon and Forest Hills in 1958

Alice Marble
Collections of the International Tennis Hall of Fame & Museum

Dale G. Caldwell

1957 Gibson's Wimbledon Victory Parade
Photo by Max Peter Haas, Collections of the International Tennis Hall of Fame & Museum

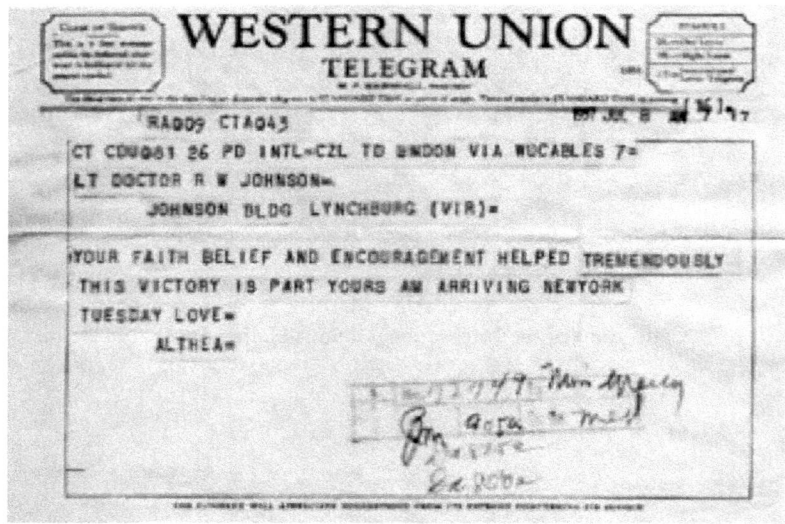

Telegram from Althea to Dr. Johnson
Courtesy of Lange Johnson

1958 Gibson receiving the trophy for the Ladies Championship
Photo by Reuters, Collections of the International Tennis Hall of Fame & Museum

Dale G. Caldwell

HIS PROTEGE—Dr. Robert W. Johnson, 1422 Pierce St., displays newspaper hailing Althea Gibson for her victory in world's amateur tennis championships at Wimbledon, Eng., last Saturday. He is also holding telegram from New York Mayor Robert F. Wagner, inviting him to attend reception today in honor of Althea. It was under Johnson's guidance Althea rose from obscurity to the pinnacle of tennis fame. (James Murdock Photo)

Lynchburg Negro Surgeon Played Major Role In Althea's Victory

By JAMES MURDOCK

For Althea Gibson, first Negro to win a Wimbledon tennis championship, it was a long time between tears.

Eleven years in fact—from the dusk of a 1946 mid-August evening in an empty grandstand at Wilberforce, O., to the famed center court at Wimbledon, England, last Saturday, when she curtsied before Queen Elizabeth II to receive the gold platter symbolic of the world's champion woman tennis player.

The story of those two times Althea cried — the first time in defeat, the second in glory — was told yesterday by Dr. Robert W. Johnson, Lynchburg Negro surgeon — and the man who is responsible for Althea's rise from tennis oblivion to champion.

For it was on Johnson's Lynchburg courts that Althea was transformed from a hard-hitting but erratic young player into a smooth, poised expert with a racquet.

She accomplished this under Johnson's guidance every summer from 1946 until she graduated

noon. She was playing another Negro girl who "lobbed" Althea's smashes through weary set after set. Finally Althea lost her temper, began to whale at the ball, and lost the match. Her New York sponsors became disgusted.

But Johnson, by then an accomplished player in his own right and a keen judge of potential talent, had seen something: he had seen speed, poise, a freedom of movement (coordination) that was just about perfect. Althea's only problem, as he saw

it, was thinking. She had a lot to learn, but the ability to learn was there, he was convinced.

When he found her after the tournament, sitting alone in the stands and her eyes red from crying, he asked her: "How would you like to play at Forest Hills?"

Forest Hills is the mecca of all tennis players. In 1946, no Negro had ever played in the United States Lawn Tennis Association (USLTA) at Forest Hills.

"Go away, don't kid me now," Althea sobbed.

Johnson convinced her he was not kidding. He laid it on the line: she had the ability, but she had to work hard. He was willing to take her in tow, give her a home, and supervise her training program.

Althea accepted. She returned to (Continued on Page 33; Column 4)

Local paper credits Dr. Johnson
Courtesy of Lange Johnson

CHAPTER 15: Breaking the Barriers Exhibit Panel 3

Panel 3 of the Breaking the Barriers Exhibit picks up in 1960 at the point where the previous panel ends. The panel presents general black history and black tennis history from that point until 1975 when Arthur Ashe wins Wimbledon.

Ashe and Dr. J

When Dr. Johnson received a recommendation from Ron Charity of Richmond for skinny 11 year- old Arthur Ashe, little did he realize that he was about to receive the answer to his dreams—a black junior who could win the USLTA Interscholastic Championship. Precocious tennis skills aside, what drew Dr. Johnson to Ashe was the youngster's ability to handle defeat and set-backs. As the youngest of the troupe, he was routinely trounced on Dr. J's backyard court by the older players. Taking it in stride, he would learn from each encounter and lose by a little less the next time.

Eventually, as his body and tennis skills developed, he began beating those who had previously dominated him. With Dr. J taking him to ATA junior events, Arthur began a long list of age group championships. In 1960, at age 17, Arthur won the ATA National men's singles championship, as well as the 18 and under title. Dr. Johnson's dreams were fulfilled when Arthur won the 1961 USLTA Interscholastic Championships in Charlottesville, Virginia.

Dale G. Caldwell

1960 ATA Junior Championships
Courtesy of Bill Davis

Bill Davis

Coming out of Tennessee A&I, where he briefly teamed with Bob Ryland, Bill Davis captured the 1958 and 1959 ATA National Men's Singles title. A 17 year old Arthur Ashe would claim the crown for the next three years until his USTA and Davis Cup play curtailed his ATA involvement. Bill Davis quickly filled this void by winning the ATA singles title 3 out of the next 5 years. Davis would go on to win a total of 11 ATA singles and doubles championships, winning the 1962 Mens doubles with his younger brother Robert.

Bill Davis, 1957 NYC Public Parks Championships
Courtesy of Bill Davis

ATA National Doubles Winners – Bill and Bob Davis
Courtesy of Bill Davis

Bonnie Logan

Bonnie Logan's name appears 19 times on the roll of ATA Champions, including seven consecutive times as National Women's Singles Champion (1964-70). Bonnie and Ann Koger were the first two African Americans on the Virginia Slims tour. Unless supported financially by a corporate sponsor or family, it was very difficult to survive on the professional tour. Lacking this support, Bonnie's professional career was prematurely curtailed. More than a decade later, when Zina Garrison was ranked No. 7 in the world and Lori McNeil was No. 13, neither had a clothing endorsement.

The lack of support was not only financial. At the highest levels, tennis was still a white sport. Whether in the locker room, on the court, in the press box or in the stands, most of the faces were white. As one touring black pro put it, "The black faces stood out like small specks in an otherwise all white background." Knowing that very few fans

Bonnie Logan – photo by Jim Thornton
Courtesy of Bonnie Logan

were cheering for you was hard; knowing that those few who were cheering viewed you as a representative of your race added an additional burden.

King Arthur

In 1963, while a student at UCLA, Arthur was named to the US Davis Cup team – the first African-American to be chosen. In 1965 he won the National Intercollegiate Singles Championship and with teammate Ian Crookenden won the doubles. 1968, a year of social and racial turmoil in our nation's history, was ironically a triumphant year for Arthur.

He won 10 of 22 tournaments and 11 of 12 Davis Cup matches. He became the first black man to win the US Nationals Singles Championship and followed this by winning the inaugural US Open Championships as an amateur. Arthur Ashe would cap his career with an immensely popular win over heavily favored Jimmy Connors in the 1975 Wimbledon Championships.

Arthur Ashe, 1968 US (Longwood)
Photo by Ed Fernberger,
Collections of the International Tennis Hall of Fame & Museum

Breaking The Barriers

Juan Farrow

As the five year-old next door neighbor of Dr. Johnson, Juan Farrow started his tennis career by picking up balls on the court and practicing with a broom handle. When he was seven he started playing in ATA tournaments and by nine he was winning them. Having won the ATA 12 and under singles in 1968 and the 12 and under singles and doubles in 1970, Juan and Dr. J were ready for better competition. Juan entered and won the 1970 USLTA National 12 and under singles title. In 1972 he moved up and won the USLTA National 14 and under singles. Dr. Johnson's insistence on complete control of the ATA Junior Development Program and his increasing success in placing Juniors in USLTA events created jealousy and resentment among some of the ATA leadership.

Juan takes pride in pointing out that he once beat John McEnroe in the Juniors just weeks before McEnroe reached the semi-finals at

Dr. Johnson and Juan Farrow
Courtesy of Lange Johnson

Wimbledon. Juan went on to attend Southern Illinois University and win three NCAA Division II singles titles. On the professional circuit, Juan struggled to find and retain sponsors and his professional career never flourished. Like several other great black players who were to follow, Juan experienced the pressures of being labeled the "next Arthur Ashe."

Newspaper article comparing Farrow to Ashe
Courtesy of Lange Johnson

Arthur at Wimbledon – Photo by Ed Fernberger,
Collections of the International Tennis Hall of Fame

Breaking the Barriers Exhibit Closing Statements

Arthur Ashe's amazing victory at Wimbledon in 1975 was an important milestone in the history of the ATA and black tennis. Althea Gibson proved that a black woman was capable of winning the United States national tennis championships as well as Wimbledon (considered by many to be the world championships of tennis). Arthur Ashe, with his Wimbledon victory (and 1968 US Open victory) proved that a black man was capable of winning both tournaments as well. As seen in this exhibit, the ATA was the foundation of their success. Unfortunately, there were many others who, if given the chance, could have won these championships. All tennis fans have suffered because racism deprived America and the world of many great champions.

Fortunately, because many barriers of exclusion have been broken, the world of professional tennis has become much more diverse. However, the administrative leadership of the sport does not reflect this diversity. Therefore, the next great challenge is to identify black leaders who are as talented in the board room as Gibson and Ashe were on the court. The ATA will likely play an important role in identifying a new generation of black tennis champions and black administrators who can take the sport to the next level of success.

Facing the Future

"As someone who grew up playing tennis with Arthur Ashe, Jr., I experienced first-hand the hurdles that blacks had to overcome. While hurdles still exist for blacks in America, I believe that the ATA will continue to be an important part of the tennis world."

Willis Thomas, Jr.
President of the ATA
2006-2007

Arthur Ashe, 1975 Wimbledon Gentlemen's Champion
photograph by Russ Adams.

The Breaking the Barriers Exhibit has become the most popular touring exhibit in the history of the International Tennis Hall of Fame because it does an excellent job of honoring forgotten heroes of the game and the American Tennis Association (ATA). The ATA has earned an important place in both tennis and American history because it effectively opened doors of opportunity to blacks who were denied access to the tennis opportunities afforded whites. The local chapters of the ATA still have deep roots in communities of color. The ATA therefore has the potential to play an important role in the future of tennis by identifying and nurturing young players of color who otherwise would not be exposed to the great sport of tennis. My hope is that this exhibit will help the ATA accomplish more in its future than it has in its incredible past.

—Dale G. Caldwell, co-curator of the "Breaking the Barriers" exhibit, first African-American president of the USTA Eastern Section, only African-American to serve as a USTA section president and later as a USTA board member, former ATA nationally ranked junior player

CHAPTER 16: Black Tennis Hall of Fame Inductees

The Black Tennis Hall of Fame (BTHOF) was founded by Dale Gilbert Caldwell in 2007 to ensure that "The incredible accomplishments of individuals who broke through barriers of race and class in tennis will now remain a part of tennis history forever." In his initial announcement on the founding of the BTHOF, Dale said: "My hope is that generations of future tennis players and fans of all races and backgrounds will be inspired by the unique ways in which inductees overcame personal and societal challenges to achieve extraordinary success in the sport."

The individuals elected to the BTHOF fall into one or more of the following three categories:

Player Category

Players are elected to the BTHOF based on their success on the tennis court and the significance of their historical tennis achievements in the black community and around the world.

Contributor Category

Contributors are elected to the BTHOF based on their unique contributions to tennis; and the historical significance of their tennis related achievements in the black community and around the world.

Dale G. Caldwell

Pioneer Category

Pioneers must have an outstanding record of success on the tennis court or have made exceptional contributions to the sport of tennis during segregation and prior to the United States civil rights legislation in 1964.

Included below is a copy of the original press release announcing the creation of the Black Tennis Hall of Fame, Incorporated:

BLACK TENNIS HALL OF FAME FOUNDING

For Immediate Release
Contact: Dale G. Caldwell
November 30, 2007
Phone: 732-208-9808

New Brunswick, NJ – The Black Tennis Hall of Fame (BTHOF) was founded today by Dale G. Caldwell to work with the American Tennis Association (ATA), the International Tennis Hall of Fame and Museum (ITHOF), the United States Tennis Association (USTA) and other organizations to honor the achievements of those individuals who have succeeded in tennis and life in spite of the many racial barriers that they faced. As a Co-Curator (with Art Carrington) of the ITHOF exhibit *Breaking The Barriers: Honoring the ATA and Black Tennis Pioneers* Dale Caldwell had an opportunity to work closely with ITHOF Museum Director Gary Cogar, Art and an incredible Advisory board to develop this outstanding exhibit which was viewed by over 26,000 people in two weeks at the 2007 US Open. In developing this exhibit, Dale discovered that the only way to fully honor and recognize all of the key individuals who have broken through the barriers of race and class to achieve success in tennis was to create the BTHOF.

Tennis has become the world's second most popular sport largely because of the geographic, cultural, stylistic and racial diversity of its professionals. The sport has developed passionate fans of different backgrounds because of this diversity. Unfortunately, diversity was not always encouraged by the sport's leadership. Most people are familiar with the tennis and life successes of Althea Gibson and Arthur Ashe. However, because of racial discrimination in tennis and many parts of the world, few people know the incredible story of the talented players of color who were not allowed to compete in major tennis tournaments because of their race.

For over fifty years, prior to Gibson's victories, blacks had been competing in club and regional tournaments. Banned from entering segregated events, African-American tennis enthusiasts in 1916 formed their own organization, the American Tennis Association (ATA), to provide blacks with the opportunity to play competitive tennis on a national level. Their struggle to gain equal access to tennis paralleled the struggle of all blacks to gain equal access to American society.

The BTHOF has developed a state-of-the-art website that will enable viewers to take a virtual tour through both tennis and black history. The BTHOF website can be accessed through the Internet addresses: www.blacktennishalloffame.org or www.blacktennismuseum.org. The inaugural class of Hall of Famers will be inducted into the Black Tennis Hall of Fame during the 2008 ATA National Tennis Tournament on Thursday Evening August 7th in Miami, Florida. Players, Contributors and Organizations will be elected to the BTHOF based on the significance of their historical tennis achievements in the black community and around the world.

# # #

The Black Tennis Hall of Fame Logo

The Black Tennis Hall of Fame, Inc. logo was designed by Dale Caldwell and drawn by his younger brother Paul Douglass Caldwell in 2008. The logo includes a drawing of Dr. Walter Johnson, Althea Gibson and Arthur Ashe, Jr. Dr. Johnson was the legendary coach of Althea Gibson (the first African-American female world tennis champion) and Arthur Ashe (the first African-American male world tennis champion). Dale felt that it was appropriate to honor the first people who transcended race to achieve global greatness in tennis. The color of the logo is red, black and green. The color red was chosen to symbolize the blood that was shed for equal rights, the color black was chosen to represent the color of the people fighting for equal rights, and the color green symbolized the bountiful land of a society where vegetation and equal rights flourish.

Breaking The Barriers

The Inaugural Class of 2008

American Tennis Association (ATA): When tennis first arrived in the United States it was played at exclusive private clubs that only allowed white Protestant members. These clubs operated "White Only" private and United States National Lawn Tennis Association (USNLTA) tennis tournaments and events that excluded black players. However, the creation of modified (and eventually public) tennis courts in black neighborhoods led to the growing popularity of the sport among many of the most influential people in the black community. These individuals loved the sport so much they created black tennis clubs and tournaments (open to both black and white players) in black communities across the United States. Since black players were not allowed to play in the USNLTA tournaments they had to create their own organization.

Members of the Association Tennis Club in Washington, DC and the Monumental Tennis Club of Baltimore conceived the idea of a national tennis organization of African Americans. Meeting on Thanksgiving Day, 1916 at the YMCA in Washington, DC, members from the major black tennis clubs founded the American Tennis Association. H. Stanton McCard was elected the first president. The ATA was founded to serve as the governing body of black tennis in the United States. Their primary focus was on organizing an annual ATA National Championship as well as a series of tennis tournaments in black communities in and between New York and Los Angeles. The ATA was inducted into the inaugural class of the Black Tennis Hall of Fame for being the first black sports organization in America, the oldest operating black sports organization in the US, and, the launching pad for most of the best African-American tennis players in history.

Arthur Ashe: Ashe was born in Richmond, Virginia on July 10, 1943 to Arthur Robert Ashe, Sr. and Mattie Cordell Ashe. He won the ATA National Boys 12 singles title in 1955, the ATA National Boys 16 Singles title in 1957, 1958 and 1959, the ATA National Boys 18 Singles title in 1960, and, the ATA Men's Singles title from 1960 to

1963. Ashe won the United States Lawn Tennis Association (USLTA) boys National Interscholastic Singles Championship in 1961. He was awarded a full scholarship to the University of California at Los Angeles (UCLA) in 1962. In 1965, Ashe won the National Collegiate Athletic Association (NCAA) Men's Singles National Championship and led the UCLA team to the National Collegiate Team Championship. After graduating from UCLA with a Business Administration degree in 1966, he served in the U.S. Army for three years.

He was the first African-American man to win a Grand Slam tennis tournament and be recognized as one of the best tennis players in the world. In 1968, Ashe won the Men's Singles Championship at the very first U.S. Open. In 1970, he became the first African-American man to win the Men's Singles division of Australian Open. In 1975, he became the first African-American man to win the Wimbledon Men's Singles title. His life is celebrated more than many other outstanding athletes because of his commitment to making a difference in the world*. Ashe's commitment to social justice and health and humanitarian issues left a mark on the world as indelible as his tennis was on the court. He was a natural leader who was a member of the board of directors of Aetna, the chairman of the board of the Black Tennis & Sports Foundation (the leading advocate for black sports interests), and, the Arthur Ashe Safe Passage Foundation, which introduced tennis, health and mentorship to more than 20,000 inner-city youngsters. In addition to being inducted into the Black Tennis Hall of Fame in 2008, Ashe was inducted into the International Tennis Hall of Fame in 1985 and the Eastern Tennis Hall of Fame in 1988. As incredible as Ashe's accomplishments were on the tennis court, his global influence in the area of human rights was even more significant. Ashe's most notable international activism centered around his protest of Apartheid in South Africa. However, he also fought against racial discrimination and for the rights of refugees for most of his adult life.

Breaking The Barriers

Althea Gibson: Gibson was born in Silver, Clarendon County, South Carolina on August 25, 1927 to Daniel and Annie Bell Gibson. Her parents were sharecroppers on a South Carolina cotton farm until, in 1930, the Great Depression influenced them to move to 143rd street in the section of New York City called "Harlem." She was an active participant in the local Police Athletic League (PAL) program as a child. She learned paddle tennis in this program and became the New York City women's paddle tennis champion in 1939 at age 12. People from her Harlem neighborhood were so impressed by her paddle tennis skills that, in 1940, they paid for a membership and tennis lessons at the prestigious Cosmopolitan Tennis club in Harlem. Her tennis skills advanced rapidly and, in 1941, she won the ATA New York State Girls Singles Championship. In 1944 and 1945 she won the ATA Girls 18 National Championships. In 1946, she lost in the Women's Singles Final of the ATA National Championships. However, this loss motivated her to work harder on improving her tennis game.

This intense focus on improving her tennis skills helped Gibson win the ATA Women's Singles Champion every year from 1947 to 1956. She was also the Mixed Doubles Champion with Dr. R. Walter Johnson in 1948, 1949, 1950, 1952, 1953, 1954 and 1955. "Althea," as she was affectionately known in the black tennis community, was the first to break the color barrier of the USLTA in 1950 and played in the U.S. National Tennis Championship in Forest Hills. She became the first African-American player to play in Wimbledon in 1951. She went on to win the French Open Championship in 1956 and subsequently won both the U.S. National Championship and Wimbledon in 1957 and 1958. These victories were especially historic because the winner's trophy was presented to her by Queen Elizabeth. She retired from Tennis in 1958 and played for a while with the Harlem Globetrotters. Gibson was selected as Associated Press "Female Athlete of the Year" in the year 1957, the first black ever to receive this honor. In 1958, Gibson wrote her autobiography *I always wanted to be somebody*. She also broke the color barrier in golf, launching her golf career in

1964 and joining the Ladies Professional Golf Association (LPGA). In addition to being inducted into the Black Tennis Hall of Fame in 2008, Gibson was inducted into the International Tennis Hall of Fame in 1971 and the Eastern Tennis Hall of Fame in 1988.

Tally Holmes: In 1917, Tally Holmes made history at the historic Druid Hill Park, in Baltimore, MD by becoming the first ATA National Men's Singles Champion. He followed that title with ATA Men's Singles Championships in 1918 and 1921. In addition, he was a finalist in the Men's Singles Championship in 1920, losing to B.M. Clark, a Jamaican who was the first black to play at Wimbledon. Holmes also won the ATA Men's Doubles Championship in 1917, 1918, 1921, 1922, 1924, 1925 and 1927.

H. Stanton McCard: In 1916, Dr. McCard made history as the first president of the newly formed American Tennis Association. He was a passionate tennis player, physician and surgeon and a leader in Baltimore's black medical community. McCard was selected as the first president of the ATA because of his reputation as an outstanding physician and the respect he had in and beyond Baltimore. The founding presidents of organizations are charged with the task of leading the development of the organization's initial mission, vision, values and strategic plan. In addition, they are ultimately responsible for developing a marketing plan for the organization and managing the egos of the people who want to be the next president. McCard was selected for induction into the Black Tennis Hall of Fame because his initial leadership of the ATA laid the groundwork for the success of the organization for many decades into the future.

Lucy Diggs Slowe: Born in Berryville, Virginia on July 4, 1885, Slowe made history as the winner of the first ATA National Women's Singles Championship in 1917. This victory made her the first African-American woman to win a major sports title. On January 15, 1908

Slowe and nine other women founded the Alpha Kappa Alpha Sorority, Incorporated. This organization has become one of the most influential associations of black woman in the world. In 1919, she worked with District of Columbia officials to create the first junior high school in the system. Slowe served as principal of this school for three years. In 1922, she became the first Dean of Women at Howard University. In 1923, Slowe became  the founder and president of the National Association of College Women. In 1929, she founded the Association of Deans of Women and Advisors to Girls in Negro Schools (NAWDACS).

Dr. Walter Johnson: Dr. Johnson (who was affectionately known as "Dr.J") was the legendary coach of International Tennis Hall of Fame and Black Tennis Hall of Fame Inductees Althea Gibson and Arthur Ashe. In addition to coaching the two best black tennis players in history, Dr. J taught many of the most promising junior players on the

American Tennis Association (ATA) tennis circuit at his home in Lynchburg, Virginia. In addition to teaching players conditioning and strategy, he taught his players how to deal with racism, bad line calls and to always maintain their dignity and composure. He was recognized in the black community as the "Father of the ATA Junior Development Program."

Dr. J's coaching on tennis, racism and life helped Ashe and Gibson combine to win 8 Grand Slam singles titles (Gibson 5, Ashe 3); 7 Grand Slam doubles titles (Gibson 5, Ashe 2); and, 1 Grand Slam Mixed Doubles title (Gibson 1). In addition to being a great coach, he was a gifted doubles player. He and partner Althea Gibson won the ATA National Mixed Doubles Championships in 1948, 1949, 1950, 1952, 1953, 1954 and 1955. In addition to being inducted into the Black Tennis Hall of Fame in 2008, Dr. Johnson was inducted into the International Tennis Hall of Fame in 2009.

Rev. W. W. Walker: Rev. Walker is credited with being an early pioneer in the growth of tennis in the black community. As a member of the Chautauqua Tennis Club in 1898, he was the founder of the first interstate black tournament. This seminal event was held in Philadelphia and attracted the best black tennis players in the area. The event's first champion was Thomas Jefferson of Lincoln University. In the second year of the tournament in 1899, Rev. Walker defeated Henry Freeman of Washington, D.C. for the championship after a closely contested battle.

Rev. Walker, continued his leadership in the sport and became known as one of the first black tennis historians. In the 1931 program of the American Tennis Association, he describes three distinct periods in the evolution of black tennis. Walker states that the first major innovation among black tennis players was the "the chop and net game." In this style, players would continually slice the ball and come to the net. He confidently explains that he introduced this tennis style and that it dominated play in the earliest days of black tennis (from 1899 to 1900). Walker goes on to say that players from the West Coast demonstrated a less conservative style of play that was rare in the more conservative from the East Coast. Walker states that the top West Coast players had a bolder, more "convincing" and aggressive style of play. He credits Edgar G. Brown with introducing this style of play consisting of an early version of the "top-spin and base line game." The third period in tennis was introduced by a group of talented young players in the early 1900s who perfected the aggressive top-spin and baseline style. However, they also had strong volleys. This "modern" black player of the 1930s was equally at home on the base line or at the net. Walker was inducted into the Black Tennis Hall of Fame in the inaugural induction year for his leadership in establishing the first major black tennis tournament and role as the first black tennis historian.

Breaking The Barriers

The Class of 2009

Wilbert "Billy" Davis: Born on January 6, 1930, Davis was the winner of 11 National Tennis Titles over a period of 33 years. He won the Boys 16 ATA National Singles and Doubles Championship in 1945; the Boy's 18 ATA National Championship in 1948; the Men's ATA National Singles Championship in 1958, 1959, 1963, 1966 and 1967; the Men's ATA National Doubles Championship in 1954 and 1962; and, the Men's ATA 45 Singles National Championship in 1978. Davis played for and graduated from Tennessee A&I. In addition to being one of the best black players in the country for many years, Davis was a mentor to Arthur Ashe and one of the most influential black tennis leaders in the country. Davis was 13 years older than Arthur Ashe and one of the best black tennis players that a young Arthur Ashe had ever met. Davis was one of the tennis leaders that provided the advice Ashe needed to become a world champion. He also  supported the expansion of tennis programs for black youth around the country. In addition to winning the ATA National Men's Double's titles together in 1962, Billy and his brother Bob (who was inducted into the Black Tennis Hall of Fame in 2014) played an important role in influencing future players and growing the sport in the black community.

Zina Lynn Garrison: In 1990, Garrison reached the Wimbledon Women's Singles Final and became the second black woman (2008 Inductee Althea Gibson was the first) to reach a Grand Slam Final. She was also the first African-American to serve as captain of the U.S. Federation Cup Team (2004) and the Women's US Olympic Team (Bejing 2008). It was clear from her early tennis success in life that she would become one of the most talented black players in history. She was an extraordinarily successful junior player. In 1977, at the age of 14, Garrison won the USTA Girls 18 National Championship. In

1981, she won the US Open and Wimbledon Junior Championships and became the number 1 junior player in the world.

Garrison also won the 1979 and 1980 ATA Women's Singles Championships and the 1980 and 1981 ATA Women's Doubles Championships before embarking on an outstanding professional career that resulted in her becoming the number 4 player in the world. Garrison's career highlights include: winning the 1987 Australian Open Mixed Doubles Championship and the 1988 and 1990 Wimbledon Mixed Doubles Championships; Runner-up in the 1990  Wimbledon Singles Championship; Runner-up in the 1987 and 1992 Australian Open Women's Doubles Championships; Runner-up in the 1989, 1990 and 1993 Australian Open Mixed Doubles Championships; winning a Gold Medal in Women's Doubles in the 1988 Seoul Olympics; and, a Bronze Medal in Women's Singles in the 1988 Seoul Olympics.

Bonnie Logan: In the 1970s, the Virginia Slims tennis tournaments comprised the vast majority of high profile events on the women's professional tennis tour. In 1971, Logan, a Durham, N.C. native, made history by becoming the first African-American woman to play in a Virginia Slims Tournament. She became a legend in the black tennis community because of her dominance of the American Tennis Association (ATA) National Championships during the 1960s. From 1964 to 1970, Logan captured seven consecutive ATA women's singles titles. In addition, in 1968, Logan captured the Eastern Carolina Closed Championship in both singles and doubles. Two years later she accomplished the same feat at the North Carolina State Closed Championship.

Breaking The Barriers

Logan was a talented junior player who won the Maryland Girl's 14 and Under Championship, the Girl's 16 and Under Championship and the Girl's 18 and Under Championship in consecutive years. Her emergence into the tennis world as a star came as no surprise because she spent much of her early playing career taking on men and older more experienced players. As a student-athlete at Morgan State University in Baltimore, Logan was so much better than the players on the women's tennis team that she petitioned to join the men's team — and won. She went on to play #2 for the men and won her flight in the Central Intercollegiate Athletic Association Tennis Championships. She spent her last two years of college focused on playing against women and later competed in the NCAA Championships. Logan finished her college career lettering in five sports and, in 1983, she was inducted into the Morgan State University Athletic Hall of Fame.

Logan is a tennis playing legend because of her victories in the 1964, 1965, 1966, 1967, 1968, 1969 and 1970 ATA Women's Singles Championships. Only Althea Gibson (10) and Ora Washington (8) have won more ATA National Women's Singles Championships than Logan. In addition to her singles titles, Logan won one ATA Women's Doubles title and four ATA National Mixed Doubles titles.

Jimmy McDaniel: In 1940, McDaniel was part of a tennis match that is considered by many to be one of the most significant sporting events in history. The importance to racial progress of Kenny Washington breaking the National Football Leagues (NFL) color barrier in 1946 and Jackie Robinson breaking the Major League Baseball (MLB) color barrier in 1948 is recognized throughout the world. However, few people know about the historic 1940 tennis match in New York City between the undisputed white world champion of tennis Don Budge and the undisputed black champion of tennis Jimmie McDaniel.

A lot has been written about Kenny Washington of the Los Angeles Rams becoming the first African-American to sign a contract with an NFL team in the post-World War II era (on March 21, 1946)

and Jackie Robinson of the Brooklyn Dodgers who became the first African-American to play a MLB game (on April 15, 1947). Yet, little attention has been paid to another important date in sports history that preceded both of those seminal events. The date was July 29, 1940 and the event was a match between the ATA champion Jimmie McDaniel and the first man to win all four of the world's most important tennis championships in the same year, Don Budge. Incredibly, in 1938 Budge became the first man to win tennis's "Grand Slam" (the Australian, French, Wimbledon and US Men's Singles Championships) in the same year. McDaniel won the ATA National Championships in 1939; however, because he was black, he was not allowed to play in the same international championships as Don Budge.

On this historic date in 1940, the black champion James (Jimmy) McDaniel and the white champion John Donald (Don) Budge squared off in front of 2,000 spectators at Harlem's Cosmopolitan Tennis Club. The match was sponsored by Wilson® Sporting Goods, which had a sponsorship contract with Budge. The timing of the match was perfect because Budge was in the middle of a five-year run as the world's number one-ranked tennis player and McDaniel was virtually unbeatable in the ATA circuit.

As the best white tennis player in the world during a period of intense segregation, Budge deserves tremendous credit for agreeing to play this match. He had nothing to win and everything to lose. Tennis was a sport that was controlled on and off of the court by the wealthiest people in the world. The sport was rampant with discrimination by both race and class. If Don Budge, who dominated a rich white sport, were to lose to Jimmie McDaniel, than a monumental barrier of both race and class would have been shattered. It was inconceivable to think at the time that a poor black kid could beat the best white player in a rich white person's sport. Budge's willingness to play McDaniel was one of the most courageous feats in sports history.

McDaniel's success on the ATA circuit made him the greatest black tennis player of the pre-World War II era. He won the 1939, 1940, 1941 and 1946 ATA Men's Singles and Doubles Championships. Between 1939 and 1941 McDaniel won thirty-eight of the forty-three ATA tournaments he entered. However, Budge's international playing experience (and comfort playing on clay tennis courts) gave him a significant advantage and he won the match by a score of 6-1, 6-2. Al Laney, the well-known tennis columnist for the "New York Herald Tribune" (and 1979 ITHF Inductee) wrote that it was likely that McDaniel "Could hold his own against the current crop of white players if he were able to play a few tournaments in which they competed."[16] It is rumored that Budge stated, "Jimmie is a very good player, I'd say he'd rank with the first 10 of our white players." Neither the victory nor the score was as important as the historic reality that this seminal match broke through important barriers of race and class.

Robert Ryland: In 1959, Ryland broke through barriers of race and class by becoming the first African-American to become a tennis professional. His success in both ATA and integrated amateur tournaments around the country made him one of the best known black players in the US. His fame led sports promoter Jack Marsh to ask Ryland to make history by joining his professional tennis circuit which included legendary tennis players Pancho Gonzalez (who was inducted into the International Tennis Hall of Fame (ITHF) in 1968), Lew Hoad (ITHF Inductee in 1990) and other top pro players. Ryland accepted and another barrier of race and class was broken when he played his first pro match in Cleveland in 1959.

Ryland started playing tennis at age nine. He was taught by his father and the iconic Mrs. C.O. "Mother" Seames (one of the first nationally known black tennis coaches) of the Chicago Prairie Tennis Club in Chicago, Illinois. Ryland had a talent for the sport and quickly rose to stardom by winning the Illinois State High School Championship in 1939, beating Jimmy Evert (Chris Evert's father) on the way to the title. In addition, in 1939, he won the ATA Boys 18 and under Singles Championship. In 1944, he played in a historic exhibition tennis match at the Cosmopolitan Club with legendary player Alice Marble (1964 ITHF Inductee) against Dr. Reginald Weir and Mary Hardwick. Ryland and Marble won the match 10-8. In 1946,

---

[16] Al Laney "2,000 Negroes," "New York Herald Tribune", July 30, 1940.

he won the Men's Singles Championship in the Detroit Public Parks integrated tournament. In 1947, he lost to the number one ranked U.S player Ham Richardson 4-6, 5-7 in the Pacific Southwest Championship. In 1952, he won the integrated Los Angeles Industrial City Championships. In 1955 and 1956 he won the ATA Men's Singles Championship in addition to being a finalist four other times.

Playing for Wayne State University, Ryland was the first black man to play in the National Collegiate Athletic Association (NCAA) tournament, advancing to the quarterfinals in 1946. Ryland was so admired in the black tennis community that a 14 year-old Arthur Ashe said his only dream was "To be good enough to beat Bob Ryland." In 1955, Ryland received a nomination by the ATA to play in the USLTA Nationals at Forest Hills. At the age of 35, with no experience on grass, he lost in straight sets in the first round. Clearly, Ryland might have done well in the US Nationals if he had been allowed to play it in the prime of his tennis career. In the 1960's, he worked briefly at the St. Albans Tennis Club in Washington, DC where he gave tennis lessons to some of Washington's elite. He later coached Venus and Serena Williams when they were juniors, and touring pros Harold Solomon and Leslie Allen. In addition, he taught tennis to many celebrities including Bill Cosby, Dustin Hoffman, Barbra Streisand and Tony Bennett.

George Stewart: Born in Panama in 1923, Stewart was the first black man to play in five US National Championship tournaments. Stewart and Dr. Reginald Weir became the first black men to play at the U.S. National Championships in 1952. Even though they both lost in the first round, tennis history was made by their appearance in the tournament. In 1957, Stewart won his first round match at the US Championships by beating Hal Treveen of the US 6-3, 6-3, 6-1. However, he lost in the round of 64 to Donald Thompson of the US 5-7, 3-6, 4-6.

Stewart was one of the best black tennis players in history. He won the ATA Men's Singles Championship in 1947, 1948, 1951,

1952, 1953, 1957 and 1964. In addition, Stewart won the ATA Men's Doubles Championship in 1948, 1949, 1951, 1956 (with Dr. Hubert Eaton) and 1957 (with John Chandler).

Malivai Washington: In 1996, at the Wimbledon Championships, Washington became the second African-American (BTHF 2008 and ITHF 1985 Inductee Arthur Ashe was the first) to reach a Grand Slam Final. He was an All-American tennis player at the University of Michigan before turning pro in his junior year of college. Washington became an extremely successful professional player who reached a career high of number 11 in the world and had wins over many tennis legends including: Andre Agassi, Boris Becker, Stefan Edberg, Jimmy Connors, Michael Chang, Gustavo Kuertan, Ivan Lendl and John McEnroe.

He has become as successful in his retirement as he was on the tennis court. He is the founder and driving force behind one of the most effective community tennis programs in the country, the Malavai Washington Kids Foundation in Jacksonville, Florida. In 2005 and 2008, the foundation was named the United States Tennis Association (USTA) National Junior Tennis League (NJTL) Chapter of the Year for its outstanding work "developing champions in classrooms, on tennis courts and throughout communities." In 2009, Washington received the Arthur Ashe Humanitarian of the Year Award during the ATP World Tour Awards. In addition, in 1997, Washington received the Boys and Girls Clubs of America CARE Award and, in 1998, he was honored with the Arthur Ashe Athletic Association Leadership Award.

Ora Washington: Many people consider Ora Washington the greatest woman athlete of all time and speculate that if she played when tennis was integrated she would have been the best woman's tennis player in the world. Washington was born on January 16, 1899 and grew up in the Germantown section of Philadelphia. In 1924, she was encouraged by a local coach to take up tennis to help her deal with the grief she was feeling because of the death of one of her sisters. She clearly had a gift for playing tennis and started winning matches soon after she began playing the sport.

Washington played tennis competitively for 12 extraordinary years in the ATA and became a champion just five years after she first picked up a racquet. She won the ATA Women's Singles Championship in 1929, 1930, 1931, 1932, 1933, 1934, 1935 and 1937. The legendary Althea Gibson is the only person to win more ATA Women's Singles titles. In addition to her singles championships, Washington won the 1929, 1930, 1931, 1932, 1933, 1934, 1935, 1936, 1937, 1938, 1939 and 1940 ATA Women's Doubles Championships (most of these titles were won with her frequent singles rival Lulu Ballard). She also won one ATA Mixed Doubles Championship.

Washington's athletic success was not limited to the tennis court. She initially played basketball with a Philadelphia team named the Germantown Hornets. In 1930, this team had a 22-1 record and won the national women's basketball team title. In 1931, Washington was the star player on a Hornet team that won 33 consecutive victories. She then played with the Philadelphia Tribune basketball team from 1932-1942 and became one of the most versatile and successful players in basketball history serving as the coach, center and leading scorer. This incredible team won 11 Women's Colored Basketball World Championships in a row.

Her success on the tennis court led many to believe that she was the best women's tennis player in the world, while her prowess on the basketball court led many to consider Washington to be the best women's basketball player in the world.

Arthur Ashe wrote in *A Hard Road to Glory* that Washington "May have been the best female athlete ever." She was so gifted she could practice while she played. Washington once said, "I don't believe in long warm-ups. I'd rather play from scratch and warm up as I went along." Between 1927 and 1933, Helen Wills Moody (1959 ITHF Inductee) won an incredible 180 straight matches without losing a set.

Breaking The Barriers

During that winning streak, when black players were not allowed to compete in major tournaments, she won an incredible 14 Grand Slam Singles Championships. However, in spite of her extraordinary success in "White Only" tournaments she refused to play Ora Washington. Her refusal to play Washington made Don Budge's willingness to play Jimmie McDaniel (see Jimmie McDaniel biography) all the more impressive.

Washington's success on the tennis court convinced members of President Franklin D. Roosevelt's administration to build hundreds of public tennis courts in urban neighborhoods across the United States to introduce tennis to the black community. Tragically, she never received the international recognition she deserved, and while working as a housekeeper, coached young people on the public tennis courts in Germantown, Pa. where she began playing tennis. In addition to being inducted into the Black Tennis Hall of Fame in 2009 Washington was inducted into the Women's Basketball Hall of Fame in 2009.

Reginald Weir: The bio photo on the right shows Dr. Reginald Weir (l) and Desi Margetson, designer of the first indoor, air-supported structure for tennis. In 1948, thirty-seven year old New York City resident Dr. Reginald Weir submitted an entry to participate in the USLTA National Indoor Championship held at the 7th Regiment Armory in New York City. Black players were not allowed to play in USLTA tournaments. However, tournament officials never thought that a doctor would be black so they accepted Dr. Reginald Weir's entry without question. They were surprised when Dr. Weir arrived at the tournament. However, it was too late for them to deny his entry into the tournament. Much to their disappointment he won his first-round match. Weir therefore made history by becoming the first African-American to play in a USLTA National Championship.

He lost in the second round to Bill Talbert (1967 ITHF Inductee). New York tennis historian Nancy McShea wrote in Weir's Eastern Tennis Hall of Fame biography that "After the match Talbert said to future Wimbledon Champion Dick Savitt (1976 ITHF Inductee), 'What a class act he is; it's too bad he didn't get a chance to play more (national) tournaments in his prime. He's very quick and a very good volleyer.'" Weir had tried to play in a USLTA national tournament several times starting in 1929 when he was refused entry into the national junior indoors that were held at the 7th Regiment Armory. In his book, *A Hard Road to Glory: A History of the African-American Athlete*, Arthur Ashe wrote that the National Association for the Advancement of Colored People (NAACP) protested the USLTA's denial of Weir's tournament entry in 1929 because he was black and received the following reply from the USLTA: "...The policy of the USLTA has been to decline the entry of colored players in our championships...In pursuing this policy, we make no reflection upon race but we believe that as a practical matter, the present method of separate associations (USLTA and American Tennis Association) should be continued."

Even though it was late in his tennis playing career, Weir took Pancho Gonzalez (1968 ITHF Inductee) to three sets in a later tournament. Weir was also an incredible person off of the court. He was an extraordinary physician who, in 1935, became one of the first black medical school graduates of New York University Medical School. In just four years, Weir became an assistant in surgery at NYU Medical Center, in 1941 started a private practice and served as one of the first African-American surgeons in Governor's Hospital on the Lower East Side.

In 1952, Weir and George Stewart became the first black men to play in the U.S. National Championships. Even though they both lost in the first round, tennis history was made by their appearance in the tournament. Weir was considered the best black tennis player in the world in the 1930s because he won the 1931, 1932, 1933, 1937 and 1942 ATA Men's Singles Championships.

Prior to these victories he was a star player on the integrated City College tennis team in New York. Weir was inducted into the Eastern Tennis Hall of Fame in 1999. In addition, he won several national USTA age group titles and was recognized numerous times by the USTA for his contributions to tennis.

Breaking The Barriers

The Class of 2010

Rodney Harmon: In 2008, Harmon made history by becoming the first African-American to coach the men's United States Olympic tennis team and led the group during the Bejing Olympics. He also made history by becoming the first black director of Men's High Performance Tennis for the USTA in 2002. He had an extraordinary junior and professional tennis career. In 1978, at the age of 17, Harmon won the ATA Men's Singles Championship. In 1979, he won the USTA Boy's National Hard Court Doubles Championship and the Boys National Clay Court Doubles Championship.

While a student at the University of Tennessee, he partnered with teammate Mel Purcell to win the 1980 Men's NCAA Doubles Championship.

In 1982, he became the second African-American (Arthur Ashe was the first) to reach the Quarterfinals of the US Open. He was named PTR Professional of the Year in 1988. As the Head Men's Tennis Coach for the University of Miami, he was named Big East Men's Tennis Coach of the Year in 1996 and 1997. Harmon received the International Tennis Hall of Fame Tennis Educational Merit Award in 2008 and was inducted into the Intercollegiate Tennis Association (ITA) Hall of Fame in 2010.

Ann Koger: In 1973, Koger made history by becoming one of the first black women to play on the Virginia Slims Women's Professional Tennis Circuit. She had an illustrious junior and collegiate career and became one of the best tennis players in the world in the 1970s. Koger learned to play tennis in Baltimore's legendary Druid Hill Park under the guidance of her mother Myrtle Koger (a member of the Baltimore Tennis Club and founder of the Netmen Coed Tennis Club of Baltimore). She worked very hard on her tennis skills and won the ATA National Girls 12 and Under Championships in 1961. Ann and her sisters Patricia and Carol were among the first black tennis stars in the Mid-Atlantic Section of the USTA. The three sisters collected more than 100 trophies in these tournaments.

Koger was a star student-athlete at Morgan State University where she was a four-year letterman in basketball, field hockey, volleyball and tennis. From 1969 to 1972, Koger followed Bonnie Logan as the second female member of the Morgan State Men's Tennis Team where she was second in singles and first in doubles. Incredibly, she placed second in the Central Intercollegiate Athletic Association's (CIAA) Flight I Men's Doubles Championships. In addition, Koger and Logan became the first black women athletes to represent a historically black university in a national collegiate tournament.

In 1968, Logan won the ATA National Women's Doubles Championship and in 1973 and 1974 she won the ATA National Mixed Doubles Championships. Since 1981 Koger has been the Women's Tennis Coach at Haverford College. She also made history in college basketball by becoming the first woman to officiate an NCAA Division I men's basketball game.

2010 was a special year for Ann Koger, In addition to being inducted into the Black Tennis Hall of Fame that year, Koger was inducted into the USTA Middle States Hall of Fame and received the Philadelphia Sports Legends Award.

Leslie Allen: In 1981, by winning the Avon Championships of Detroit, Allen became the first African-American woman to win a major pro tennis tournament since Althea Gibson won her last tournament in 1958. She beat Hana Mandlikova (a 1994 ITHF Inductee who throughout her career won the women's singles titles at the Australian, French and US Opens) 6-4, 6-4. Previous winners of the tournament included Billie Jean King, Chris Evert, Martina Navratilova and Evonne Goolagong. Allen also made history by becoming the first African-American Woman in a French Open Mixed

Doubles Final. Allen and Charles Strode lost the final to Barbara Jordan and Eliot Telscher 2-6, 3-6, however they made history, nonetheless.

Allen graduated from the University of Southern California with a Bachelor of Arts degree in speech communications. She was a key member of the 1977 USC Women's National Championship team. On the women's professional tennis tour Allen reached a high ranking of number 17 in the world, making her the highest ranked college graduate in the history of the women's tour. Allen also won the ATA Women's Singles Championship in 1977. She currently runs the Leslie Allen Foundation which teaches young people how to succeed in tennis and life and introduces them to behind the scenes careers in professional tennis. Allen was inducted into the Eastern Tennis Hall of Fame in 2016.

Oscar Johnson: In 1948, Johnson broke through barriers of race and class by entering and winning the integrated USLTA sanctioned Long Beach Junior Open tennis championships in Southern California. This victory qualified him to make tennis history in 1948 by becoming the first African-American to enter a USLTA national junior tennis championship. To the great surprise of the white USLTA tennis officials, Johnson went on to make even more significant history by winning the National Junior Public Parks Tournament at Griffith Park in Los Angeles. Johnson therefore became the first African-American to win a USLTA Sanctioned National Junior Championship.

Johnson went on to be a star junior player on the USLTA tennis circuit. However, he frequently faced discrimination at various tournaments throughout the country. Tragically, at events like the 1948 National Junior Indoor tournament in St. Louis, he was forced to hear crowd members yelling racial slurs at him while he was playing. In spite of these challenges he did well on the court. In the St. Louis tournament he lost in the Quarterfinals to a young man named Tony Trabert (a 1970 ITHF Inductee) who would later become the number 1 player in the world.

Johnson won the ATA Men's Singles Championship in 1950 and was the USLTA Missouri Valley Men's Singles Champion in 1953. In addition, he and Althea Gibson were the first black mixed doubles team to compete in the US Nationals. They reached the quarterfinals of the tournament in 1951 losing to Lou Hoad (1980 ITHF Inductee) and Maureen Connolly (1968 ITHF Inductee).

Johnson was drafted to serve in the Korean War and did not get a chance to play competitive tennis for two full years. His incredible athleticism enabled him to rekindle his game and in 1953, he made history once again by becoming the first African-American tennis player to play in the National Hardcourt Championship. That same year he was able to reach the second round of the US Nationals where he lost to Joseph Davis of the US 8-6, 9-7, 3-6, 4-6, 4-6. Johnson was so good as an adult player that in 1954 tennis legend and promoter Jack Kramer (1968 ITHF Inductee) offered him a contract to become a professional tennis player. Unfortunately, he snapped a tendon in his elbow and had to stop playing for a year. Johnson never fully recovered from the injury and never signed that contract. He is one of the many black tennis players who likely would have become international tennis stars if it were not for the widespread racial discrimination in the sport.

The Class of 2011

Ms. Isadore Channels (Izzy) – In the early 20th Century, the ATA National Championships was one of the most significant events in the African-American community in the United States. People were so anxious to see the best black tennis players they would travel from around the country (and parts of the Caribbean) to the site of the tournament each year. The winners of the men's and women's titles were national heroes. The first twelve years of the ATA Women's Singles Championship was dominated by the following four black tennis icons: Lucy Diggs Slowe (winner in 1917 and 1921), M. Rae (winner in 1918, 1919 and 1920), Lulu Ballard (winner in 1925, 1927 and 1928) and Channels who won the Championship in 1922, 1923, 1924 and 1926.

Channels was born in Louisville, Kentucky on February 1, 1900. In addition, to being an extraordinary tennis player she was also an outstanding basketball player. Channels became a legend in tennis in the black community by becoming the first woman to win four ATA Championships. She also was an excellent doubles player who won the 1924 ATA Women's Doubles Championship.

Ms. Flora Lomax-Bray – In 1938, Lomax won her first ATA Women's Singles Championship. She would go on to win the Championship in 1939, 1941 and 1942. She was an outstanding doubles player who won the ATA Women's Doubles Championship in 1942 and the ATA Mixed Doubles Championship in 1937 and 1940. She played during the "Golden Age" of black tennis where history was being made by stars like Ora Washington, Jimmie McDaniel, Reginald Weir and the Peters Sisters.

Lomax is shown in the photo with Jimmie McDaniel after winning the New York State Mixed Doubles title at the Cosmopolitan Tennis Club in August 1940. Lomax was a darling of the black press who referred to her as the "glamour girl of tennis." They commented on her "pretty white pleated tennis shorts" and socializing with Joe Louis and some of the most famous black celebrities of the day. Lomax is still considered one of the most glamorous champions of women's tennis.

Ms. Lulu Ballard – In 1936, Ballard made history by winning her tenth ATA Women's Doubles Championship. She was an outstanding singles player who won the ATA Women's Singles Championship in 1925, 1927, 1928 and 1936. However, she proved that she was one of the most talented women's doubles players in history by winning the ATA Women's Doubles Championship in 1925, 1926, 1927, 1928, 1929, 1930, 1932, 1934, 1935 and 1936. In addition, she won the ATA Mixed Doubles Championship in 1938. In all likelihood, Ballard would have won many more ATA Singles Championships if she had not played during the time of the incredible Ora Washington. She won her second and third championship the year before Washington won her first championship and she won her last championship in 1936, the year between Washington's seventh and eighth championships. The photo at the right photo was taken at the Pennsylvania Championships in 1939 after her loss to Ora Washington.

Lori McNeil – In 1994, McNeil shocked the tennis world and made history by beating the legendary Steffi Graf 7-5, 6-4 in the first round at Wimbledon. This was the first time in Grand Slam history that a defending champion lost in the first round. Incredibly, this was not the first time that McNeil had beaten Graf in the first round. In the 1992 WTA Tour of Champions, McNeil beat Graf 7-5, 7-6 (7-5). It was the first time since 1985 that Graf lost in the first round of a tournament.

McNeil played on the women's professional tennis tour for 19 years and won a total of 10 singles titles and 33 doubles titles. She reached a career high ranking of number 9 in singles in 1988 and number 4 in doubles in 1987. McNeil never won a Grand Slam singles title. However, she won the 1988 French Open Mixed Doubles Championship with Jorge Lozano and reached the semi-finals of the 1987 US Open (after beating Chris Evert in the

Quarterfinals). She also reached the semi-finals of the 1994 Wimbledon where she lost to eventual champion Conchita Martinez.

McNeil was an extremely talented junior player. In 1978, she won the ATA Girls 14 and 16 Singles Championships. McNeal won the ATA Girls 14 Doubles Championship with Zina Garrison in 1977 and 1978. In 1979, she won the ATA Girls 18 Singles Championship in addition to the US National Girls 18 Doubles Hard Court Championship with Garrison. McNeil won the US National 18 Doubles Indoor, Hard Court and Clay Court Championships with Garrison in 1980. In 1981, she teamed with Garrison once again to win the US National 18 Doubles Indoor and Hard Court Championships. McNeil is one of the most talented black players in history. Her success on the court paved the way for players like Venus and Serena Williams.

Dr. Robert M. Screen – In 1976, as the head coach of the Hampton University men's tennis team, Dr. Screen made history by becoming the first African-American tennis coach to win a NCAA national championship. That Hampton University team won the NCAA Division II National Championship. He coached the Hampton team to another NCAA Division II Championship in 1989. In addition, he led the Hampton team to 1,068 victories making him the all-time winningest coach in NCAA Division I history. In the photo, Dr. Screen accepts his induction certificate and trophy from Black Tennis Hall of Fame Executive Director, Bob Davis, and Founder Dale Caldwell.

From 1985 to 1994, the Hampton Pirates finished as the number 2 ranked tennis team in the NCAA Division II an amazing six times under Dr. Screen's leadership. He also coached the men's team to two Historically Black Colleges and University (HBCU) National Championships and three Virginia Collegiate Championships. His men's tennis teams won seven Mid-Eastern Athletic Conference

(MEAC) titles. Dr. Screen was also the successful coach of the Hampton women's tennis team which won four MEAC titles.

In addition to being an excellent coach who led the tennis team for more than four decades, Dr. Screen was an extraordinary chair of Hampton's Department of Communicative Sciences and Disorders which trained more African-American speech pathologists than any other college in the country. He was a 1953 graduate of Hampton who was inducted into the Hampton University Athletics Hall of Fame in 2009.

Ernie Peterson – In 1968, Peterson began his tennis coaching career with the Boston Parks and Recreation Department. He left that position to coach at the Franklin Field Tennis Center in the Dorchester Section of Boston. He played an instrumental role in helping to establish the legendary Sportsman's Tennis Club as one of the most successful urban tennis programs in the United States. This program successfully kept students from poor households to stay off of the streets, avoid crime and become productive citizens.

In 1976, Peterson founded the Peterson School of Tennis in the College Park, Georgia which expanded on his tremendous work in Boston. This program enhanced the lives of thousands of young people in the Atlanta area. After Peterson's death on April 10, 2010, USTA Executive Director Gordon Smith stated, "Ernie not only developed great players, he developed great human beings. Our thoughts and prayers are with Ernie's family." His daughter Jewel, who was also a student, played on the WTA circuit and took over leadership of the School after his death.

The Class of 2012

Katrina Adams – Althea Gibson was the first African-American to enter and win the US Nationals. Arthur Ashe was the first person to win the US Open. On January 1, 2015, Katrina Adams made equally important history by becoming the first African-American to serve as the chairman of the board, chief executive officer (CEO) and president of the United States Tennis Association (USTA) – the organization that owns and operates all official US national championship tournaments and the US Open. The USTA is the governing body of tennis in the US. Adams was selected because of her successful 10 years of service on the board and instrumental role as First vice president of the board in 2013-2014. Her selection for this role is particularly significant in an organization which had a history of openly discriminating against African Americans by preventing them from participating in their events.

Adams is also the first former professional tennis player to serve as the chairman, president and CEO of the USTA. She was an accomplished professional tennis player who won 20 WTA Tour doubles titles and one ITF singles title. Her 1988 -1999 career high rankings include #8 in doubles and # 67 in singles both in 1989. After retiring from professional tennis, Adams successfully transitioned into coaching and broadcasting. In the coaching arena, from 1999-2002, Katrina served as a national tennis coach for the USTA, coaching and mentoring junior and professional tennis players in all aspects of their careers. Her television career began as a commentator for BET's coverage of the United Negro College Fund Celebrity Golf and Tennis Challenge from 1999-2001. In addition, Adams provided analysis on the international feeds of the 1999 Pilot Pen and Lipton Championships, as well as ESPN's coverage of the 1999 Bausch and Lomb Championships. Since that time, she has served as a tennis analyst for the Tennis Channel and a contributor to *Tennis* Magazine.

Off the courts, Katrina has helped provide strategic direction for the WTA Tour and professional women players worldwide, serving four one-year terms as a player representative on the WTA Tour board of directors and participating in the integration of the WTA Tour, ITF and Players Associations. She also served five two-year terms on the WTA Tour Players Association board of directors in the posts of vice president and treasurer and chairman of the anti-doping committee. Since 2005, Adams has served as the executive director of the Harlem Junior Tennis and Education Program where she helps local children learn tennis and succeed in school and life.

Born and raised in Chicago, Adams started playing tennis at the age of six on the public parks tennis courts. She is pictured here with the Black Tennis Hall of Fame Founder Dale Caldwell and Executive Director Bob Davis. Adams earned a tennis scholarship to Northwestern University where she studied communications and became the Intercollegiate Tennis Association  (ITA) Rookie of the Year in 1986. In 1986 and 1987, she teamed with her college doubles partner Diane Donnelly to amass an incredible two year doubles record of 72-5. In 1987, Adams became the first African-American to win the NCAA Doubles Championship. Adams and Donnelly did not lose a set on their way to the collegiate championship. They were both named to the NCAA All-American team twice (1986 and 1987). Adams was inducted into the Northwestern University Hall of fame in 1998, the USTA Midwest Section Hall of Fame in 2005, the Chicago District Tennis Hall of Fame in 2008 and the Eastern Tennis Hall of Fame in 2015.

David Dinkins – In 1990, David Norman Dinkins made political history by becoming the first and, to date, only African-American Mayor of New York City. He is a passionate tennis fan who has shaped tennis history by using his influence as Mayor to clear barriers to the US Open's growth. In 1994, Mayor Dinkins and his administration negotiated a property lease agreement in Flushing Meadows, New York that benefited both the USTA and the City of New York. This agreement has increased the net profitability of the tournament and enabled it to have a greater positive economic impact on New York City than all of the Yankees, Mets, Rangers and Knicks home games combined. It is one of the reasons that the US Open in Flushing Meadows, Queens is the most financially successful tennis tournament in the world.

Breaking The Barriers

The lease agreement was just one of the ways that Mayor Dinkins has been one of the most important contributors to tennis in New York City. One of the challenges that the US Open faced in Queens was the considerable noise of airplanes taking off from nearby LaGuardia Airport. The players and fans constantly complained about the noise of the planes. Mayor Dinkins and his well-respected administration convinced the Federal Aviation Administration (FAA) to establish special takeoff procedures at La Guardia Airport for the entire 14 day US Open tennis tournament. This change helped to make the tournament even more popular with players and fans. Attendance at the US Open has made it the largest annually occurring sporting event in the world.

Mayor Dinkins is the first African-American to serve six consecutive terms on the USTA board of directors. In this capacity, he played a vitally important role in promoting the growth and development of tennis throughout America (especially in African-American communities).

In the picture below, Mayor Dinkins receives his Black Tennis Hall of Fame Induction Sculpture from Black Tennis Hall of Fame Founder Dale G. Caldwell and Executive Director Bob Davis. Mayor Dinkins was vice-president of the board of the Black Tennis and Sports Foundation and, as a board member of the New York Junior Tennis League, helped to develop the largest community tennis program in the world. He is also on the Advisory board of the Black Leadership Forum and the board of the Nelson Mandela Children's Fund where he promotes the growth and development of tennis in communities of color around the world.

Mayor Dinkins is a living legend who has dedicated his life to helping children, providing leadership in good government and promoting the growth and development of tennis in African-American communities. For the last two decades he has been a true "Tennis Ambassador" supporting efforts to promote tennis in black communities around the world. He was a trusted and cherished friend of the late Arthur Ashe and also deserves to wear the title "Citizen of the World." He has won hundreds of awards for his tremendous leadership and community service. Mayor Dinkins was inducted into the USTA Eastern Tennis Hall of Fame in 1993. Every year he is honored by the New York Open professional tennis tournament when they celebrate *David Dinkins Family Day* on the first Saturday of the tournament.

Ulysses "Pete" Brown – For more than 50 years, legendary "Coach Pete Brown" was one of the leading grass roots tennis program developer in the urban communities of Los Angeles. His influence went well beyond Southern California. Coach Brown became one of the most respected grass roots tennis coaches in the United States. He specialized in inspiring and developing young tennis players in a way that made them great people off of the court. Coach Brown was often called the "Patriarch of West Coast Tennis." He was recognized around the United States for his extraordinary work developing quality

tennis players and people. In 1979, he won the Martin Luther King Community Service Award. In 1987, he won USTA/USPTA Southern California Community Service Award and the California Community College Tennis Coaches Association Coach of the Year Award. In 1989, he won the Outstanding Teacher of the Year Award. That year he also won the Congressional Tribute for Lifetime Achievement and Community Service Activities – Recorded in The House of Representatives Congressional Record on 11/21/89. In 1995, he won the Southern California Tennis Association Lifetime Achievement Award. In 2000, he was inducted into the California Community College Tennis Hall of Fame.

Coach Brown passed away in September 2010. He was so respected by the communities he served that volunteers created the annual Pete Brown Tennis Classic to "Honor the Legacy of Coach Ulysses 'Pete' Brown." In the picture, Willie Emerson accepts the award for the late Coach Pete Brown from Dale G. Caldwell and Bob Davis.

Mark Manning – In 2002, when Manning became the chairman of the board, president and chief executive officer (CEO) of the USTA Northern California board of directors, he made American tennis history by becoming the first African-American president of a USTA Section. The USTA was founded in 1881 and grew to establish 17 sections across the country. Each of these sections are focused on growing the sport of tennis in a particular region of the country. They are governed by an independent board of directors that is led by a volunteer who is board chair, president and CEO of the organization. Over time the budgets and scope of these sections have grown so that they all have a full-time staff and executive directors that report to the CEO and board of directors. The Section president therefore has a great deal of influence over tennis. It took 121 years before Manning broke through barriers of race and class to become the first African-American to lead one of these 17 sections.

A former City of Oakland, California fireman, Manning founded and ran the Elmhurst Youth Tennis Center in inner-city Oakland and spent many years using tennis as the vehicle by which he could have an incredibly positive impact on urban youth. Many of the USTA Northern California Diversity Scholarship recipients have credited Manning for their success on the court and in the classroom. Manning was also a leading voice for "minority

participation" in tennis. He served on committees and worked with the late Oakland Mayor Lionel Wilson toward that end.

Manning was a member and chair of the USTA NorCal Junior Council. In addition, he was a recipient of many USTA national, sectional and community awards. In 1992, Manning was honored by USTA NorCal with the Service to Tennis Award, which recognized his significant contributions to the game of tennis over a period of many years. In 2013, Manning was inducted into the USTA Northern California Tennis Hall of Fame.

Tennis was a central part of Manning's life and sadly, on March 29, 2012, he passed away at the age of 53 while on a rail journey with some of his tennis students to Reno. In many ways it was fitting that Manning passed away while on a tennis trip with some of the young people he mentored. He was a true innovator and champion for the youth of Northern California. The picture on the left depicts Manning's

sisters, Cleo Simon and Lillie Ferguson speaking during Manning's (posthumous) Black Tennis Hall of Fame Induction ceremony.

Margaret "Pete" Peters and Matilda Roumania "Repeat" Peters

Known affectionately as "Pete and Repeat," the Peters sisters dominated the ATA Women's Doubles circuit by winning 14 ATA Women's Doubles Championships. They won the ATA National Women's Doubles titles in 1938, 1939, 1940, 1941, 1944, 1945, 1946, 1947, 1948, 1949, 1950, 1951, 1952 and 1953. The Peters sisters were known for their powerful slice serves, strong backhands and tremendous consistency. They have been inducted into the Black Tennis Hall of Fame as a pair because their ATA Doubles Championship victory streak of 1938 to 1941 and 1944 to 1953 will likely never be broken. They will be remembered as one of the most dominant doubles teams of all times.

Breaking The Barriers

The Peters sisters were both born in Washington, D.C. Margaret was born in 1915 and Roumania was born in 1917. They both graduated from Tuskegee in 1941 with physical education degrees and spent most of their professional lives as teachers. In addition to being a doubles star, Roumania Peters was also a successful singles player who won the 1944 ATA Women's Singles Championship. In 1946, she won her second ATA Women's Singles Championship and became the only African-American woman to beat Althea Gibson in a major tournament.

The sisters did not receive widespread recognition until they were in their 80s. The USTA honored the legendary players during the 2003 Federation Cup quarterfinals in Washington, DC on July 19th and 20th. They were both inducted into the Mid-Atlantic Section Tennis Hall of Fame on November 15, 2003.

Ronald Charity – In addition to being the best black tennis player in Richmond, VA. in the 50 s, Ron Charity is recognized as being the man who first discovered and encouraged a young Arthur Ashe. After learning to play tennis in Richmond's Brookfield Park, Ashe, at the age of 7, attracted the attention of Charity, who was

serving as a part-time tennis coach at the time. Charity was so impressed with Ashe's game and attitude that he arranged for him to spend the summers at the Lynchburg home of Dr. Walter Johnson who received widespread recognition as the coach of Althea Gibson. Dr. Johnson became Ashe's coach and mentor and, with Charity and a few others, became the architects of the American Tennis Association's formal Junior Development Program. Charity was also instrumental in the creation of a network of families who offered family to family (no-cost) housing to players traveling on the ATA circuit. In the top photo, Charity is pictured with Dr. Whirlwind Johnson in 1964. In the middle photo, Charity flashes his legendary smile. In the bottom photo, Ron's son Khris Charity accepts the Black Tennis Hall of Fame Induction Trophy from Dale G. Caldwell and Bob Davis.

The Class of 2013

Lucille Freeman – Those individuals who have worked behind the scenes to support black tennis legends are often overlooked. Lucille Freeman was a pioneer in the Washington, DC area for black players.

She served as hostess to many up and coming tennis players – providing room and board and transportation during their visit to the ATA tournament in Washington DC. Freeman exemplified everything that is good about tennis as she imparted the love of the game to her sons, Clyde (who became president of the ATA), Harold and Thomas. She became a legend herself by becoming the primary contact person for black tennis in the Washington, DC area. Freeman's nomination and induction into the Black Tennis Hall of Fame is particularly pleasing to many of the black tennis legends who are still alive because they were among the hundreds of beneficiaries of her hospitality and generosity.

Breaking The Barriers

Virginia Glass – In 1991, Glass made history by becoming the first female president of the American Tennis Association (ATA). She served as president for two two-year terms. In addition, Glass was the first woman of color to serve on the USTA executive committee. In 1969, she co-founded the Mountain View Tennis Club in San Diego, CA and was one of the original founders of the San Diego District Tennis Association. Glass's long service with this influential organization included serving as president and at-large board member. She was also one of the original founders of the San Diego Umpires Association and served as a West Coast editor for *Black Tennis* Magazine. In 1988, Glass won the Women's 60-and-over division of the International Tennis Federation Veterans Championship. In 2008,  Glass received the "Lifetime Achievement Award" from the Southern California Tennis Association (SCTA) for her work with local tennis organizations and Community Development.

Glass served on the ATA's junior development committee and as a board member of the Black Tennis & Sports Foundation. Over the last 70 plus years, she has volunteered at virtually every level of organized tennis both in the ATA and the USTA. In addition to her volunteer work, Glass was a very successful tennis parent who is the proud mother of Sidney and Luis Glass, both of whom were top junior players in the USTA Eastern Section. Sidney Glass played tennis at the University of Wisconsin and Luis Glass went on to be an All-American tennis player at UCLA. In 2010, Glass was inducted into the San Diego Tennis Hall of Fame.

Sydney Llewellyn – Nicknamed "Mr. Tennis," Llewellyn coached and managed many of the best black tennis players in the country during and immediately after racial segregation in the sport. The players he worked with included: Althea Gibson, Arthur Ashe, Wilbert Davis, Robert Davis, Arthur Carrington, Donald Ringgold, Tom Jones, Michael O'kala, Louis and Sydney Glass and many others. Llewellyn was born in the Caribbean and worked as a New York City taxi driver when he first came to the US in 1930. He started teaching tennis at the courts in Harlem (affectionately called the "Jungle") in the mid-1940s. These legendary courts are located at 151st Street and 7th Avenue. Llewellyn also became a member of the Cosmopolitan Tennis Club where he lectured and taught many outstanding black tennis players.

Llewellyn played an important role as Althea Gibson's touring manager and coach. He helped to guide her to five Grand Slam titles (1956 French, 1957 and 1958 Wimbledon, and, 1957 and 1958 US). He also started her professional tennis career by arranging for her to get paid to play matches before the Harlem Globetrotters basketball games. In 1983 Llewellyn married Althea Gibson. However, their marriage ended in divorce in 1988.

Llewellyn was a tennis innovator in every sense of the word. He wrote a fascinating article called "The Theory of Correct Returns" which described a unique winning strategy for tennis. Llewellyn was an inventor who developed a product called "Equiform." This elastic cable device helped players achieve ideal stroke production. In addition, he founded the first prize money tournament for African Americans in Myrtle Beach, South Carolina. Llewellyn also originated the "Turkey Tournament," an event designed for players that had never won a tournament. He made history by becoming the first black United States Professional Tennis Association (USPTA) certified teaching professional. Llewellyn received a lot of awards throughout his life. However, one of the most prestigious was his induction into the USTA Eastern Tennis Hall of Fame in 1993.

John Harding Lucas II – In 1976, as a student at the University of Maryland, Lucas made history by becoming the first African-American to be selected to the collegiate All-American teams in both basketball and tennis. Born in Durham, North Carolina in 1953 to two educators, Lucas learned at an early age that he had talent in both tennis and basketball. He broke basketball legend Pete Maravich's all-time

Breaking The Barriers

North Carolina high school scoring record. In addition, at 17, Lucas was named to the Junior Davis Cup tennis team. He received more than 350 college scholarship offers to play basketball and/or tennis. However, he chose to attend the University of Maryland because he wanted to play both sports at a school with a strong basketball and tennis team. Schools like UCLA wanted him to focus on either basketball or tennis. Lucas was an extraordinary collegiate basketball star who became the all-time high scorer in the University of Maryland's basketball history and won the Atlantic Coast Conference Singles Championship in tennis in 1974 and 1975.

Lucas represented the U.S. and won a bronze medal at the FIBA World Basketball Championships in 1974 and a gold medal at the Pan American Games in 1975. In spite of his extraordinary success on the basketball court by the time he graduated from Maryland, Lucas was still undecided as to which of the two sports he would pursue. However, when he was chosen in the first round of the 1976 National Basketball Association (NBA) draft by the Houston Rockets he chose to pursue a full-time professional basketball career. Lucas played in the NBA for 14 years and was a member of the 1986 Houston Rockets team that made it to the NBA finals, where they lost to the Boston Celtics. He is also currently 24th on the all-time career assists list. Lucas served as the head coach of the San Antonio Spurs (1992-1994); vice president and general manager of the Philadelphia 76ers (1994-1996); assistant coach of the Denver Nuggets (1999-2002); and, head coach of the Cleveland Cavaliers (2002-2004).

Lucas did play some professional tennis during the off-season of his pro basketball career. In addition to serving on the Black Tennis & Sports Foundation board, he competed in seven Grand Prix professional tennis tournaments. In 1973, in the Louisville, Kentucky Grand Prix tournament, Lucas lost in the round of 64 to Geoff Masters of Australia 1-6, 0-6. In the same tournament, Lucas and John Whitlinger lost to Bill Bowrey and Dick Crealy of Australia 1-6, 4-6 in the round of 32.

In the 1973 Merion, PA Grand Prix tournament he lost to Jeff Austin 4-6, 4-6. In that same tournament, in the round of 16 doubles event, Lucas and Vic Seixas lost to John Paish of Britain and Jeff Simpson of Australia 6-3, 1-6, 3-6. In the 1979 San Jose Grand Prix tournament, he lost in the Round of 32 to John James of Australia 3-6, 2-6. In the 1979 Raleigh Grand Prix tournament, he lost in the round of 64 to Gordon Jones of the US 1-6, 1-6. In that same tournament, Lucas and Fred McNair IV lost in the semifinals to John Austin and Billy Martin 5-7, 1-6.

Lucas had success playing World Team Tennis with the San Francisco Golden Gaters in 1976 and the New Orleans Sun Belt Nets in 1978. In addition, in 1975, he was the head coach of the Houston Wranglers, a team that included tennis legend Steffi Graf as its star player. In the 1980s, Lucas also coached legendary professional tennis player and 2011 Black Tennis Hall of Fame Inductee Lori McNeal.

James "Jimmy" Smith – Smith was one of the founding members of the Sportsman's Tennis Club (STC) in Boston, Massachusetts and served as the Head Coach and CEO of the organization for several years. The Sportsman's Tennis Club brought tennis into the lives of thousands of Greater Boston residents young and old since it was founded in 1961. This extraordinary youth program improved the lives of participants by helping them develop their academic, health and social skills. Hundreds of the young men and women  graduating from the STC program have attended college on full or partial tennis scholarships. Thousands more participants have discovered strength, courage and self-determination off the courts as added benefits of their work on the court. Club founders Jimmy and Gloria Smith were true innovators in community tennis. In 1989, they organized a Sportsman's USA/Soviet Union Goodwill Tennis Tour which enabled STC juniors to travel to and to play in the Soviet Union.

Breaking The Barriers

STC is legendary for more than its tennis programs. In 1998, Harvard University's Men's Tennis Team made history by playing its first match in the poorest section of Boston against Penn State at Sportsman's Tennis Club. It is estimated that more than 40,000 youngsters have benefitted from the STC activities and events. These unique programs helped participants learn valuable lessons about tennis and life. When growing up in Boston, Jimmy played just about every sport except tennis. He learned to love the game the game later in life and became determined to play tennis even though it was almost unheard of among urban blacks at the time. He described tennis as "Opening the doors to a whole new world." His focus and determination opened those doors to tens of thousands of children whose lives have been enriched due to his vision.

Both Jim and Gloria have passed away, but the Sportsman's Tennis Club continues to provide leadership and guidance to the children of Boston. Jimmy Smith received a lot of awards throughout his life. However, his induction into the USTA New England Tennis Hall of Fame in 1993 was one of his greatest honors.

Bessie Stockard – In 1971, Stockard won her first and only ATA Woman's Singles Championship. She went on to win 12 ATA national titles in a combination of events including: women's singles, women's doubles, mixed doubles, senior woman's singles and doubles. She was one of the best tennis players in the country and had an opportunity to play on the Virginia Slims women's professional tennis tour from 1971 to 1974. Stockard was twice chosen to represent the Mid-Atlantic tennis team in the Mid-Atlantic Sears Cup. She qualified and represented Washington, DC on two occasions in the Senior Olympics. She was tennis coach for the Montgomery College Women's Intercollegiate tennis team and led that team to two NCAA national championship tournaments. Stockard is a two-time Regional XX Tennis Coach of the Year and is founder and director of the Bessie Stockard Girls and Boys Three-Sport

Camps. This camp provided basketball, tennis and swimming training for participants.

Stockard was inducted into the Eastern board of Officials Hall of Fame in 1998, the Tuskegee University Sports Hall of Fame in 1993, the District of Columbia Sports Hall of Fame in 2012, and the USTA Mid Atlantic Section Hall of Fame in 2013. She made history by becoming the first African-American female tennis player to integrate the Bitsy Grant Tennis Club (Atlanta, GA) and the Kenwood Country Club (Bethesda, MD).

The Class of 2014

Edgar G. Brown - Brown was an extraordinary tennis player who was the ATA Men's Singles Champion in 1922, 1923, 1928 and 1929. He was also one of the earliest practitioners of topspin, which dominates modern tennis. Brown also has the dubious distinction in the ATA of receiving a one year suspension for refusing to play due to darkness. He believed that continuing to play as the sunlight began to fade hindered play and further, could result in serious injury. So he refused to play a match and was suspended for a year.

Brown was one of the leading tennis activists of his day. He felt strongly that black players should not be content with winning ATA championships. Brown openly expressed his belief that there should be a strong societal push to allow black players to enter white only tournaments like the US Nationals at Forest Hills and Wimbledon. Unfortunately, he was not successful in convincing the white governing bodies to integrate these tournaments when he was a player. However, he became a legend of black tennis because of his extraordinary talents on the court and his fight to eliminate tennis segregation off of the court by advocating for more black tennis administrators.

Breaking The Barriers

Bob Davis – In 2008, Davis made history as the first executive director of the Black Tennis Hall of Fame. In this capacity, he has managed the day-to-day operations of this organization dedicated to recording and promoting tennis history. Born in New York City, Davis was a 2-time ATA National Champion. He won the Boys 18 ATA Junior National title in 1961. In addition, he won the ATA Men's Doubles Championship with his brother in 1962, 2009 Black Tennis Hall of Fame Inductee Billy Davis. A Life member of the ATA, Davis competed in the U.S. National Championships at Forest Hills, was the USTA Mixed Doubles National Champion in 2006 and the ATA 70 and over Men's Doubles Champion in 2015.

Off the court, Bob leased the largest private tennis club in New York State in the '70s and managed his family-owned sleep-over tennis Academy in the 80s. He then helped to create and was national program director for the Ashe/Bollettieri "Cities" Tennis Program (ABC) which later became the Arthur Ashe Safe Passage Foundation. As CEO, this program introduced tennis to more than 20,000 inner-city children and provided health screenings, tutoring and academic support to these children in 10 U.S. cities across America. Once the Safe Passage Foundation closed its doors, Bob created Black Dynamics, Inc., which offered scholarships for the most talented minority youth to the IMG Bollettieri Tennis Academy. The founding belief of Black Dynamics was that youngsters needed world class competition in order to reach world class performance. Two alumni of Black Dynamics represented the United States on the Federation Cup Team. Bob then created the Panda Foundation, Inc. (www.thepandafoundation.com). The Panda Foundation, modeled after the extremely successful Safe Passage Foundation, provides introductory tennis instruction to more than 500 urban youth each year. These underserved youth also receive dental and health related services as well as mentoring by local professionals. All Panda programs are free to the children. Bob also coaches professional players and served as the coach of the Jamaican Davis Cup Team in 2013.

Dr. Hubert A. Eaton, Sr. - In 1932, at the age of 15, Eaton made history by being the first African-American to win the North Carolina Interscholastic Tennis Championships. In 1933, he proved he was one of the best black junior players in the country by winning the Boys 18 ATA National Championship. Eaton added to his legendary status by becoming the Colored Intercollegiate Athletic Association (which is now called the Central Intercollegiate Athletic Association or "CIAA") Singles Champion in 1936. Eaton and George Stewart won the ATA Men's Doubles Championship in 1948, 1949, 1951 and 1956. In 1946, Dr. Eaton took Althea Gibson into his home, providing the structure and discipline that allowed her to attend and graduate from High School. He provided tennis instruction on his home tennis court and, along with Dr. Robert Johnson, directed her early ATA career. Eaton was a successful ATA president during a critical period in the organization's development. He served in this role from 1960 to 1970 and helped the organization maintain relevance at a time when tennis was becoming integrated.

Eaton was an excellent student. He graduated from Johnson C. Smith University in 1937 and wanted to go to medical school in North Carolina to continue his education. Unfortunately, African Americans were not admitted to any of North Carolina's medical schools. He therefore attended the University of Michigan and earned his M.D. in 1942. Eaton actively fought for integration both on and off of the tennis court. In his native Wilmington, N.C., Dr. Eaton led efforts to desegregate Wilmington College (forerunner of the University of North Carolina, Wilmington), the YMCA, the Municipal Golf Course and the County Library System. He served on the board of Trustees of the University of North Carolina, Wilmington, serving as chairman in 1981. Dr. Eaton ran for a seat on the New Hanover County board of Education in 1952, 1954 and 1956. He lost those races but made history by becoming the first African America to run for public office in New Hanover County since the 1890s. Dr. Eaton was a leading local civil rights activist and sued New Hanover County to provide equal funding for black public schools. This successful litigation led to the eventual desegregation of the County School System. In 1984, Eaton was inducted into the North Carolina Tennis Hall of Fame for his accomplishments as a tremendous tennis player and outstanding leader.

Mary Etta Fine and Eva Belle Bracy - Mary Etta was born in Kansas City, Kansas in 1924. Two years later her sister Eva Belle was born. Their older brother, Leo introduced both girls to tennis. The sisters were extraordinary players who won the ATA National Women's Doubles championship in 1955, 1957 and 1958. Mary Etta also won the ATA Mixed Doubles National Championship in 1951 with her brother and mentor Leo and the ATA Women's Singles Championship in 1958. During the height of her tennis career, Mary Etta became Althea Gibson's dear friend and fiercest rival.

Both sisters graduated from college with degrees in education and became school teachers in the Kansas City area. Eva Belle Bracy started playing tennis at the age of 14. She was fortunate to have her sister Mary Etta and her brother Leo as hitting and training partners. She was a spirited and determined athlete, however, and played several other sports. In addition to the National titles that she earned with her sister, Eva's son Theron played college tennis on scholarship at Kansas City Kansas Community College and Baker University.

Richard Hudlin - Richard made history by playing tennis for the University of Chicago from 1926 to 1928. He served as captain of the 1928 team, establishing himself as the first African-American to serve as captain of a tennis team at a "Big Ten" college. This accomplishment is made even more remarkable when one realizes that Richard was the only black man on the team from 1926-1928. But, he didn't stop there. In 1945 he filed a lawsuit against the Muny

Tennis Association of St. Louis to open public tennis facilities to all players, most particularly to players of color. He won the legal battle, thus enabling Blacks to participate in tournaments at St. Louis municipal facilities. Champions Althea Gibson and Arthur Ashe spent time with Mr. Hudlin in St. Louis honing their skills at the Armory tennis courts. On the slick, lightning-fast wood surface, Arthur was transformed from a backcourt player into a serve-volley specialist, a game that would serve him well during his professional career.

Arthur completed his final year of High School at Sumner High under Mr. Hudlin's tutelage. Mr. Hudlin spent 36 years as the coach at Sumner High School. In addition, he served as the president of the Muny Tennis Association and was the first black member of the St. Louis District Tennis Association. In addition to coaching Ashe and Gibson, Hudlin coached Bruce Foxworth and Juan Farrow. He was a champion as well as a champion maker. Hudlin was a teacher, leader, mentor, supporter, donator and defender. He passed away in 1976, living long enough to see both Althea Gibson and Arthur Ashe win the U.S. Open and the prestigious Wimbledon titles. In 1992, Hudlin was inducted into the St. Louis Tennis Hall of Fame. In 2015, he was inducted into the USTA Missouri Valley Tennis Association Tennis Hall of Fame.

Lendward Simpson - In 1964, Simpson made history by becoming the first African-American to win the USLTA Eastern Boy's 14 singles title at Forest Hills. This was a particularly significant achievement because he defeated future pro tennis legend Dick Stockton in the finals. This extraordinary accomplishment enabled Simpson, ate the age of 15, to become the youngest male to ever compete in the US National Championships at Forest Hills in 1964. He also played in the US National Championships in 1965 and 1966. In 1967, he continued his extraordinary junior career by winning the

ATA National Boys Singles and Doubles Championships. Simpson was able to use his exceptional tennis talents to enhance his education. He attended Cheshire Academy on a tennis scholarship and played #1 singles, and because of his extraordinary tennis accomplishments, was the first person inducted into their athletic hall of fame. In 1967, Simpson won the National Prep School Championship. He was one of the best players in the country  throughout his junior career as evidenced by his top 10 national ranking in the USLTA in every junior age group for both singles and doubles.

While at Eastern Tennessee State University, Lenny played #1 singles for three years and was ranked #1 in the Ohio Valley Conference for three consecutive years. In 1964 and 1965 Simpson and Luis Glass won the ATA Men's Doubles Championship. In addition, Simpson and 2009 Black Tennis Hall of Fame Inductee Bonnie Logan won the ATA National Mixed Doubles Championship four consecutive times from 1967-1970.

In 1974, Simpson made history once again by becoming the first African-American to play World Team Tennis, signing with the Detroit Loves. He was inducted into the North Carolina Tennis Hall of Fame in 2012 and the Greater Wilmington Sports Hall of Fame in 2013. Simpson continues to give back to the tennis community and support future tennis champions. The not-for-profit tennis program that Simpson currently leads serves more than 200 children per week in the Wilmington, North Carolina community.

Henry Talbert – Tennis is one of the most popular sports in the world because of incredibly talented athletes and extraordinary administrators. Unfortunately, tennis fans rarely recognize those individuals who, behind the scenes, do the hard work that enable talented tennis players to become legends. Henry Talbert is one of those individuals who, quietly behind the scenes, helped to diversify the leadership of the sport and grow the game. After graduating from

 UCLA and serving in Vietnam, he became the National Urban League's director of veterans affairs. A life-long tennis player with a game developed on the public park courts in Los Angeles and at Dorsey High School, Talbert began his legendary service to the USTA in 1974. He made history by becoming the first African-American to be a USTA administrator on the national level.

Talbert demonstrated his extraordinary leadership skills by developing and running successful national tennis programs in the USTA's headquarters in New York City, Princeton, NJ and White Plains, NY. He felt a calling to leave the USTA national office and become the executive director of the USTA Southern California Section in 1997. He held that position until he retired in 2013. 2002 ITHF Inductee Pam Shriver, who is part of the broadcasting team for the Australian Open television, said from Melbourne, "I feel fortunate to have known Henry for decades from East coast to West coast. Henry's love of tennis was only surpassed by his love of family and friends."

Talbert set a moral, ethical and quality standard that tennis leaders, along with everyone in the game, should aspire to achieve. He was a caring and loving individual who opened doors of opportunity for most of today's new crop of US tennis administrators and mentored every African-American who held leadership positions in the USTA.

His passing in January of 2014 was treated in the world of tennis administrators the same way the passing of a pro player who won all four of the Grand Slam Championships would be treated by tennis fans. He was a true gentleman who raised the bar of administrative leadership in the sport of tennis.

The Class of 2015

Nick Bolletieri – In 1978, Bolletieri purchased a 23 acre tomato farm to start the Nick Bollettieri Tennis Academy. He has become a tennis legend by expanding on the high-performance tennis camp model made popular by coaching legends like Harry Hopman and John

Newcombe. In a relatively short period of time after the camp opened, he was able to convince some of the United States' best junior players to come to the camp to compete against each other. Young players like Andre Agassi, Jim Courier, Chip Hooper, Pete Sampras, Martin Blackman, Maria Sharapova, Monica Seles, Anna Kournikova and many others helped to make the camp the legendary success it has become. Over the years there have been a lot of high-performance tennis camps. However, the Nick Bolletieri Tennis Academy is arguably the most successful of all time because it includes ten world number 1 players among its alumni. These players included Andre Agassi, Boris Becker, Jim Courier, Martina Hingis, Jelena Jankovic, Marcelo Rios, Monica Seles, Maria Sharapova, Serena Williams and Venus Williams. In addition, Bolletieri alumni and former professional player Martin Blackman is the Head of Player Development for the USTA.

Establishing a world class tennis training camp was not enough for Bolletieri. He had a personal passion for growing the game in nontraditional communities. In 1987, after meeting with Arthur Ashe to discuss the lack of black tennis players on the professional tennis circuit, he and Ashe decided to create the Ashe/Bollettieri "Cities" Tennis Program (ABC). This unique national tennis organization established well-run instructional programs in urban communities across the United States. The programs were operated in Albany, New York; Kansas City, Kansas; Kansas City, Missouri; Los Angeles, California; Newark, New Jersey; and, New York, New York. The program was later renamed the Arthur Ashe Safe Passage Foundation and ran for 13 years. During this time more than 20,000 students from urban communities were taught tennis, tutored and received health education. Many of those students have paid forward what they learned in this program and are teaching in or supporting urban tennis programs around the world.

Bolletieri was inducted into the Tennis Industry Hall of Fame in 2012, the United States Professional Tennis Association (USPTA) Hall of Fame in 2013 and the International Tennis Hall of Fame in 2014. He was inducted into the Black Tennis Hall of Fame (BTHOF) in 2015 because of his legendary commitment to growing tennis in urban and black communities in the United States. He invested hundreds of thousands of dollars of his personal money and valuable time to ensure that this program was a success. Thanks to Ashe and Bolletieri's efforts in this program, which was led by BTHOF executive director Bob Davis, tens of thousands of young people graduated from college, received college scholarships, became great tennis players and most importantly, became productive citizens of the world.

Angela Buxton – In 1956, Buxton made history by winning the French Woman's Doubles Championship with Althea Gibson. She therefore played an important role in helping Althea Gibson become the first African-American to win a Grand Slam tournament doubles championship. Buxton and Gibson went on to win the Wimbledon Women's Doubles Championship that year as well. In 1953 and 1957, she won the Women's Singles title at the Maccabiah Games for Jewish athletes. People of Jewish descent were not admitted to the All England Lawn Tennis Club where Wimbledon was played until 1952. In addition, they faced discrimination on the world tennis tour. The racism that Gibson experienced and the anti-Semitism that Buxton experienced brought them together on the tennis tour. When they won the Wimbledon Women's Doubles Championship one British newspaper used the unfortunate headline "Minorities Win" to call attention to their victory.

Buxton was an excellent singles player who reached the 1956 Wimbledon Women's Finals. Prior to that accomplishment, she won the English Indoor title, the London Grass Court singles championships and the English Hard Court Doubles title with Darlene Hard. She reached the semi-finals of the Women's Singles division of French Championships in 1956 (the same year she and Gibson won the Women's Doubles Championship).

Buxton was inducted into the International Jewish Sports Hall of Fame in 1981 and the National Jewish Sports Hall of Fame in 2014. She was inducted into the Black Tennis Hall of Fame to honor her for risking the alienation of her peers by providing the friendship, guidance, support and encouragement that Althea Gibson needed to become the first black global tennis champion. Her love for Gibson was so deep that Buxton led the charge to raise money for Gibson when she was very sick and destitute near the end of her life.

Dale Gilbert Caldwell – In 2007, Caldwell made history by founding the Black Tennis Hall of Fame (BTHOF) in New Brunswick, New Jersey. This organization, which has been managed by Executive Director Bob Davis since 2009, has become the premier black tennis history organization in the world. Prior to this accomplishment, in 2006, he made history by becoming the first African-American to serve as the president and chief executive officer (CEO) of the USTA Eastern Section that was responsible for growing tennis in New York State, Northern New Jersey and Southern Connecticut. When he led in the hiring of D.A. Abrams, the USTA Eastern Section became the first and only section ever led by an African-American

president and CEO and an African-American executive director. In 2011, Caldwell made history by becoming the first and only African-American to serve as a Section president and CEO and then as a member of the USTA board of directors.

Caldwell's father, the late Reverend Gilbert Haven Caldwell, Junior knew and marched with Dr. Martin Luther King, Junior. Consequently, he grew up around the Civil Rights Movement and developed a deep passion for black history in the United States. His love for tennis and positive experience playing in the ATA junior circuit inspired him to use his influence as the first black president of the USTA Eastern (one of the most powerful sections in the USTA) to convince the International Tennis Hall of Fame (ITHF) to honor the black players who were not allowed to compete at the highest levels of tennis because of their race. In 2006, shortly after becoming Section president, Caldwell, wrote letters to the ITHF President Tony Trabert and the ITHF Executive Director Mark Stenning describing how Major League Baseball has successfully honored Negro League baseball players. In the letter, he encouraged them to consider developing an exhibit to honor black tennis players and the American Tennis Association (ATA). In addition, he reached out to legendary tennis columnist and commentator Bud Collins to encourage him to speak with Trabert and Stenning about Caldwell's exhibit idea.

His efforts paid off and the ITHF agreed to develop the exhibit with the museum director developing the exhibit and Caldwell as the curator. Former ATA champion Art Carrington was one of the players that Caldwell admired most when he was growing up. When he learned of Carrington's passion for tennis history he convinced the ITHF Museum Director Gary Cogar to allow Carrington to serve as Co-Curator of the Exhibit. Cogar, Caldwell and Carrington made history by developing the legendary ITHF touring exhibit on black tennis history called "Breaking the Barriers." This exhibit, which includes an award-winning film, was introduced at the 2007 US Open where 35,000 people viewed it. It is historic because it is the first major exhibit to chronicle the history of black tennis from the late 1800s to the 1970s. It has become the most successful touring exhibit in ITHF history.

Caldwell has become an internationally recognized tennis historian because of his curation of the *Breaking the Barriers* Exhibit; co-authoring the book *Breaking the Barriers* with the ITHF in 2016; and, co-authoring the book *Tennis in New York* with Nancy Gill McShea in 2010. In 2013, he founded the *New York Open* tennis tournament at the legendary West Side Tennis Club in Forest Hills. This tournament has become the professional tennis championship of New York City. In 2015, he founded the Global Tennis Alliance, LLC which has established a series of independent professional tennis tournaments around the world called the *"Open Tennis Tour."*

He is also an accomplished player who earned national rankings as a junior in the 18 and under division of the ATA and in the 40 and over division of the USTA. In addition, he has been a certified Professional 1 with the United States Professional Tennis Association (USPTA) for 40 years and certified teaching professional with the Professional Tennis Registry (PTR) for 5 years. In 2010, he was awarded the *Tennis Educational Merit Award* by the ITHF for his volunteer work on the *Breaking the Barriers* Exhibit and with the USTA.

Arthur "Art" Carrington – In 1972, Carrington made history by participating in the first televised ATA Men's Singles Championship match. He lost an incredibly close five set match to Horace Reid that was televised on Boston Public Television. Legendary broadcaster Bud Collins was the color commentator for that historic match. Carrington may have lost that match; however, he went on to win the ATA Men's Singles Championship in 1973. He was an extremely talented

player who was a frequent practice partner of Arthur Ashe. In addition, throughout Carrington's professional tennis career, he competed against and/or practiced with legendary players Bjorn Borg, Vitas Gerulaitis, Rod Laver and other top professional tennis players at the time. In addition, he coached Vera Zvonareva who, under his tutelage became the number 2 women's tennis player in the world.

Carrington was recruited to Hampton College (now Hampton University) because of his tennis skills and, in 1965, became the first student to receive a full athletic scholarship. In 1966, his freshman year, he lost in the finals of the Central Intercollegiate Athletic Association (CIAA) Championship. However, he went on to win the CIAA Championship three years in a row. After graduating from Hampton in 1968, Carrington became the first head tennis pro hired at the Westfield Indoor Tennis Club in Westfield, New Jersey.

Carrington was a tennis legend on the tennis court because of his smooth tennis strokes. However, since retiring from professional tournament play, he has become one of the best known black tennis historians. His enthusiasm for black tennis history is contagious. He currently has the largest collection of "Negro Newspapers" covering the ATA National Championship. Carrington, also made history by co-curating, with Dale G. Caldwell, the International Tennis Hall of Fame (ITHF) touring exhibit on black tennis history entitled "Breaking the Barriers." This exhibit, which includes an award winning film and debuted at the 2007 US Open where 35,000 people viewed it, is the first major exhibit to chronicle the history of black tennis from the late 1800s to the 1970s. It has become the most successful touring exhibit in ITHF history. In 2009, Carrington published the book *Black Tennis, An Archival Collection: 1890-1962*. This popular book featured fascinating newspaper accounts of the ATA, tennis pioneers and black tennis clubs.

Carrington is currently the president of the New England Tennis Association (NETA). He runs the Carrington Tennis Academy based at Hampshire College in Amherst, Massachusetts. Since founding the tennis camp in 1980, the academy has helped more than 2,000 students improve their tennis skills.

Breaking The Barriers

Marcus Freeman – In 1977, Freeman made history by publishing *Black Tennis Magazine* (now called *BT Magazine*), the most successful black tennis magazine in history. This publication has covered many of the most important events and people in modern black tennis history. Freeman spent much of his career as a school teacher and administrator. However, late in his career, Freeman became the Head Tennis Pro and Manager of the Kierst Tennis Center in Dallas, Texas. When asked what prompted him to publish *Black Tennis Magazine*, Freeman stated, "One major tournament in the state of Texas was won by a couple of black youngsters who were victorious in both singles and doubles, but received no coverage in the media. It appeared at the time that the news media intentionally omitted the names of these

black youngsters because of their race. This led me to conclude that this type of racial discrimination occurred throughout the United States. This discovery convinced me to create *Black Tennis Magazine* to correct this wrong." The magazine was supported financially by advertisements from local banks, sporting goods stores, tennis equipment manufacturers and other businesses.

Freeman achieved his goal of creating a magazine that filled an information void in black tennis. The magazine has been, for decades, the leading source of information about black tennis. The first edition of *BT Magazine* was focused on covering major tournaments in Texas and the Southwest. The magazine was initially an 8 page publication in newspaper format that primarily covered players in the Southwest Athletic Conference (SWAC), which was composed of Prairie View A&M University, Texas Southern University, Southern University, Alcorn A&M and Mississippi Valley State University. Freeman later decided to highlight black tennis players who had the potential to succeed in the predominantly white USTA tournaments. He was therefore able to publish stories about many of the most promising young black players in public schools, colleges and universities.

Starting with the coverage of the ATA national Championship in New Orleans, Louisiana in 1977, the magazine had interesting stories of the most prominent people in black tennis throughout the United States. Some of the players that were profiled in early editions of *BT Magazine* included: 2008 Black Tennis Hall of Fame Inductees Althea Gibson and Arthur Ashe; 2009 BTHOF Inductee Zina Garrison; 2010 BTHOF Inductee Leslie Allen; 2011 BTHOF Inductee Lori McNeal; 2013 BTHOF Inductee John Lucas; 2015 BTHOF Inductee John Wilkerson; the 1975 ATA and 1975 National Association of Intercollegiate Athletics (NAIA) Men's Singles Champion Benny Sims; 1976 and 1977 ATA Men's Singles Champion Terence Jackson; 1978 ATA Singles and Doubles Championship Finalist Cedric Loeb; Juan Farrow, 1978 NCAA Division II Men's Singles Champion; and, Herbert Provost, Texas Southern University tennis coach and SWAC Coach of the Year in 1971-1972.

In 2000, the magazine became a 32 page publication and added legendary tennis teaching professional Vic Braden to its staff. This change made the publication more popular than ever. It included sections on general tennis news, pro tennis, instruction, college tennis, the ATA and junior development. The 2013 edition of *BT* Magazine featured the First Lady of the United States Michelle Obama and described her efforts to influence more Americans to adopt a healthy lifestyle which included playing lifelong sports like tennis. This 104 page issue was the largest ever produced. Thanks to Freeman's efforts, the world has a written record of many of the most important stories in black tennis over the last 50 years.

Chip Hooper – In 1986, Hooper became the second African-American man (behind Arthur Ashe) to earn a global top 20 ranking. On April 19, 1982, Hooper achieved a career high ranking of number 17 in the world in Singles. On December 8, 1986 he reached a career high doubles ranking of 18 in the world. An extraordinary tennis player with one

of the most powerful serves in tennis history, Hooper was the best African-American men's tennis player on the professional tennis tour for many years.

He was one of the most successful black junior players in history. In 1971, his USLTA national rankings included number 3 in Boy's 12 Singles and number 1 in Boys 12 Doubles (with Juan Farrow). In 1977, Hooper was ranked number 17 nationally in Boys 18 Singles in the USLTA. He was twice named to the US Junior Davis Cup Team and, as a two-time All-American at the University of Arkansas, was the top seed in the 1981 NCAA Championship. Hooper was the first Arkansas student-athlete to achieve the nation's number 1 ranking in singles. He captured the Southwest Conference titles in 1980 and 1981 and won the Intercollegiate Tennis Association (ITA) National Indoor Championship in 1981.

Hooper joined the ATP professional tennis tour in 1982. During his tennis career he won five pro men's doubles tournaments and was a finalist in two pro men's singles tournaments. Hooper's most memorable tournament was the 1982 US Indoor Championships where he had wins over Peter Fleming, Roscoe Tanner and John Sadri before losing to 1998 ITHF Inductee Jimmy Connors in the semi-finals. After retiring from pro tennis, Hooper became a successful coach of top players. He is best known for coaching former world number 1 Jelena Jankovic. Hooper is a true tennis innovator who is now running a program called Black Belt Tennis (BBT) which integrates martial arts theory and practice into the sport of tennis. This approach is designed to integrate the proper balance of intelligence and force. In 2003, Hooper was inducted into the Arkansas Razorback Hall of Honor.

John Wilkerson – In 1971, Wilkerson won the ATA Men's Singles Championship. This accomplishment was extremely impressive because he started playing late in his youth. Born in San Antonio, Texas, Wilkerson was a senior in high school when he first picked up a tennis racket. John's brother and his friends played tennis on weekends and they frequently tried to convince him to come along. He refused to join them for many months. However, he fell in love with the sport the one day in 1957 that he decided to go with them to the tennis courts. The next week he tried out for his Wheatley High School

tennis team and, because he was a natural athlete, beat all of the players on the team. Incredibly, Wilkerson went on to win district and state titles in singles and doubles that year. He was given a tennis scholarship to Prairie View A&M. However, he dropped out of school to join the US Army. He later attended Texas Southern University (TSU), and, in 1972, won the Southwest Athletic Conference (SWAC) Singles and Doubles Championship.

After graduating from TSU, Wilkerson became the tennis director at MacGregor Park in Houston, Texas and developed a passion for teaching young people about tennis and life. In 1977, he started coaching two 11year-olds named Zina Garrison (2009 BTHF Inductee) and Lori McNeil (2011 BTHF Inductee) at the MacGregor Park tennis courts in Houston, Texas. Wilkerson would coach these players throughout their tennis career and become one of the best known black coaches in pro tennis. Under his tutelage, these players would go on to become two of the best black professional tennis players in history.

In 1981, Zina Garrison became the first African-American to win the Wimbledon and US Open Junior Titles. That year she became the number one 18year-old player in the world. In her first tournament as a professional, the 1982 French Open, she had an amazing run to the quarterfinals where she was beaten by 2000 ITHF Inductee Martina Navratilova. On November 20, 1989, Garrison reached a career high singles ranking of number 4 in the world. She also reached a career high doubles ranking of number 5 on May 23, 1988. On July 4, 1988, McNeil reached a career high singles ranking of number 9 in the world. In addition, on November 9, 1987 she reached a career high doubles ranking of number 4 in the world.

Wilkerson is a board member of the Houston Tennis Association and is currently the tennis director for the Zina Garrison All Court Tennis Academy. In this role, he has helped more than 100 youths receive college scholarships. He was inducted into the Texas Tennis Hall of Fame in 2002 and the Texas Black Sports Hall of Fame in 2009.

The Class of 2016

Martin Blackman – Martin first rose to prominence as one of the best juniors attending the Nick Bollettieri Tennis Academy, where he played with Andre Agassi, Jim Courier and David Wheaton. He reached the semi-finals of the US Open Boy's 16's where he defeated Michael Chang and Petr Korda. Blackman reached the doubles semi-finals of the tournament with MaliVai Washington. He won the 1986 USTA Boy's 16 National Championships in both singles and doubles (where he partnered with Michael Chang). He was a finalist in the USTA Boy's 18's National Championships in 1986. As a student at Stanford, he was a member of two NCAA Championship teams. He played on the professional tennis tour for seven years where he reached a world high ranking of number 158.

He became the coach of American University in 1998 and, during his time there, he was named Conference Coach of the Year three times. Blackman led the team to three conference titles, two NCAA appearances and their first national ranking. In 2004, he became the director of the Junior Tennis Champions Center in College Park, MD. He led the center for five years and helped them identify and develop some of the best juniors in the country.

Blackman served two terms on the USTA board of directors from 2003-2004 and 2005-2006. However, he made history by becoming the first African-American to be the General Manager of USTA Player Development where he leads the US's efforts to recruit and develop the next generation of American professional players. He has contributed to the growth of tennis in the Black Community through his efforts to identify and develop some of the best black players in the country.

Marcel Freeman – Marcel was the number 4 player in the USTA 18 and under division and number 1 in the Boys 12's and 18's in the USTA Eastern Section. He was a 4-time All-American for UCLA from 1979 to 1982. He played number 1 on the UCLA team his senior team, was ranked number 1 in the nation and was named the ITA Player of the year in 1982. He was also a member of the US Junior Davis Cup Team.

In 1985, he won the Nancy, France Men's Doubles tournament with teammate Rodney Harmon. His best Grand Slam result was reaching the 3rd round of the 1986 US Open. Freeman had wins over Stefan Edberg, Harold Solomon, Tim Mayotte, Ilie Nastase, Johan Kriek and Peter Fleming. He reached a career high world singles ranking of number 46. He was inducted into the ITA Hall of Fame in 2012 and the USTA Eastern Section Hall of Fame in 2016. Marcel served as Chanda Rubin's coach and helped her reach number 6 in the world. He also coached Lindsey Davenport, Mark Knowles, Janet Lee and Martin Blackman. He lives in Hollywood, California and teaches tennis in Beverly Hills, California.

Bryan Shelton – In 1984, Bryan Shelton won the Alabama High School singles championship. He played on the tennis team of the Georgia Institute of Technology in Atlanta where he won the 1985 Atlantic Coast Conference (ACC) title. Also in 1985, he won the US Amateur Championships. Shelton and Ricky Gilbert were ACC Doubles Champions in 1986. In 1988 he was named All-American. Shelton graduated from Georgia Tech with a BS degree in

Industrial Engineering in 1989 and was inducted into the Georgia Tech Athletics Hall of Fame in 1993.

Shelton won the 1991 and 1992 Newport Hall of Fame Championships and reached the Mixed Doubles final at the 1992 French Open partnering with Lori McNeal. He reached the highest world ranking of 55 in singles in 1992 and 52 in doubles in 1994. He retired from the pro tour in 1997 and became a USTA National Coach from 1998 to 1999. In 1999 he became the Head Coach of the Georgia Tech Women's Tennis Team. He was named ACC Coach of the Year and 2002, 2005 and 2007. His team won the 2005, 2006 and 2007 ACC Championships. In 2007, the team won the NCAA Women's Tennis Championship by defeating UCLA in the finals. Shelton was named the Intercollegiate Tennis Association (ITA) Coach of the Year in 2007. He has been the University of Florida Men's Tennis Head Coach since 2012.

The Class of 2017

James Blake – James Blake has been one of the most successful African-American male players to play professional tennis. He earned nearly $8 million in professional prize money and had a record of 366-256 on the professional singles tennis tour. He achieved a ranking of number 4 in the world in 2006 and number 31 doubles. He was a member of the victorious 2007 US Davis Cup Team and won the Hopman Cup in both 2003 and 2004. During his career he took a page out of Arthur Ashe's playbook and developed a reputation as a gentleman and a class act on the professional tour. His popularity helped to increase interest in tennis in all communities of color (especially the African-American community). He founded and operates his charity, the James Blake Foundation, which invests in medical research. He has also been the chair of the USTA

Foundation which supports the growth of tennis in underserved communities. He is a frequent volunteer at events in urban tennis programs. Without question, he has been one of the most influential black tennis players in history.

James Ciccone – James served as the American Tennis Association's pro bono general counsel dating back to the 1990s without compensation or expenses, for a period of over 20 years. Celebrating its centennial anniversary, this term of service represents more than 20 percent of the life of the organization. He advised five American Tennis Association presidents, boards of directors and executive committees, repelled two hostile takeover bids, supervised national elections involving  controversy and competing factions in the interest of preserving unity, re-wrote the organization's constitution and bylaws, established the historical preservation committee in the interest of protecting the rich legacy of black tennis, established the dispute resolution committee as an alternative to litigation between members as a condition of membership, established the advisory committee as a vehicle to involve financial leaders in organizational affairs to commit financial resources to the organization and expertly settled litigation that threatened the existence of the organization.

He also protected the Southern Section, including the Alabama, Arkansas, Florida, Georgia, Louisiana, Mississippi, North and South Carolina and Tennessee, the Southwestern Section, including Nebraska, New Mexico, Oklahoma and Texas, the New York and New Jersey sections, and the Caribbean section. James developed a son, Vincenzo Ciccone, who represented the organization as the men's open singles national champion, the number one ranked player, a college all-American, and a member of the Jamaica, W.I. Davis Cup Team. James plans to publish his fiction masterpiece, *Nobody Stays*. It is a trilogy containing metaphors relating to tennis history and other topics. Look for it!

Breaking The Barriers

Yannick Noah - Yannick is the only male player of African descent to win the French Open. His career high ranking was number 3 in the world in 1986. His professional match record was 476 wins and 210 losses. He won a total of 23 professional singles tournaments and 16 professional doubles titles. He became the second most popular (globally) male tennis player of African descent. His personality and success on the court inspired people of color around the world to take up tennis. He has been very active in charity work and supports the charity Enfants de la Terre, a charity created and run by his mother. He also founded Fete le Mur in 1996, a tennis charity for young people living in underserved communities. He has recently become a popular musician and continues to tour the world.

Richard Williams – Richard, the father of Venus and Serena Williams, has developed two of the finest players ever to strike a tennis ball. He took tennis lessons from a man known as "Old Whiskey" and decided his future daughters would be tennis professionals after seeing Virginia Ruzici play on television. He wrote a 78-page plan and started giving lessons to Venus and Serena when they were four and a half and began taking them to public tennis courts. Soon after that he got them into Shreveport tennis tournaments. In 1995, Williams pulled them out of a tennis academy and coached them himself. Defying conventional wisdom and much criticism, Richard stayed true to his faith and belief in his daughters.

This faith was rewarded when Serena won the US Open in 1999 and Venus beat Lindsay Davenport to win the 2000 Wimbledon title. After that victory, Richard shouted "Straight

Outta Compton" (in reference to a song by N.W.A. based on that area in Los Angeles) and jumped over the NBC broadcasting booth, catching Chris Evert by surprise and performing a triumphant dance. Evert said that the broadcasters "Thought the roof was coming down." History will recognize Richard Williams as one of the greatest tennis coaches in history.

The Class of 2018

D.A. Abrams – D.A.'s accomplishments as an administrator are voluminous. He has been one of the most influential African-American leaders in tennis. As the first executive director of the USTA Missouri Valley Section from 1997 to 2000 and the second African-American executive director of the USTA Eastern Section from 2006-2012, Abrams did an extraordinary job of leading the day to day operations of these two influential sections. In Missouri Valley, he advocated for greater diversity and increased participation in the sport. In the Eastern Section, he worked closely with Section President Dale Caldwell (inducted into the Black Tennis Hall of Fame in 2015) to grow the game of tennis. It was the first and currently only time that an African-American president & CEO worked with an African-American executive director to lead a USTA Section.

At Eastern, Abrams established "Grow the Game" funding to aid member organizations in promoting and developing the growth of tennis. A record $1.5 million was allocated to be invested in local tennis programming. Under his leadership, he increased USTA Junior Team Tennis Unique Players from 692 to 6,393 in 2010. This was an amazing 820% increase during the period. The increase was particularly significant because it was far above the USTA's growth of 52% over the five-year period. In addition, the Section increased USTA Individual Membership 13% from 43,606 in 2005 to 49, 255 in 2010.

Breaking The Barriers

As chief diversity & inclusion officer of the USTA (a department started in 2012), D.A. played a critically important role in diversity and inclusion in tennis. His experience includes defining and implementing the following official statement from the USTA: *"Diversity & Inclusion is a strategic priority of the USTA and one of our core values. Diversity allows us to touch all of America and Inclusion allows All of America to touch us. Our diversity and inclusion philosophy is designed to match the "Needs" of our customers with D&I related solutions."* D.A. did an outstanding job of helping the leadership of the USTA understand that the only way to achieve their strategic growth objectives is by embracing diversity. In this role, D.A. convinced the USTA to support the important work of the Black Tennis Hall of Fame. His efforts helped the organization become the most successful organization celebrating black tennis history. D.A.'s accomplishments over the decades have enabled the diverse American population to not only participate, but to flourish in the game of tennis.

Ronald Agenor – With an ATP high ranking of #22, Ronald sustained one of the longest careers in the history of the game (19 years). He had victories over some of the world's greatest players of his generation including, Agassi, Connors, Annacone, Rosset, Leconte, Forget, Curren and Pat Cash, just to name a few. He reached the quarter finals of the French Open in 1989 and the fourth round of both the US Open and French Open in 1988.

After retiring from the game, Ronald started his tennis academy in Los Angeles, CA. and trained aspiring professionals, juniors, juniors seeking college scholarships and adults. He is the son of a former Haitian Diplomat at the United Nations and Minister of Agriculture of Haiti. He is the youngest of a family of six children and learned how to play tennis in Congo (Ex Zaire) in 1974 and discovered competitive tennis in Bordeaux, France. Ronald is also an Ambassador for Peace and Sport, an organization under the High Patronage of SAS Prince Albert II of Monaco.

Desmond Margetson – Desmond was born in New York City on May 3, 1926. He was a nationally ranked player in the late 1940's and early 1950's. He captained the New York University tennis team and played #1 singles for the team. He worked for 59 years as an engineer in almost every engineering field: civil, aeronautical, mechanical, chemical, electronic, human factors and computer applications, to name some. Des was an inventor. Many of the inventions of which he was most proud were created for the companies that employed him and were often classified. One of his original designs later won an award at an Air Force competition.

Between 1950 and 1954 he reached the round of 16 four times at the USTA Indoor National Championships and in 2000 was inducted into the New York University Athletic Hall of Fame. In 1957 *World Tennis* magazine introduced Desmond as the "Father of Indoor Tennis" when he introduced the concept of the "Tennis Bubble" allowing for all-weather tennis. "The New York Times" again recognized him for his tennis bubble concept. He received a Lifetime Achievement Award from the USTA in 1957 for his contributions to tennis.

The Class of 2019

Nathaniel and Frankyln Jackson – These brothers from Laurinburg, North Carolina were extraordinary pioneers of black tennis. These brothers were the American Tennis Association (ATA) Men's Singles doubles champions in 1931, 1933, 1934, 1935, 1936 and 1938. In 1934, Nathaniel was the ATA National Men's Singles Champion. His brother Franklyn was the ATA National Men's Singles Champion in 1935 and 1937. Nathaniel was one of the most talented players on Dr. Hubert Eaton's Wilmington, North Carolina home tennis court. It was here that he had a chance to hit and practice with world champion Althea Gibson. He also introduced the game of tennis to the legendary Lendward (Lenny) Simpson (who was inducted into the Black Tennis Hall of Fame in 2014). It is rumored that he beat world champion Fred Perry on Dr. Eaton's tennis court.

Chanda Rubin – Rubin became a professional tennis player in 1991 at the age of 15 and played on the WTA Tour for 16 years. She reached a career high ranking of #6 in the world in singles and #9 in the world in doubles. She won 7 WTA Tour singles titles and 10 doubles titles, including the Australian Open doubles title in 1996. In singles, she reached the semi-finals of the Australian Open and reached the quarterfinals of the French Open three times. In doubles, she also reached the finals and semifinals of the US Open in back-to-back years, as well as the semifinals of Wimbledon. Her competitive fire and work ethic gained her

wins over many other top players like Jennifer Capriati, Gabriela Sabatini, Arantxa Sanchez, Martina Hingis, Amelie Mauresmo, Justine Henin, Lindsay Davenport, and Serena Williams. She has competed in record-setting matches, the most memorable being when she came back and won after being down 5-0, 40-0 in the 3rd set against Jana Novotna at the French Open.

Chanda was a member of the 1996 and 2004 US Olympic Teams as well as the US Fed Cup team from 1995-1997 and from 1999-2004, helping the US to take the title in 1999. She was also an accomplished junior player, winning the Wimbledon girls' singles title and rising to No. 2 in the world junior rankings in 1992. She has won various awards for her accomplishments on the court and for her work with numerous charities. She was inducted into the Southern Tennis Hall of Fame in 2009, the Louisiana Tennis Hall of Fame in 2012, and the Louisiana Sports Hall of Fame in 2013. Although she became a professional as a junior in high school, one of Chanda's fondest memories is of staying in school and graduating with her class.Currently, Chanda works as a broadcast analyst for Tennis Channel as well as being a real estate professional and motivational speaker. She served three terms as a director-at-large on the United States Tennis Association (USTA) board of directors as well as terms on the USTA International Committee and the ITF Juniors Committee. She has a degree from Harvard University Extension School, in the field of Economics, with a minor in Finance.

Awards

Louisiana Sports Hall of Fame Inductee 2013
Louisiana Tennis Hall of Fame Inductee 2012
Southern Tennis Hall of Fame Inductee 2009
International Lawn Tennis Danzig Trophy 2008
Gene Scott Renaissance Award 2008
USTA Service Bowl Award 2003
Hormel Foods/Family Circle Player Who Makes A Difference Award 2002
Arthur Ashe Leadership Award 1997
USA Magazine's Most Caring Athlete Award 1998
WTA Most Improved Player Award 1995

Breaking The Barriers

1996 US Olympic Committee Female Athlete of the Month and thereafter Female Athlete of the Year
USTA Female Athlete of the Year 1996
ATA Athlete of the Year 1995

Richard Russell – Richard is the only Jamaican to qualify and win matches at all Grand Slam Championships. He was the youngest national champion at age 16. A founding member of the ATP (Association of Tennis Professionals) in 1966, he achieved the distinction of holding the record of winning a first round match at the Australian Open 6-0, 6-0, 6-0. He represented the Jamaican Davis Cup and had wins over Arthur Ashe and Charlie Passarel in 1966 and a singles win over Eric Van Dillon in the 1970 Davis Cup tie versus the West Indies. He also had a  singles win over Dennis Ralston at the Caribe Hilton in San Juan, Puerto Rico.

Richard was the director of Tennis at the Half Moon Club in Montego Bay and was responsible for bringing tennis luminaries Ilie Nastase, Bjorn Borg, Jimmy Connors, Pancho Gonzales and Pancho Segura to participate in celebrity events at the Half Moon Club. In 2002-2003 he was the circuit chairman to Jamaica, hosting 2,000 plus world class Futures players, their coaches and family members from all over the world by creating and running 22 men's professional tournaments in a record-breaking series of events which had never been attempted in the Caribbean. Richard is the chairman/director of the Russell Tennis

Academy at Hillel Academy, Campion College and Campion Deep Dene.

In 2011, he became chairman of the All Island High School tennis championships and director of Tennis Jamaica. Richard is the father to three sons, all of whom are involved in tennis: Craig Russell is the Project Manager responsible for the family Tennis Court Building Operation; Ryan Russell, a Wimbledon junior semi-finalist and world ranked ATP Pro Player at age 19. He and his brother, Rayne are the two leading High School teaching professionals. Rayne and Ryan are formers of Jamaica's Davis Cup Team.

Benny Sims – Mr. Sims, a native of Beaumont, Texas, has had over 40 years of extraordinary success in the game of tennis as a player, coach, administrator, mentor and spokesperson. After attending Texas Southern University, where he was a two-time All American, and American Tennis Association (ATA) Men's Singles Champion, he embarked on the professional tour. Sims soon relocated to Boston, Massachusetts where he went on to coach, working with Jim Smith at Sportsmen's Tennis Club, which reached national acclaim under their direction. He then moved on to Harvard University and became the first African-American assistant tennis coach in the Ivy League. After his time at Harvard, Sims was appointed head tennis pro at the famed Longwood Cricket Club, and was then recruited by the late Arthur Ashe to serve as a National Coach for the USTA Player Development program. Sims was the first African-American to hold both of these positions. Sims is perhaps best known for coaching Chanda Rubin (who was also inducted into the Black Tennis Hall of Fame in 2019). Partnering in 1998, under Sims' tutelage, Chanda Rubin reached a ranking of #7 in the world on the women's professional tour. Benny Sims Jr. currently resides in New Jersey with his wife and has two adult daughters.

Theodore Thompson – Thompson was born in Hubbard City, Texas in 1907. He moved with his family to Washington, DC at the age of 6. Ted was an extraordinary athlete who graduated from Wilberforce University where he starred in both tennis and basketball. He won the ATA National Mixed Doubles title in 1931, the Men's Singles title in 1925 and 1927 and the Men's Doubles titles in 1917, 1919, 1921, 1922, 1924, 1925, 1926 and 1927. Theodore partnered seven times to win these doubles titles with Tally Holmes, (winner of the inaugural ATA Championship in 1916) and once with Eyre Saitch. Ted passed away on August 9, 1963. He was an extraordinary tennis player who, if given the opportunity, could have been one of the best tennis players in the world.

Phil Williamson – Williamson is an accomplished and respected professional with more than 10 years of experience in every aspect of tennis coaching. He is a success-oriented individual as well as a team-builder. Phil sees challenges as opportunities with a performance record in developing players to reach their potential on the junior collegiate and tour level. A self-motivated leader, adept at facilitating projects in a fast-paced and detail-oriented environment,he is also an effective communicator who relates well to diverse groups of people at all levels within an organization.

A native of New York, Phil graduated from Mount Vernon High School in 1983 and Columbia University in 1987 with a Bachelor of Arts in Economics. While at Columbia he became one of the few African Americans to be the #1 player at an Ivy League School. In 1984 he helped Columbia University capture its first IVY League title in over 12 years and then repeated the feat three years later before graduating. He was ranked 45th in Head

Intercollegiate Tennis Standing and an Intercollegiate Tennis Association (ITA) rank of #31.

Phil played on the Association of Tennis Professionals (ATP) Tour from 1987 to 1993 reaching his highest singles level of #294 in August of 1992 and highest doubles level of #133 in August of 1989. He participated in numerous ATP events including the US Open (1985, 1986, 1987-89, 1991-1993, 1997), Wimbledon (1989, 1992), Australian Open (1992), Newport International Hall of Fame (1992) NYTL/SOBRO Bronx Challenger doubles quarterfinalist and the Shawmut US Pro Championships (Boston 1989) doubles finalist. He also represented Antiqua in Davis Cup and other national events to include the Pan American Games (Argentina 1995 - played #1 singles), Davis Cup (played #1 singles and doubles), El Salvador 1996, Bermuda 1997, Bolivia 1998 and Panama 1999.

His tennis teaching experience includes positions as program director with the Harlem Junior Tennis Program; director of tennis, Tennis Club of Riverdale; director of tennis, Hudson Valley Health and Tennis Club; head coach and school advisor for Academy Players, Ross School Tennis Academy; and as a personal coach. Phil currently holds life memberships with the United States Tennis Federation (USTA) and the American Tennis Association (ATA). He is also a member of the United States Professional Tennis Association (USPTA) with an Elite Pro rating. He served on the board of the ATA 2000-2002; a New York delegate for the ATA New York Tennis Association 2000-2002; ran NYTA tournaments at USTA National Tennis Center 1999-2001; and a member of the board of directors of the Jerry Alleyne Memorial Foundation.

Epilogue

I wrote this book to demonstrate to readers why tennis has been, and will continue to be, one of the most interesting human endeavors in the world. Very few other activities have the rich recreational and professional history of tennis. There are just a handful of truly international sports that have the same level of popularity and economic impact. No other sport has these elements while providing relatively equal opportunities for both men and women. Tennis has been an extremely important part of my life. I began this book by sharing my family's unique tennis journey and the role that tennis has played in my life. Everything that I have ever accomplished has been rooted, in one way or another, in my tennis experience. I was inspired to research the amazing history of the sport because of the important role it has played in my life.

I was surprised to find in my research that this simple sport of hitting a ball back and forth has been the pastime of kings, presidents, celebrities and peasants. Leaders of the sport have not only been at the center of major world events, they have helped to shape history. The early days of tennis were built around economic, social and racial exclusion. However, the sport, like society as a whole, has made tremendous strides in the areas of diversity, inclusion and equity. Serving as the curator with Art Carrington of the International Hall of Fame *Breaking the Barriers* exhibit was one of the things that I am most proud of in my life. I worked very closely with museum director Gary Cogar to put together an exhibit that honored players and administrators that were excluded from many aspects of the sport because of their race. I became so obsessed with this project that I founded the Black Tennis Hall of Fame to permanently record the amazing accomplishments of people who overcame barriers of race and class to succeed in the sport. I am grateful to Bob Davis and D.A. Abrams for being the first people willing to take the organization to the next level. I am also grateful to the wonderful board of the Black Tennis Hall of Fame (BTHOF) who have generously given their time and expertise to grow the organization. The core of this group includes Bob Davis, D.A. Abrams, Art Carrington and the current executive director Shelia Curry. I am also grateful to Todd Martin the CEO of the International Tennis Hall of Fame (ITHF), Doug Stark the Hall of Fame museum director and Nicole Markham the curator of collections. These leaders of the BTHOF and the ITHF are making important history by recording it.

I am convinced that the future of tennis is very bright because the COVID-19 pandemic has, surprisingly, inspired new people to play the sport. The global pandemic has killed or hurt tens of millions of people, closed millions of small businesses and reduced participation in many different sports. However, in a strange way, the pandemic has increased recreational focus on tennis.

Medical experts state that, in order to avoid getting sick from any virus, people should keep a safe social distance away from one another. They should stay at least six feet away from other people and should wear a mask. People have been prevented from going to the gym and have been forced to avoid team sports. They are actively seeking new ways to exercise their mind and body. Families that had never before considered playing tennis have taken up the sport because it is the perfect social distance activity. Players are more than six feet away from one another and stand at opposite sides of the net. In many areas of the world, tennis courts are busier than they have been for many years. I am convinced that people will continue to play tennis in record numbers long after the pandemic is contained.

The major professional tennis tournaments continue to generate more interest than ever. This signals that tennis fans have maintained their passion for the sport in spite of the global health challenges. I would like to end this book by thanking you for joining me on this incredible journey through the world of tennis. I hope that my writing inspires you to follow the sport more closely and consider playing the game that has changed my life. Perhaps it will change your life too.

For sales, editorial information, subsidiary rights information or a catalog, please write or phone or e-mail

Absolutely Amazing ebooks
Manhanset House
Shelter Island Hts., New York 11965-0342, US
Tel: 212-427-7139
www.absolutelyamazingebooks.com
bricktower@aol.com
www.IngramContent.com

For sales in the UK and Europe please contact our distributor,
Gazelle Book Services
White Cross Mills
Lancaster, LA1 4XS, UK
Tel: (01524) 68765 Fax: (01524) 63232
email: jacky@gazellebooks.co.uk

www.ingramcontent.com/pod-product-compliance
Lightning Source LLC
Chambersburg PA
CBHW050548160426
43199CB00015B/2573